FINDING THE LIGHT IN THE DARKNESS: RECLAIMING MY FREEDOM AND IDENTITY

Sabina Harmony

Published by New Generation Publishing in 2024

First Edition

Paperback ISBN: 978-1-83563-513-1
Hardback ISBN: 978-1-83563-514-8

www.newgeneration-publishing.com

New Generation Publishing

Chapters

This book is a true story of my lived experience and life thus far, while some details such as names of people have been changed to protect the privacy of the individuals involved, the core events are accurate.

Trigger Warning:
This book includes content that contains graphic scenes of torture, grievous bodily injury, sexual assault, domestic violence, and references to suicide and death. Due to the varying forms of abuse throughout, such as assault, drug addiction, and criminal activity, there are multiple references to mental health and its symptoms.

If you find yourself relating to anything in this book or would like to learn more about coping mechanisms and techniques to help heal, there is a second book that includes both the story and all of the helpful tools and therapeutic techniques I found beneficial.

However, this book is not intended as a diagnostic tool for any of the conditions explored. The information provided is a generic overview and should not be used as a substitute for specific medical advice. Please seek an individual consultation with a registered medical professional if you feel any of the topics covered are relevant to you.

If you find yourself overwhelmed with heavy emotions or triggered, please take some time for self-care. This could include:

- Grounding exercises, such as deep breathing or mindfulness meditation

- Taking a walk in nature or a calming environment

- Journaling to release and process your thoughts

- Engaging in creative activities, like drawing, painting, or music

- Spending time with a pet or loved one who brings you comfort

- Doing something physically relaxing, such as taking a warm bath, stretching, or practicing yoga

- Listening to soothing music or an uplifting podcast

- Reaching out to a supportive friend, therapist, or helpline if needed

- Taking breaks and caring for your mental well-being is important as you navigate this material.

Dedication

This book is dedicated to all the Angels that God has sent to me through the tough process of writing this book and all the people who made my journey to ministry and freedom from the bondage of Child Sexual Abuse and neglect possible so that I was able to live to tell this tale.

I dedicate this book to both my parents who lived a life of unresolved trauma. To my siblings, and my three beautiful children, who gave me my purpose, to my grandchildren. It is my hope that may they grow up in a world free from abuse and may this be a legacy for them, their children, and their children's children.

I dedicate this book to my readers, anyone suffering at the hands of abuse and the readers who simply seek understanding.

To the people who helped me survive and saw in me the goodness that I lacked the ability to see in myself. Those who counselled me to recognise the tools I needed to heal from the shackles of abuse. go through the arduous task of putting pen to paper and producing this memoire which I hope shall bring healing to many that read it.

I recognise as I forgive others, I ask for any hurt that has been caused to anyone unbeknownst to me and by me, to also be forgiven.

Introduction

This story is my story, the story of my pain and the abuse I have endured. My favourite part of the story is that it is still going. I am still here, the rest is still unwritten, the possibilities endless. With experience comes understanding and I have chosen to share that with you, my reader. You are either here, holding my book because the topics covered are true to your own tribulations or, you are seeking an understanding, so you can assist someone dear to you. Either way, I am glad we found each other.

We start at the beginning of it all, childhood. Each of us, despite the difference in experience, are uniquely shaped by the tales of our earliest days. Some haunted by those early memories, others not so. No story is ever the same, but the basis in many ways can be. It's that idea that we are so alone, and no one can understand that drove me to put pen to paper. The idea that we should keep the tough times to ourselves because nobody wants to hear it, or they wouldn't get it, even if they are willing to listen, a taboo I long to re write. We are never alone; we are unique but not isolated in kind.

There are ten main types of abuse, it is never simple nor is it linear. It is, by design, isolating and to a degree, humiliating, typically not the topic of choice for most. I found myself at a point in my life where this just screamed out to me, what about the victims? People find themselves not knowing what to say to us, attending therapy can initially be too daunting of a task, self-healing can seem impossible and often a level of assistance is required. It becomes a whirlwind, extremely overwhelming and knowing where to start or who to turn to is a task that may be repeatedly put off.

As a psychodynamic therapist myself, I often hear people in their initial stages of therapy saying things like you just won't understand; the truth is, I do, more than most in some areas and for that I want to share my story. I too had to learn; it wasn't just me that these things were happening to.

Going back to the ten main types of abuse, we often find self-help books or articles are subjective and designed to focus on one of the above. Indicators of abuse and behaviours exhibited are not exhaustive and quite often, individuals are subject to several types of abuse at the same time, it's even possible that this is happening and going undetected by the victim. I for a long time thought some of the things that were happening to me, were normal or my fault.

My story is a culmination of the things I was exposed to, the things that were forced upon me, physically and emotionally. Not exclusive to a partner but my parents, my siblings, people that crossed my path in life but also, my understanding of the whys and the struggles that led these people to treat me the way they did.

All the characters in my book, are fighting their own battles. When I came to realise that, seeing my abusers as victims, I knew I was halfway to healing. It is by no means easy to look at these individuals and well, sympathise, in fact, you don't have to sympathise, but to understand is powerful. For example, my dad was sexually abused but he also had a gambling addiction that caused my family real pain, given I am one of four. My mum, she didn't have it easy growing up, but then, she made sure I didn't either, the monster, he raped me for 10 years. I was subjected to betrayal of friends, colleagues, and the church I was a part of for years. My list is a long one.

I mentioned that abuse isn't linear, neither is healing. The idea can seem quite simply unthinkable and completely out of the question. It doesn't have to be the case, from someone who felt for many years exactly that way, I now know healing is possible - you just need the tools. Strength is already proven, you are still here and if you are supporting someone else, please remember that they have made it this far.

You will come to learn, whilst seeking my own answers, I have found many wonderful books along the way, all from which have left me with tools to share and use alike. I have left you a list for further reading and hope my journey will inspire you to continue yours. I want to leave you with this quote from Peter A.Levine;

"I have come to the conclusion that human beings are born with an innate capacity to triumph over trauma. I believe not only that trauma is curable, but the healing process can be a catalyst for profound awakening - a portal opening to emotional and genuine spiritual transformation. I have little doubt that as individuals, families, communities and even nations, we have the capacity to learn how to heal and prevent much of the damage done by trauma. In so doing, we will significantly increase our ability to achieve both our individual and collective dreams."

And, as Martin Luther King Jr. said, "As my sufferings mounted, I soon realised that there were two ways in which I could respond to my situation - either to react with bitterness or seek to transform the suffering into a creative force. I decided to follow the latter."

Chapter One

Is She Breathing?

"For I know the plans I have for you," declares the Lord, "plans to prosper you and not to harm you, plans to give you hope and a future."

Jeremiah 29:11

"Is she breathing? Looks like an overdose with all the drugs and alcohol… what's her name?"

"Sabina, Sabina Harmony." "Check her ABC's" "Airways clear" "Breathing?"

"Shallow and ineffective" "Get a SATs probe on her"

"We need a 100% oxygen mask on her now, get ready to ventilate"

"Circulation?"

"She's pale, lips are blue, she's cold." "What's her pulse?"

"40 and irregular, weak radial pulse" "Check her blood pressure"

"BP is 90/53 ..."

"Right, check GCS"

"GCS 4 - pupils are pinpoint, fixed and unresponsive."

"I'll get a line in. Draw up Naloxone and we need to give fluids now! I'll also need a full set of observations to rule out other reversible causes."

"OK, respiration 6, temperature 35.6, still unresponsive"

"Empty vials of oxy... pregab— paracetamol... amitriptyline and zopiclone... nearly empty bottle of vodka"

"Try to find out how much of each she's taken to tell Toxbase, get an ECG on her now, heart rate is rising, now 120."

"Get us P1 backup. She needs sedation to protect her airway, she's already vomited, with her SATS and respiration rate, we need to ventilate"

"Her end tidal CO_2 is only 3.6, the BVM and mask isn't enough. I am going to upgrade her airway to an I-gel."

"Do you want an NP or OP airway first?"

"No, she's in need of a more advanced airway, we can't waste any time."

"Call it in... blue light it..." "4511 to Control..."

"Control to 4511... go ahead."

"Got a thirty-six-year-old female. Name, Sabina Harmony. Currently unresponsive, GSC 4. Empty pill boxes – Oxycontin, Pregabalin, Paracetamol, Amitriptyline and Zopiclone and a nearly empty bottle of Vodka. Likely taken together about an hour ago, estimated 12:30am. Evidence of vomit. The scene is safe and has good access."

"Her vitals?"

"Respiration 6, SATS 88%, 95% on 1.5 litres of oxygen - heart rate is irregular 40 to 120, BP is 90/53, GCS 4, pupils are pinpoint, a 1, temperature is 35.6, and BM is 5.0."

"OK, what have you given her?"

"We've put two lines in, 0.9% saline and 250 mils of fluid, 400 mcg of Naloxone intranasally to no effect, end tidal CO_2 is now 4, was 3.6 and ventilating with I-gel"

"Copy that, back-up dispatched, ETA 5 minutes."

****

As I start to become aware, I can hear voices and beeping noises, barely audible, like whispering. I can make out they are talking about me but have no idea why. Looking up at a bright light, I am strangely drawn to it. Through the haze, I can make out the doctors and nurses, my brother George crying and my friend Dawn leaning over me, sobbing. "Wake up... we love you. Why didn't you ask for help? You could have asked us for help." Suddenly, I realise I am above them all, looking down, on them and myself.

Everything is brighter, clearer. Lights Flashing. Beeping and whirring noises become sharper, a sharpness I have never known before. I could see the intricate details, showing me how it was all made. I could see the energy, how it congregated into form and matter. I gasped at the realisation and just like that, immediately I am lifted, up into an overhead fluorescent light. Then, somewhere beyond, drew me in. And then… distance. Why didn't you ask for help are the last words I heard as the sobs, the flashing, beeping, and rushing around become fainter and fainter. More distant, as I drift... drift away.

I felt someone take hold of my hand, and a voice. "There is a lot I want to show you." Then, I saw myself, the times in my life that I chose to wipe from my memory and bury deep down inside. Things I could not forgive; the hurt, the pain. I saw all the unforgiveness, bitterness, hate and the anger in my heart. All the people that had betrayed me, abused me, sexually, physically, emotionally, spiritually. Those who had lied to me, hurt me. All the people I did not forgive. In that moment, I realised I was still holding on to the anger, the resentment. I thought I had forgiven, and I had tried. I had tried to let go, of all the horrible emotions, the negative experiences but it all culminated as I realised in that moment, the toxic piece's I had been carrying for so long had become me. Driving me to this moment, pushing me, pushing me to the point of wanting so badly for it all to end. I had tried to take my own life.

Then there were the screams, as I was guided into what can only be described as a dark cave. It was cold, filled with feelings of pain and anguish. Thousands of people, all shapes and sizes, colours, and cultures. Scrambling in despair, so much sadness. Unable to communicate with each other, their mouths agape in agony, as if they were exploding and on fire with torment, to be continued indefinitely. No way out.

The voice began to explain as it held firmly onto my hand, these people are now reaping what they had sown. They too had lots of unforgiveness in their hearts, bitterness, anger, resentment. All mirroring their pain and past.

I could no longer feel my hand being held and it went dark again. I was terrified and now alone. The panic of not knowing what to do or what this now meant, for me. Am I to become one of the figures I had just seen? I looked around, desperately searching for something... Anything. All I could think of, to find some comfort in that dark moment was 'The Lord's Prayer'. The word's flashing before my eyes.

Our Father, who art in heaven, Hallowed be thy name

Thy kingdom come; thy will be done On earth as it is in heaven

Give us this day our daily bread And FORGIVE US

Our trespasses…

I paused. Forgiveness! How could I be forgiven? I had just tried to take my own life!

I cried out, "Forgive me Lord! Forgive me, Lord!" Over and over, and over again as the prayer continued to flash before my eyes.

Appearing in front of me were their faces. One by one, they flashed before my eyes. All the people who had hurt me and robbed me in my life. At this point, I knew I was not just praying but I was having a conversation. A conversation with a higher being. The visions and flashbacks of every incident that had caused me to feel pain. I saw the people, the people I needed to forgive. I finished the prayer.

"For thine is the kingdom, the power and the glory, forever and ever, in Jesus' name, Amen."

In that moment, I knew I was in the presence of God. Intermittent feelings of light and love flowing through me, in waves, each one building on the last. Each time overwhelming me, deeper into feelings of unconditional, nonjudgmental love, forgiveness and acceptance.

I felt unworthy. I remember thinking, but how can you love

me after all that I have done? At this point I was told I needed to forgive myself and the voice called out "With unforgiveness in your heart you cannot enter the Kingdom of God." Then came another wave of light, this time followed by love, forgiveness, and acceptance of myself. An overwhelming rush of love moving through me, entirely. Seeing myself the way my creator saw me. Sobbing and crying, the tears wouldn't stop but, they were tears of love, love like I had never known or experienced before. Every time a thought of unworthiness, or guilt, my sinfulness or shame rose up in me, another wave of love would crash over me. Like a storm, the tears poured as I let go of the hatred that had been brought upon me.

As He took my hand, transitioning me from the dark place I had just witnessed, a blazing light, like a whirlpool began spinning, getting bigger and bigger. The vision became clearer as I started to see thousands of people, beaming, facing towards something brighter. I could hear the most beautiful and angelic music. The figure holding my hand called it a gathering of saints. They weren't angels, they didn't have wings, but they looked angelic to me. With their hands raised high and facing a light brighter than before, I could feel the presence of my ancestors. There were colours I had never seen on earth and unlike the sun, this light didn't hurt my eyes in anyway. I was drawn to it, to look directly at it and I just wanted to get closer.

In this moment, I was filled with joy as the light's presence surrounded me. The angelic voices compelling me to move closer, but the figure held back my hand and said I could not go. Instead, He guided me to a field where everything seemed so truly alive. The plants, the flowers and the trees in perfect correspondence, harmony. The flowers synchronised as if swaying in a slight summers breeze, dancing to the sound of the saintly song. Radiating through me, tranquillity, and perfect peace. It was paradise times a trillion, there are no words with the power to encompass just how amazing it was. Everything now seemed so clear, as if my heart and mind had transpired beyond what we know in this life. I could see, smell, hear, so clearly and I wanted to stay forever.

I was awestruck as the light began to open. Radiantly it moved towards me, I was encircled by its glory. I could make out a figure, but I couldn't see a face as it dazzled in the light. As the figure moved aside, it was like a window had opened before me, it was stunning, majestic and it was, what had to be, paradise.

I felt as if I could finally stop running. I had found what I was searching for, and I was home. Immediately I saw the faces of my three children: Gabriel, Mary and Abel. The figure suddenly stepped in front of me and again the voice said "Sabina, now is not your time." I cried out, in protest, for what I had just seen, "No, please, let me stay! I want to stay!"

"Sabina, there is work to be done. With unforgiveness in your heart, you cannot enter the Kingdom of Heaven. Now is not your time."

Chapter two

Mum and Dad

"Whoever welcomes one of these little children in my name welcomes me; and whoever welcomes me does not welcome me but the one who sent me."

Mark 9:36-37

Early August 1975 - Birmingham, England. Entering the world 6 weeks premature. Mum's placenta had stopped feeding me, no longer supplying the nutrients I needed. Weighing just two kilos (4.5 pounds) Mum wasn't allowed to hold me. The technology back then wasn't as it is now. The first 6 weeks of my life were spent in an incubator, no skin-to-skin contact, no touch or affection. Perhaps my start in life explains my weak immune system. My own son was also born prematurely and in huge contrast to my own beginning, despite him being 12 weeks in comparison to my 6, I was allowed to touch him straight away. I had to be torn from his side; I was allowed to hold him from day one, with what is known as a kangaroo hug, skin to skin contact throughout, building as much of a bond as a mother could. The anguish I would feel leaving him every night, returning home to an empty crib, endlessly praying that he would be strong enough to make it home, is something I wouldn't wish on any mother.

Research has found that parents of premature babies or having traumatic stressful births, are more likely to experience mental health problems than parents whose babies arrived full- term or with no complications at birth.

These may include anxiety, depression or post-traumatic stress disorder (PTSD).

Premature babies can also have a form of post-traumatic stress after staying in the neonatal intensive care unit (NICU) or after a birth that was via Caesarean Section.

Providing a nurturing environment is a fantastic way for parents to maximise their premature baby's outcome. Trauma-Proofing Your Kids: A Parents' Guide for Instilling Confidence, Joy and Resilience by Peter A. Levine is a terrific book and highly informative.

This book assists parents and other lay caregivers in the prevention and healing of trauma by serving as a practical guide to "stressbusting" and building resilience in kids so they can easily cope with our fast-changing world.

When I was released from the NICU and considered well enough to be bought home, Mum was already pregnant with my sister. Caring for a new baby, my older brother and a battle with morning sickness couldn't have been easy. On top of that, Dad had a serious gambling addiction leaving my mum with the added anxiety of providing for us all. Did I mention she was only 23? I take my hat off to her for coping as best she could. I was just 9 months old, and a new baby comes along. Three kids, two under one, it must have been very overwhelming. Trying to get us all to sleep so that she too could have some rest herself. This was when it started, the physical abuse. She would get my baby sister to sleep and if I cried in need of anything, waking my sister up would earn me a slap from Mum - my first introduction into the world of fear.

Fast forward a few years, I was approaching my third birthday and Mum was expecting her fourth child. We moved to London, life in Birmingham was incredibly stressful for Mum, she had social services on her back as she was struggling so much with three children and Dad's gambling. We moved so she could be closer to her own family and have some much-needed support from her four sisters.

In later life, whilst doing the research for this book, I applied for my Subject Access Report from Social Services (SAR) from Hammersmith and Fulham. A report that is complete with all the information relating to my family's involvement with Social Services and Child Protection. Thirty-eight pages long and the opening line, "This family are extensively known to Birmingham Social Services."

I made a conscious decision not to go the step further and apply for the SAR from our time in Birmingham. The SAR I requested referred to Birmingham Social Services attending our home investigating reports of child abuse. An anonymous person had reported seeing my mum hitting young children. None of us kids were ever removed from the home in Birmingham, and this was a contributory factor in the move to London. I didn't, as most children do not have any memories of my childhood before the age of 2 and I didn't wish to know any more than I already did about my childhood.

I can't imagine the stress Mum was under, caring for and feeding her young family whilst subject to the pressures of my dad's gambling and carrying another child. I'm sure it didn't help with overcoming or learning how to handle her emotions. Mum didn't have good coping mechanisms; upon reflection I think she was an undiagnosed autistic. She couldn't read or write and had behavioural issues. She did, however, do such an excellent job of masking her disabilities, I didn't know she couldn't read or write until I was in secondary school. She would say things like "I don't have my reading glasses" if I needed help with my homework or "Go and ask your dad."

Her childhood was a difficult one, she would often say, "Let no spoken word over you hold you back." For whatever reason, she was rejected by her mum. Mum was the second eldest behind my Uncle Barry and the eldest female of five girls. She was also considered 'the black sheep' in the family. Mum's sister, my Aunt Julie said Mum was unhappy most of her childhood. At school, Julie remembers Mum getting the cane because she couldn't sit still on her chair, at home, she wasn't the oldest and she wasn't the youngest; she just wasn't noticed and maybe that's why she acted out and was sent to a boarding school for children with behavioural problems. Julie said Mum "was a nutter;" but she always made her laugh.

Mum's dad, Grandad Reggie Rubens, was Jewish and a Rabbi. He had a number tattooed on his arm from the Holocaust, but he never spoke about this with anyone. He was very cold and selective in how he treated his kids and grandchildren. He might give one a pound coin, and another just ten pence.

At eleven, I gave my life to Christ, and Grandad disowned me. Being a highly respected member of the local Jewish Synagogue, he felt my newly found Christian status brought shame on him and the family. However, I was not alone, when my Aunt Julie got married to Uncle Lee, she converted to Catholicism. Her marriage was even televised by the BBC, which upset Grandad greatly; he shunned her and her family excluding them from his Will. Despite the Holocaust happening two generations before my birth, its aftermath ripped through our family in an undeniable display of coldness, cruelty, and separation. Aunt Julie shared with me that Grandad would sometimes wake his children by pouring a bucket of yellowed baby bath water over them. Rancid, cold, dirty water that had been sitting outside for days, flung over kids to wake them in the morning. Mum was six or seven when she became ill and that is how she contracted polio.

Mum was in hospital in an iron lung, on and off for two years, keeping her alive. Affecting her schooling and having a knock-on effect on the rest of her life; falling behind the other kids her age. To make matters worse, Mum had severe dyslexia and after being treated for Polio she never caught up, she was functionally illiterate for the rest of her life. About a month after Mum was discharged from the hospital, she was playing outside and was hit by a motorbike as she tried to cross the road. That put her back in hospital, this time with broken legs. She didn't have it easy at all.

Age eleven, Mum was sent to boarding school. She liked being the centre of attention and at home, she wasn't, acting out, an attempt to seek the attention and love she so desperately craved and had not previously received. She acted out at boarding school too, running away with a friend, bunking together on the train whenever she had the chance. She hated that boarding school so much she would take the train home, she just wanted to be home.

At fifteen Mum left school to work as a hairdresser and at seventeen she met dad at a club called the Hammersmith Palais. They were childhood sweethearts. Aunt Julie said Mum was so happy it beamed from her face; she was a different person. On her eighteenth birthday she gave birth to my brother, Art. Not welcome in her family home any longer she moved into a mother and baby unit in Tunbridge Wells, Kent and at nineteen she got married to Dad in Fulham Town Hall. It was not long after that they moved to Meriden, Birmingham, where I was born two years later.

After leaving Birmingham and returning to London, we did move in with Mum's mum for a while in Fulham. Known only to me as Nan, I don't have any memories of living with her when we first got to London, but I do remember her being stern and mean. She had the look, like a "don't mess with me" scary, look. I don't remember her being kind or gentle, ever and she never had anything nice to say about anyone. I didn't even know Nan's name was Barbara until I was about thirteen, we no longer lived with her, and someone called the house phone asking for my Mum. I said "She's at my Nan's, would you like the number? You can call her there." Of course, they asked me for my Nan's name, and I just replied, "I don't know her name, I just know her as Nan." Isn't that strange?

It must have been very crowded when we first moved to London and stayed at Nan's, there would have been my mum, pregnant at the time, Dad, Art, Me and Jane, Grandad Frank (her second husband) and my four aunties - Julie, Molly, Trudy, and Beth. All in what I think was a small three-bedroom flat, in a block. Dad was paying Nan £100 a week in rent which was a lot of money back then, he would tell me stories of how Art had to sleep in the bottom drawer. God only knows how we all fitted in, but we did.

After having George and a stressful move, it wasn't long before our family from Birmingham came to meet the new addition to the family and see our now home. Upon the rest of the family's departure, Dad's brother, Uncle Rob decided to stay with us, for the first time. Dad was about to leave for a job in Egypt as a driver for a Sheikh and would be gone for a few weeks - Rob had nowhere else to stay and Dad convinced Mum to let him stay at ours. During this time, Uncle Rob became friendly with a man named Ted, he lived in one of the mansions opposite our house and subsequently introduced him to the family.

Whilst Dad was away, Mum quickly became agitated at the situation, but this time Dad was not there to protect me. It was always me she took any stress out on, and after being scolded by my Mum, Nan had taken me to the doctors with a cut to my ear. The GP diagnosed me with a burst ear drum, a result of the kick I had taken to the head and Social Services were once again involved in our lives.

When my brother George was born, my Mum and Dad refused to leave the hospital as Nan didn't want another baby in the house as it was already incredibly stressful for everyone there. Eventually, my parents were given a council house in Musard Road Fulham, a three-bedroom converted house on the corner of a quiet street. It had a wooden gate which swung open leading to a place designated for a car, but we didn't have a car, so we used this space as our back yard to play in. My brothers shared a room, which I think must have been an extension added to the house as there was a sewer hole in the middle of their room. In the summer it would smell and one year sewage water came up ruining the carpet and the boys got extremely sick - this being one of the reasons that later we ended up having to move.

Entering the house through the front door you were met with a small hallway, at the end were two doors. One leading upstairs to the flat above us and the other lead to our home. To the left was mine and Jane's bedroom, it was a massive room with a big bay window, likely it was previously used as a living room before the house was split into two. It had a chimney wall in the centre of the room, although now just a plastered-up wall I'm sure when the house was first built this would have been the fireplace. We only had one heater for the whole house which was placed in what was our living room; money was tight with Dad's gambling, so it was not always possible to put the heater on. Mum and Dad paid for gas and electricity by way of coin meter and oh, how I wished they had left the open fireplace. I remember greatly the extremely cold nights, especially during the winter months, sometimes sleeping with many layers on to try and keep warm. Sharing a room meant that I had my little sister Jane, she was a great way to keep warm, I would often sneak into her bed and snuggle up with her.

Following on from my burst ear drum, we were now known to our new, local child protective services, and they started by quickly finding a placement at Greyhound Road Nursery and Family playgroup for all of us. They wanted to assess Mum's parenting around all her children, it was also a place she could get advice and the staff would be keeping Social Services informed of how she appeared to be coping or any further incidents that may take place. The notes in the SAR from the time states I was "very quiet and withdrawn," apart from a mention of one time when I was behaving "out of sorts" and very unlike my usually timid self; fearful, tearful and scared.

Ted, Uncle Rob's friend, was now a frequenting figure in our lives. He would often play cricket with the boys and Dad in the summer months. There was a cul-de-sac just beside the mansions across from our house, which also sat in front of the primary school, cars didn't have access to the area and that is where we used to play. There was also big, green, iron gates which we would use as a backstop and in the summer months, stumps were painted onto the gate in white paint. Dad loved cricket, he loved playing it and watching it and down our street there was always a real sense of community; lots of young families living there. My parents were quite social, and Mum had a big family living close by, so there were always people in and out of the house.

My dad was the second of three children, each born a year apart. The eldest, Aunt Monica, born August 1950. My dad was born in September the following year, leaving Uncle Rob, the youngest of three. Born exactly one year later, on Dad's birthday. According to the records from the Archdiocese of Birmingham, my paternal Grandfather left my Nan after Rob was born. She was struggling physically with anaemia and heart problems. The notes I obtained stated the doctor had suggested she go to a convalescent home, but that was, of course, out of the question with three children to raise. I'm certain her health issues and a combination of emotional devastation, after her husband leaving them to fend for themselves, are the route of the devastating decision she ended up making. All three were bought up in Catholic Children's Homes. A heart-breaking choice for any mother to make.

I retrieved their records from the children's home. The application to Father Hudson says my grandfather left my Nan for "someone he liked better." Grandad Bill leaving Nanny Lilly made it almost impossible for her to provide a stable home for three children with her ill health. The emotional toll of abandonment made lovingly taking care of them a trying task; knowing they didn't have everything that kids need and deserve. It was mentioned in the notes my Nan was quite a nice person but rather weak with the children, allowing them to do whatever they pleased. It was clear, she couldn't handle the boys on her own, without the firm hand of a father figure. It was when Rob was four, Dad was five and Monica six that they were placed in the home. In the notes, one of the Nuns asked Nan the question, "How long do you think it will be before you're able to look after the children yourself? When do you expect them to be returned home?" Her reply, "When Monica is old enough and can help look after the boys." She was only six years old.

So off they went to live at St. Margaret's House, part of Father Hudson Homes in Birmingham. My Aunt Monica was the sweetest and still is. The gentlest, kindest and most loving soul I've encountered, I love her so much; she's an awesome aunt and a wonderful Mum to my cousins, she wouldn't say boo to a goose. She had a great relationship with my dad and despite their small, one year age gap, was like a mother to him. Dad and she were very similar in nature, and as per the homes records my nans intentions were that the boys could come out of boarding school when Monica was older because she was so great with them; she had a natural motherly way about her.

My Nanny Lilly must have worried greatly as the children were in the home, as she focused her hopes on Monica reaching an age where they could all return. Monica had taken great care of the boys even whilst they were home with my nan despite her young age. I will never forget the happiness in my dad's eyes and the smile that would beam across his face whenever he saw my aunt in later life. Aunt Monica did eventually get to go home again and live with Nanny Lilly, whilst the boys stayed at boarding school.

At some point, they were transferred to St. Edward's Home for Boys in Birmingham. It was here that they came to the attention of Father Eric Taylor. Both my dad and Uncle Rob were subjected to and became victims of sexual abuse, at the hands of Father Eric Taylor during their time at the home. My dad was one of Father Taylor's altar boys and remembers being taken to the hospital at the age of ten, maybe eleven and being diagnosed with Syphilis. The Nuns would take him regularly to the hospital for treatment and because of the ordeal Dad suffered an overwhelming phobia of hospitals.

In 1998 Father Taylor was convicted of sexual offences against boys as young as six years old. He died in prison in 2001.

In 2021, Dad was diagnosed with terminal Stage 4 anal cancer, and it was confirmed to be a direct result of the abuse he suffered as a child.

Here is just one extract from a BBC news article. One of many articles. Containing dreadful accounts, relating to that same school, shared by brave survivors. Abused in a home run by Priests and Nuns, the very people entrusted to take care of already vulnerable children and in the name of God.

Thursday, 30 April 1998, BBC UK

Paedophile Priest Jailed

Father Eric Taylor: abused boys as young as six!

A Roman Catholic priest has been jailed for seven years for sexually abusing boys at an orphanage. The offences took place at the Father Hudson Society's home in Warwickshire, between 1957 and 1965. Some of the boys were as young as six.

Father Eric Taylor, 78, was convicted at Warwick Crown Court on 16 charges of indecent assault and two more serious charges on boys at the Father Hudson's home in Coleshill, Warwickshire.

The court was told Taylor, now of Aston-By-Stone, Staffordshire, abused boys and then stood by as they were beaten by nuns for complaining about their ordeals. Taylor, who denied all the charges, was found not guilty of a further three charges.

He was jailed for seven years on the two most serious offences and five years for indecent assault. The sentences will run alongside each other.

After the jury returned their verdicts, the court was told how Taylor had previous convictions for indecent assault.

Taylor had abused four boys at his vicarage in Worcestershire in 1975.

One of the jurors broke down as the priest was convicted, the judge telling him he was a disgrace to his cloth and the church he proclaimed.

"Your victims were not only young, but they were helpless, you were the nearest thing they had to a father figure," he added.

Throughout his trial, middle-aged men gave graphic evidence of what Taylor had done to them. Some likened the regime to a concentration camp in which they were known by number rather than name.

One said: "This is a victory for justice. The forces of good will always catch up with him."

Another told the BBC about a reign of terror at the home, which he called Taylor's "harem".

However, some were not around to see Taylor sent down, having committed suicide because they could not live with what the priest had done to them.

At age of 82, the former Worcester pervert priest who was jailed for a string of sex offences against young boys died in prison.

Father Eric Taylor, who was imprisoned for seven years in 1998 after being found guilty at Warwick Crown Court of 18 sexual offences against children, was found dead in his prison cell. He was due to go before a parole board a few weeks before his death, after serving half of his sentence.

Taylor, who was branded a "disgrace to his cloth" by the trial judge in 1998, had abused boys over an eight-year period at Father Hudson's Orphanage, in Coleshill, Warwickshire. He had attacked them as they were enjoying "treats" or when they were in bed sick, and often forced children to engage in sex acts. He also frequently kissed choirboys before and after practice.

Taylor was also fined £250 by Worcester magistrates in 1975 after admitting indecently assaulting four young boys at his Tolladine Road home. He had enticed the youngsters into his house with offers of drink and cigarettes.

****

On 1 February 2001, Eric Taylor received and accepted the decision of Pope John Paul II by which he is returned to the lay state within the Catholic Church.

From that moment, he was no longer a Catholic priest.

My Dad, just before his death, shared with me some of the things he had experienced throughout this time in his life. One being what he referred to as "the red hand gang." Father Taylor would give 'special' boys a slap, marking them with a red handprint, meaning they were selected to attend a special communion with him. Here they would be offered wine and would be allowed to smoke, he would get them drunk and this is when the assaults would take place.

He told of horrid beatings and the terrible treatment from the Nuns. The embarrassment the children were subjected to if they did anything wrong, such as wetting the bed. Boys were made to stand naked in the school grounds following a bed wetting, the other children were made to point and snigger.

After doing a little research, I learnt that Father Eric Taylor had many demons of his own. One being trauma caused after being held a prisoner of war; who knows exactly how badly he was treated or even what his childhood was like, but it's often the case that children who are abused are much more likely to become adults who abuse. In fact, 30-40% of people who are abused as children, go on to become abusers. Other studies on sexually abused boys have shown that around one in five continue in later life to victimise and molest children themselves.

Dad was very different from Mum, he was always quiet and extremely nurturing, encouraging and positive in his parenting. He could always see the good in people. He was an honest man and a very poor liar; you could see right through him when he lied; written all over his face as his cheeks went red and his eyebrows white. My dad never had a bad thing to say about me, or anyone for that matter. He was always singing my praises, my biggest supporter, which made my Mum jealous. Dad loved my long, curly blonde hair and made sure I knew I was beautiful in his eyes. He was really the only constant when it came to giving me any positive, loving attention. Mum was always calling me stupid and hated that I might outshine her.

One night they got into an argument over the attention towards me. The following day, Mum sat me down and cut of all my hair. She was a hairdresser and didn't just cut it, she could have given me a nice new look. Instead, she chopped my hair until it was sticking out all over the place. The next day we had school photos, I was beside myself and when Dad got home, he was devastated.

That was the cycle; there would be an argument between my parents, and the next day, after Dad went to work, Mum would blame me for the argument. She would punish me, by having me clean the house, she would have me brush the carpet with a hairbrush until you could see footprints in the pile when you walked over it – or whatever else she could think of to make things miserable for me. If it wasn't for my dad, I don't know how I would have ever made it through my childhood. His love was unconditional.

At one time, I really wanted to be an Air Hostess. Dad encouraged me as he always did, reminding me how proud of me he was, Mum hated that but all I wanted was to be accepted, especially by my Mum. I could never measure up, I tried so hard to please her. I once asked Aunt Julie why she thought my Mum was the way she was with me, she answered quickly, "It's because you're the pretty one." I think at a point, my dad began to figure this out, so he stopped praising me as much when she was around because he didn't want to make it worse for me when he left for work. More than anything I just wanted to be loved and accepted by Mum. I just wanted her to acknowledge me, be proud of me, but I never achieved it. Never once, not a day in my whole life did my mother ever tell me she was proud of me.

I thought if I went into hairdressing like she did after my exams, rather than continuing at school, it would please her. Dad really wanted me to stay on at school, but Mum was a hairdresser and I thought if I took after her then she would be proud. Instead, it just confirmed to her what she spoke over me, that I would never make anything of myself. Mum couldn't read or write, and she was threatened by me already, so I couldn't be smarter than her too and go onto higher levels of schooling. I was however the only one in the family who finished school and completed all my GCSEs.

Maybe the things that were important to me meant nothing to her. For example, following the birth of my autistic daughter, we took part in a show being filmed by Channel 4. A documentary aired as four, one-hour long episodes and we were followed by a film crew for almost six months. It wasn't easy; the show was called "Young, Autistic & Stagestruck". After the completion of filming, I set up a support group helping families of children with disabilities. I went on to be nominated for a Community Champion Award that covered nominees from the whole of Great Britain and - I won!

I was then part of a small documentary, filmed by the Community Channel, showing the work I did supporting almost 2000 families with disabled children. Mum never acknowledged the documentary that featured my work. After my near- death experience, I was a chaplain in two prisons and a pastoral support worker in a very large church; work that I love doing, serving God and others. All I ever wanted was to hear how proud she was of me, to hear that she loved me. But nothing I ever did would ever be good enough for her.

I'm sure she did love me in her own way, she just didn't know how to show it. I came to understand Mum a lot better as I have learned more about her childhood experiences. It was very healing, and I was able to show more grace and understanding about my upbringing. It is heartbreaking, but Mum was never shown love herself. She really didn't know how to love or show affection. She wasn't loved herself, and as I've discovered, you can't give what you haven't got.

As I got older, it seemed the more I did to better myself, to make her proud, the more she resented me. I just couldn't please her. I was always left wanting.

I think as Mum saw Dad protecting me from her, she was reminded of the love that she did not get or receive in any way from her own parents. The angrier she got, the more he would protect me. I was stuck in the middle. Mum favoured the boys over the girls – it was as clear as day and everyone knew it. Everyone knew that George was Mum's favourite. She did not manage to hide all the scars of life; the stress really did take a toll on her. Her body really did keep the score of all the trauma she was carrying.

Mum had cancer twenty-one times and died on 23 July 2015 at Trinity Hospice, London. In the time I spent with her as she was dying; I think I was always waiting for her to finally say the words, "I'm proud of you Sabina". When she lay dying in a bed at the hospice, I never left her side for the last two weeks she was alive. I would hear her telling the nurses stories of all my siblings, how proud she was of them, but never once did she mention me. Still, I'm so very glad I did stay with her, as four days before she died, she gave her life to Christ. Just me and Mum while listening to the words of the song Oceans. This was a massive thing for me. She was Jewish after all, a Rubens, and her father had drummed it into her how important that was.

My father passed away in January 2023. I was with him when he received the diagnosis that would come to be his end. Not only was he told he was dying, but he also had to accept that this, after all these years was yet again another scar left behind by the actions of Father Eric Taylor. As soon as he walked out the consulting room with the doctor, he said to me, "I want to give the pope a piece of my mind". Being a safeguarding officer myself for vulnerable adults, I began my mission to seek the apology my beautiful Daddy deserved. I wrote to the archbishop on my father's behalf and at his request. It was important for me to get this apology for my dad and not just for him but also for myself.

The Church was responsible from the start; all my sexual abuse may never have happened to me if it hadn't first been done to my abuser by a Priest. I never got an apology from my perpetrator before he died, I didn't want the same for Dad, and this is where it all started. I also wanted my dad to be in the best position possible to meet our Papa God. Before my wonderful Daddy died, he got the apology from the Church that he was looking for, in writing; it wasn't from the Pope, but it was the next best thing. My job was done.

Attached is the letter I sent the archbishop;

11 November 2021

To whom it may concern,

My name is Rev'd Sabina Harmony. I am an ordained Minister and Chaplain and have served as Family Support Worker at The Nehemiah Project, a residential, supported-housing rehabilitation programme for men coming out of prison who have drug and alcohol addictions. I have also served as Chaplain in Brixton Prison, and with my husband Bob, helped run a programme called Principles for Life at Wandsworth Prison. I have served as a Safeguarding Officer and pastoral support worker, and counsellor. I also focus on inner healing and the mind, body, spirit connection through Psychodynamic Therapy and trauma healing.

I am writing on behalf of my Father, William (DOB 18/09/1951). He lived at St Edwards's Boys Home, Coleshill, Warwickshire from ages five to ten, and was a victim of sexual abuse as were many other young boys. Dad remembers falling ill and being taken to hospital by nuns at St Gilbert's School for Boys, Hartlebury, Worcestershire when he was eleven years old and being treated for Syphilis. Today, my dad is dying from anal cancer.

My dad's younger brother Rob (DOB 18/09/1952), now deceased, also lived at St Edward's Boys Home with my dad, and their older sister Monica. Rob also suffered sexual abuse at the home and then turned it on me, sexually abusing me, his niece, beginning when I was five years old and continuing until I was fifteen.

My Dad is not interested in a financial pay-out for the abuse he suffered at the hands of those he was entrusted to as a young boy. Instead, what I want for my dad, his dying wish, is an apology, some sign of remorse for causing his lifelong guilt, shame and anger, and acknowledgement of his pain: physically, emotionally and spiritually.

I cannot begin to express the anguish the Church has caused my family, robbing my dad and his younger brother of their innocence, and the ripple effect continuing into the next generation, having my own innocence stolen by my uncle because of what he experienced while under the care of priests and nuns.

I have forgiven my uncle and the Church for being the source of such pain and suffering in my family. After being diagnosed with Stage 4 anal cancer, my dad asked me to write to the Pope, especially because the medical staff stated definitively that his cancer was caused by the sexual abuse he suffered as a young boy in Father Hudson's home.

Now, I am asking the Church to hear us – my dad, my uncle, and myself – as victims crying out to be heard. I am asking for an apology, not in the form of a cheque, but a heartfelt written apology from the Archdiocese of Birmingham, compassionately acknowledging my dad's pain and suffering, and the anger and trauma he has had to live with his entire life.

Is it too much to ask the Church, God's instrument of healing, restoration, truth and love, to respond now with compassion, humility, and grace? To fulfil a dying man's, wish to be heard, and for the young boy inside to be told "it wasn't your fault"? By faith, I choose to believe it isn't. Please contact me if you have any questions or need further information. I look forward to your timely response.

In Christ,

Rev'd Sabina Harmony

It's not until we are older do we realise the impact of the way our relationships are formed with our parents and how this impacts our entire life. It also impacts the way we raise our own children and how all our relationships are formed with those around us; the way we are raised affects our whole life. It's called in the psychology field, "attachment theory". When I researched it myself as I was studying to become a psychodynamic psychotherapist, I was amazed at its findings, and it also jogged a childhood memory.

I remember at around the age of six in the very early eighties, being taken to what I think must have been a hospital setting. I remember walking there with Mum and it being in a building very close to Charring Cross Hospital, at the end of Greyhound Road, just down from the nursery setting that the Social Services had put in place for Mum to be assessed with all her children. It was not far from where we lived, in fact it was just two streets away. I remember being in a room with some toys in it and one whole wall just being one big mirror. I remember my Mum taking me, leaving me to play with what must have been a doctor and coming back a little while later. I think it may have been an assessment in "attachment theory", because I remember at the end being told by Mum, she could see everything I had been doing. I thought, oh no, have I done something wrong? Am I going to get told off or worse? A beating when I get home… I remember being quite amazed at being shown how the two-way mirror worked, by being taken into the next room to see the room I was just playing in through a big clear window.

I would really recommend looking up what your "attachment style" is. Our personality and relationship style are greatly formed by our childhood experiences and how we were parented. We adopt from our parents some of their own parenting models. These "attachment styles" drive our own relationships like scripts running in the background that we are unaware of until we are made aware of them, if ever, and we have therapy to tackle the curse of abuse. My Father fought to keep our family together; there was a very unhealthy "attachment style" running through our family, dating back to the Holocaust and the abuse that happened to my father at the Hudson home.

At the age of four, in my SAR report obtained from Social Services, there were letters addressed to the court from a social worker, about the possibility of having me put into care. My dad was due to attend court for a petty crime and the letter stated that "if Mr William Harmony was sent to prison, Sabina would be put into care for her safety". My beautiful Daddy must have been trying to protect me from what had happened to him and could possibly happen to his little girl if I was put into care by Social Services. If only he knew.

My fight for Justice

I am now in contact with the Roman Catholic Church in Birmingham after writing to The Archbishop and informing the Church of the abuse my Dad and uncle suffered. I must say, he has been most kind and gracious in his support.

After I had sent the email to the Archbishop, I went into my bathroom, I fell to my knees, crying, praying and begging for God to do something. He did, He heard my cry, and my prayer was answered within twenty-eight minutes of sending the email, The Archbishop called me back himself with an apology. That phone call was about an hour long; it was the most healing phone call of my life. I felt his compassion. I felt the Christ-like love. I could tell he cared. He didn't get his PA to reply, he was so moved by my email that he picked up the phone and called me himself. He also came to see my Dad on his death bed, a few days before he was promoted, to give him the apology in person and to ask his forgiveness, to let him know and to allow him to hear the words, "It wasn't your fault".

The most beautiful blessing I received was when he came to visit my Father, and before he left, he asked me to pray for him. Not Bob, but me, it was such an honour. I thank the Lord for using him and his beautiful spirit- filled heart, he gave me something that me and my beautiful Daddy always needed, to hear the words, it wasn't our fault and an apology.

The Archbishop felt called to hold a special mass for my Dad after his death, on Ascension Day at Southwark Cathedral. It was held in a private chapel at the side of the

Church. He asked that my dad be free from any account of the abuse that he suffered and soul injury that he had carried his whole life. I brought my friend Caroline along with me. My siblings were invited but they did not attend, understandably so – as unbelievers they are still very angry with the Church and what it did to our family. The mass was truly beautiful and so very special. We witnessed my Dad's forgiveness ceremony where I tangibly felt the breaking off and deliverance of so much generational trauma. We prayed for all my siblings and for reconciliation, which is what I know my Father would want for us.

This is the letter of apology which was sent to my Father on beautiful headed paper, which I placed in my Father's' hand when they come to collect his body from his home to be cremated:

Dear Mr William ....

I was so grateful to hear from your daughter, Rev Sabina Harmony, a few days ago in her email and when we spoke, she told me about some of the terrible and criminal abuse that you suffered as a child at St Edward's Home in Coleshill and about its continuing impact upon you and the members of your family.

I wish to offer you, on behalf of the Archdiocese of Birmingham, my sincere and unequivocal apology for all that you suffered at that time from the very people from whom you had every right to receive nothing but care and support in the name of the Catholic Church.

I also offer my heartfelt apologies for the heavy burden that you and your family have been carrying for many years because of those dreadful experiences. I feel nothing but shame that you were made to suffer in such a way.

I sincerely hope that my letter will bring you some comfort and peace of mind, and if I can offer help in any other way to you or your family, I would be grateful to know. I have no right to expect you to forgive the Catholic Church for what you have gone through, but you do have every right to hear me ask you for your forgiveness – and I do so wholeheartedly.

If it is acceptable to you, please accept my prayers for you and your family. I repeat my thanks to your daughter for contacting me and I wish you all ever blessing in the years ahead.

With my kindest wishes. Yours sincerely

Signed

Archbishop Bernard Langley.

****

Spiritual warfare is a spiritual battle. The enemy doesn't want us to be free, he wants us to be captives to our past and the pain of our trauma; he wants us to forgive; he wants our hearts full of anger and pain. He knows what separates us from God, but it's our choice to decide which father we follow, Father God or the father of lies!

Dad wrote a Will. He had nothing to leave behind as he had gambled everything away. There was only one thing listed in his will which was: "In the event of my passing, if any claim is to be made against the Roman Catholic Church, all four siblings have to agree." I pray that one day my Dad's final wish will come true, that we can reunite and have reconciliation. Both my Father and I didn't want hush money. My Daddy put it like this, "If I was to take a pay-out and I brought anything with it, even as much as a lampshade, I will always see that lampshade and know how it was brought, always reminding me of what happened!" That's why he never took a pay-out before his passing. My siblings didn't see it that way. I think it angered them as he never supported us growing up financially while we were growing up because of his gambling habit and now he had a possibility to do so with a pay-out but chose not to. My Father was also worried that my brother George would possibly spend it on drugs, possibly putting a final nail in his coffin. So, he left the will saying we all had to agree to make a claim. After his death and the sad way my siblings were treating me, I relented but 100% of my quarter share will go into the Harmony Healing Foundation to help anyone who has suffered any form of abuse or trauma.

Healing does not have to be a long process when one is afforded with the knowledge they need to get well and live a peaceful life beyond childhood trauma. I would like "Harmony Healing House Foundation" to be a place of refuge for anyone that requires trauma therapy of any kind. A safe space where people can come and find understanding, compassion, love and kindness as well as a listening ear to be heard. To be believed. It will be a place of inner healing for the mind, body and spirit. 100% of the proceeds of this book will also go into the foundation and to support helping to heal others, as well as 100% of my part of any pay-out that is split between the four siblings made to us by the church.

Chapter three

Family Life

"Whoever claims to love God yet hates a brother or sister is a liar.

"For whoever does not love their brother and sister, whom they have seen, cannot love God, whom they have not seen." – 1 John 4:20

It was a bright sunny day as we played in the garden at Greyhound Nursery, Fulham. I was just over four years old and little George was almost two. They had a chicken pen in the garden and whilst there we would be accompanied into the chicken pen to collect the eggs, which was so much fun. Inside they had a large area where various play stations would be set up, some with crafts, some with toys. I also hold joyful memories of singing the song 'Oranges and Lemons', dancing under each other's arms, held high making a bridge as a long line of children passed through. As you came out of the main play area into the garden there was a bush with small, red berries on it. Little did we know our little George had taken a liking to the berries. Just outside the nursery there was a brick wall with a built-in flowerbed and on the top were bushes. We would sometimes sit on the wall waiting for Mum to put George in his Silver Cross pram that Dad had found. Dad was a rubbish collector in Knightsbridge and all through our childhood he would bring back great treasures that people had thrown away. He would always say, "Where there is muck, there is money."

The wall was maybe two feet high, and I loved walking on top of it, I loved walking on every wall I could find as most kids do. As I sat on the wall waiting for Mum, I noticed this little orange pot and it looked to me like a lovely pot of sweeties. Being the child that never got and never asked for fear of punishment, I saw it and I claimed it as mine and I didn't want to share. I could savour these sweets for a long time, and no one would know. I didn't want to share them with Art, Jane or George; that little transparent orange pot was mine.

It was like a new two-in-one toy; sweets and a shaker or somewhere to store little treasures. After I had eaten all the sweets, I thought I could use the pretty orange pot to store precious things. I got very attached to things; I still am, but silly things that remind me of happy and special times. I'm a 'it's the little things' type of person. I keep cards and tokens of love, gifts that remind me of happy memories. Lavish things don't mean much to me. Maybe I didn't see myself worthy of nice things. I had no idea that this beautiful orange pot filled with sweets would be a life-long memory. I didn't know it wasn't a pot of sweeties. It was a pot of medicine, tablets that must have fallen out of someone's bag. So, I picked them up. Yes, it was finders' keepers in our house, but most of the time they found my stuff and kept it. That's sibling rivalry for you. There were four of us kids with just five years between us all. I was the timid, quiet, lonely little second child that felt nobody wanted her.

The walk home wasn't a long one but the whole time I was fixated on keeping my newfound treasure safe. How was I going to make sure that nobody else found my little pot of sweeties? The whole time the pills rattled around in the pot with every step I took. I walked along the walls at a much slower pace in hope nobody would hear it, I risked the wrath of mum demanding I kept up. I couldn't eat them there and then; they would have asked immediately what I was eating. The walk had felt longer than usual as I protected my findings, as soon as we arrived home everyone was so busy I could finally, safely stash my cargo. But where I thought. Maybe I could spill out the 'sweeties' and keep the special pot to put things in. Hmmm, what to do?

Not long after walking through the door, little George began throwing up. Seems he had been eating the red berries from the bush at the nursery, we could clearly see the berries and it smelled horrid. Immediately feeling sick myself but mainly sorry for my baby brother; I think I was born an empath; I've always had a gentle heart and a particular place in it for my George. When he had a poo, it was a stinky green, which further worried Mum. "What's your father going to say?". Not that it was much of a threat, my dad wouldn't hurt a fly. But I knew and I had learnt very early on, when Mum said those words, it meant that I would probably receive a whipping shortly after. From her of course, never Dad. I don't remember my dad raising a single hand to me, ever.

Whilst writing this book, I asked my siblings and like me, they don't either. Apart from one time, George was quietly playing in the kitchen, roughly nine years old; Dad and Art were watching football together. Dad had asked Art to check on George, it was just too quiet. Art found him in the kitchen, little splattered droplets of blood, everywhere. He'd taken a liking to the metal broom handle and wanting to use it as a lightsabre he attempted to strip the white coating off the pole using a sharp knife, so it looked more like the one's in Star Wars. In doing so, he had sliced his finger open, shaking his hand in the air causing the splatter as he panicked.

Art went to get Dad, leading him to the blood splattered kitchen; Dad being Dad, an empath too with a deep routed fear of hospitals, any type of medical situation, made him feel helpless. I think it was the shock, possibly triggering a memory of his own as his actions were far from normal. Turning to Art, he slapped him, and he shouted, "Sort your brother out." This is the only recollection any of us children have of Dad every raising his hand to any of us. Maybe he knew Mum dispensed enough of the beatings, most of the time, me at the receiving end.

Panic spread across Mum's face in anticipation of a trip to A&E with little George, he had poisoned himself by consuming the berries - he was too young to have known and nobody saw him eating them. Taking us all along would have been impossible for Mum, she called one of her sisters to watch over us. In the motion of all the drama, I took my special orange pot into my room with ease. I opened it up and to my delight I was met with the prettiest of pink sweeties, my favourite colour. Not believing my luck, I quickly took one, placing it in my mouth and at equal speed realising it wasn't very nice at all. I was disappointed but excited all at once, it doesn't matter that they're not the best, they're sweets. I thought my little brother may like them, that may help cheer him up...

Big mistake, very, very big mistake, what happened next went from bad to worse. Me, with the best of intentions, emptied all the sweets from the pot, pouring them into my hand George was sitting on Mum's lap. Still looking very green in complexion I was desperate to cheer him up. Approaching timidly, as I always did when Mum was in a bad mood, in the sweetest voice "Here you go George, you can have these. They will make you feel better, I saved you, my sweets. I don't want them; you can have them."

Immediately, questions came firing from Mum, asking them faster than I could process the last one asked. "What are these? Where have these come from? Why do you have them?" Questions flying around the room, my auntie had just arrived but still I felt no comfort, just fear and worry. "How many have you eaten? Where did you get them?" she repeated. I stammered, and the more I stammered the angrier Mum became, I just didn't understand what I had done wrong. Did she think I had stolen them; she was going to beat me, I didn't know what to say or do, I froze. At this point, it wasn't just Mum asking questions. "We need to know what these are and where they came from!" they demanded.

I still wanted my little orange pot, the white lid made a cool noise when you popped it open, I was attached, it was special to me, I found it. I began crying and still stammering, now choking on any attempt of words, nothing was coming out. Finally, I spat it out, I answered the question, I found an orange pot with pink sweets. The adults continued to scream and yell and then began to mention dying and needing to go to the hospital. All of a sudden, they're telling me that my pink sweeties are poison too, I had just seen what happened to little George and a different fear was setting in. All I can hear is from Mum is "Tell me, tell me, tell me!" and then the slaps arrived. "Do you want another one? If you don't tell me how many you have eaten..." SLAP! How can any child speak through tears and the slapping? At this point, I'm unsure if I said anything and now both me and George had a trip to the hospital with possible poisoning. Sometimes the less said, the better and I learnt this very early on, but not this time, saying nothing made her angrier.

On the walk to Charring Cross Hospital, Mum was still freaking out. She was relentless the whole way there, ten minutes of the same question's they had repeatedly asked me at home. Ten minutes of slapping me, screaming at me, all whilst pushing my green faced little George in his pram. I just had no idea what was going on, or how my little pink sweets had gotten me into so much trouble. I didn't feel sick or like I was about to die. Would the one I had eaten kill me?

Mum was terrible in crisis, what must have been going through her head? Looking back, as an adult and a mother myself, I can only imagine how she felt at that moment. She just wanted information. I don't remember much from the hospital, but I remember getting home and being told my pink sweeties weren't sweeties but medicine and taking medicines that aren't prescribed for you, can kill you. Mostly, I just remember the beating and the intense fear of dying like they were telling me. Through the eyes of a four-year-old, a child, this was not a fun memory.

****

My mum was petite in stature but big in personality. Her personality and her voice were much bigger than her slim build. She had a wicked sense of humour and loved being the centre of attention. But she suffered with health problems throughout her life. Aunt Julie estimated that Mum had probably spent a cumulative total of eight years of her life in and out of hospital with various illnesses. While she recovered from Polio, the effects of the disease continued to give her problems the rest of her life.

After having children, she spent the weekends going to the old folks' home and doing the ladies hair. She did it because she wanted to give back and help in the community, she would often take us with her. I have fond memories of visiting the ladies in the home. We would often get to go to Bishops Park in the summer after she had finished work, as it was right by the home. The old ladies would sometimes give us 10p to buy ourselves some sweets and Mum only charged £1.50 for their hair, oh how times have changed! This was to cover the products really; unfortunately, she had to stop because someone informed the benefits people she was working. The women in the home loved it when Mum visited, being fussed over and pampered. Everyone was sad when Mum was forced to stop. Later, she worked as a dinner lady at a school in Knightsbridge. Often, if Dad had gambled all his wages, then our dinner meals were leftovers from school lunches - so we never went hungry. Working in the school kitchens meant she could also be home with us during mid-term and the summer holiday breaks.

Mum was labelled a problem child, the black sheep of the family but that may have hidden some deeper issues. Back in those days, there wasn't much testing for Autism, even more so in girls or other testing for learning disabilities. I gained so much more understanding and respect for Mum after I was blessed with having a daughter who was then diagnosed with Autism, ADHD, PICA, PDA, Epilepsy, as well as severe learning difficulties.

Raising my beautiful daughter Mary helped me to understand Mum's difficult childhood a little better. I see my Mum in my daughter so much and it's helped me to see her in a different light today than I did then. It makes me love her even more knowing how much she must have struggled in this dark and difficult world with her disabilities. I now believe God gave me a beautiful gift in my daughter Mary, to help me understand my childhood and Mum so much more. That brought healing in itself. To understand it wasn't my fault and really it wasn't my mother's fault either. When I think about it now, my empathic heart cried out for my Mum and what she must have had to cope with growing up and becoming a mum with her disabilities. I'm also very proud of her for getting as far as she did. What a beautiful woman she was. I pray my munchkin Mary has as much of a life as Mum had. I miss her so much. I miss her laughter; I miss what joy she often brought to a room with her silly pranks. She always tried to make people laugh. She was the life of the party. She had a dark side, and she struggled a lot; if she didn't click with you, if she took a dislike to anyone, you knew about it, and she made it very clear. She had a very feisty side and a big temper, but she always tried to bring happiness to whatever room she was in, unless I was in it.

****

Summer holidays, the four of us kids were at home and Mum wasn't in a good mood. We were all running around the house and getting under her feet. I was probably about six years old at the time, about a year after the sexual abuse had started. Mum was trying to clean the house; we kept scurrying about getting in her way. We decided to play hide and seek instead, and I loved playing hide and seek. Somehow, I would feel safe crouching down hiding, thinking no one could find me. Now, I understand that this event was one of the first times I felt staggering fear, which then led to intense feelings of anxiety. I had decided to hide in the white stand-alone wardrobe in mine and Jane's bedroom, I tiptoed in and tucked down into the back corner of the wardrobe. I pulled down some clothes that were on hangers to cover me. I was tucked nicely at the bottom behind the clothes and amongst all the shoes. I shut the door and stayed there. I heard Jane counting from 1 to 10 and saying, "Here I come, ready or not." I waited and waited, but no one came to look for me. I was starting to get a bit uncomfortable, and I needed to move because I was getting a dead leg from crouching down trying to stay as still as possible. As I started to move, I felt the wardrobe moving also and with a sudden crash and bang the wardrobe had fallen, with me in it. I was trapped inside the wardrobe, unable to get out. Now that was scary enough for a six-year-old. What happened next is a memory I would love to have erased from my mind forever, because I now realise what was spoken over me has impacted my entire life. A lie spoken over me that I lived with for most of my life, until I found total healing in the three 'Rs', a three-step process to healing; the 'recognise', 'renounce' and 'replace' technique.

The first time the sexual abuse involved penetration, I was five years old. Every time it was over, I had blood in my knickers and absolutely no idea what to do with them. I was so fearful of what Mum would say if she found them in the wash. In desperation, I hid them behind the wardrobe in our bedroom. The pattern continued and this became my hiding place, this is where I hid the abuse, in the form of a pile of blood-stained knickers. As I lay trapped inside the wardrobe, my hiding place no longer a secret. The bloodstains had dried to a dark brown colour with time.

The loud bang as the wardrobe came crashing down brought everyone rushing into the bedroom. Mum and Art lifted the wardrobe up enough for me to squeeze out. Mum was screaming and shouting. As I crawled out of the wardrobe, Mum grabbed me by my hair, dragging me out and I was met with a massive slap around the face. Screaming and shouting, "What the f**k are you doing?" I cowered away in fear, trying to cover my face. Whenever she moved around me and lifted her arm, I would flinch, thinking it was going to be a slap, because you would get a slap out of nowhere, for no reason at all. If there was a reason, she would use objects like wooden spoons, belts, you name it. If it could be picked up, it could be thrown at us. Sometimes you wouldn't know what it was for; you never saw it coming. Mum's go-to tool was the wooden spoon. Art was always the smart one; once he decided to hide all the wooden spoons after Mum hit him with one, breaking it over him while doing so.

My sister and I, frantically trying to tidy up the mess created as everything had fallen out of the wardrobe; Mum was not happy at all, she had been cleaning the house only now to find the contents of the wardrobe on the bedroom floor. Mum's face was bright red; she was screaming, shouting, slapping and trying to tidy up all at the same time. As she was sorting through the mess, she found the pile of knickers. She went ballistic! I mean wild, crazy, scary!

Mum picked up the knickers and started shouting "What the f**k are these?!? You dirty, dirty bitch! You f**king dirty stinking bitch, why are you hiding all your shitty dirty knickers behind the wardrobe?! You f**king disgusting filthy animal! You dirty, nasty bitch ..." With each angry scream came a slap, a punch and then kicks. As I lay there, curled up into a ball trying to protect myself. Then she grabbed a fist-full of my hair, wrapped it around her hand, lifted my face, and hissed, "Look at me! F**king look at me, you nasty, dirty bitch!" She grabbed a pair of the dirty knickers and began rubbing them in my face, like rubbing a puppy's nose in their mess. All the while the beating continued – slaps, punches, kicks, pulling me around the room by the hair; from the floor to the wardrobe, from the wardrobe to my bed. As she threw me on the bed she screamed, "You stay there, you f**king, dirty bitch... you filthy f**king, dirty bitch! If I ever find you hiding your dirty, stinky shitty knickers behind wardrobes again… In fact, if I find anything at all behind it, anything that should not be there… You will f**king know about it!" I knew what that meant! "You will surely know about it!" Still haunts me to this day.

"Don't hide your shitty, dirty knickers anywhere! You put your filthy, stinky, shitty, dirty knickers in the wash bin with the rest of your dirty washing! You take them off, you put them straight into the wash! Are you that f**king stupid, you don't know where to put your dirty washing?! Are you really that thick, you dirty, filthy f**king bitch!"

Every time she said it her face would contort with disgust, with hate in her eyes, like the punishment still wasn't enough. I was so scared. But there was absolutely nothing I could do. I couldn't run, I couldn't hide, I just had to take it.

Then she started screaming and shouting, "In fact, use the f**king toilet paper to wipe your ass, you dirty bitch!" My Mum had a very filthy mouth and there wasn't a sentence without a swear word.

"You're six years old and you don't know how to wipe your f**king ass?! What's wrong with you child? When you don't wipe your ass properly, you will stink! No wonder they call you fleabag at school and nobody wants to play with you, that's why they all run away from you! What do you expect if you shit your f**king knickers!"

She just kept repeating, "Tramp! F**king filthy tramp! You're a tramp, a filthy f**king dirty tramp!" Another slap, another kick, another yank of my hair. "You not wiping your f**king ass properly, you filthy dirty bitch, your gonna make my house stink of shit! You are nothing but a f**king piece of shit! You stinking piece of shit! I don't want to see or hear a word from you the rest of the summer holidays!"

These words have impacted my entire life. I have lived with the lie that I'm nothing but a piece of shit, never ever good enough. And I tried, right until her last breath in the hospice when she was promoted to be with our Lord and Maker. I believe this is part of the reason I have allowed people to walk all over me because I thought so little of myself. I believed the words my Mum spoke over me. But that is not who I am. I am a child of GOD, a princess of the Almighty King of the Universe! He loves me more than words can ever say. And now I rest in the comfort of knowing who I really am but to get there I needed to go through a lot of processing, forgiveness and therapy. I had to repent of partnering with that lie and living in that lie for so long, I had to walk into the truth of my identity; the truth always sets us free. No child should ever be treated that way. It wasn't my fault!

Mum used to say, "Sabina brought herself up; the rest were dragged up." And in a way, she was right. I never felt that I fitted in. I did the most chores, was punished the most and received the most beatings. I was the black sheep; picked on and targeted. So, I spent time with other friends and their families. She raised Art, Jane and George as best she could. It's true, I really did bring myself up. With the help of many different and beautiful people, many different influences. But all my life I wanted to be dragged up like the rest of my siblings, I wanted to feel a part of a family, but I never did.

The first family that took me under their wing was the Bambury family. I met Ruth in nursery at Sir John Lillie Primary School and we were in the same class together all through primary school. I was probably five or six when I went away with them for the first time. They would take me

48

on holidays, I remember Gabrielle, Ruth's Mum would buy clothes for me. We would wear matching clothes and pretend we were twins, even though we looked nothing alike.

Life at Ruth's was fun. She had two brothers, lots of nice things, all the latest toys and a beautiful bedroom. We were like sisters. The boys would play fun tricks on us, and it seemed like we were always laughing. Looking back, I think it was so much fun because at the Banbury's I felt safe and free. I never would have guessed that Ruth's brother would get with my aunt and go on to have a child with her, in a way making us real family; but that was many years later.

The Banbury family were wealthy and well known in the community. Ruth's dad managed a football team, Ruth and I would pretend to be cheerleaders as we watched from the side lines every Sunday, come rain or shine. We even made our own pompoms and dance routines. We were only young but both Ruth and I had a crush on a young man called Franky. There was a song in the charts, which went something like "Franky, my baby, will you remember me…" We would both sing it and perform a cheerleader dance on the sideline of the pitch, in the hope he would notice us.

After every game, Ruth's dad would take us to the pub with the team and he would buy us a tomato juice. We would feel so grown up. On the way home, we would visit the shellfish stall and take back lots of yummy shellfish to Ruth's house. We would sit for hours peeling prawns and using a pin to get the winkles out, dipping them in vinegar and eating them. Ruth's dad, Lee, was deeply involved in Freemasonry. Every year they would attend the formal ball, dressed up beautifully, the photos hung proudly all around the house. Many showed them with very well-known people, one featured the former Prime Minister Margaret Thatcher. I think they were quite high up in the Freemasonry circles.

I spent nearly half my time living with the Banbury's from age six to ten. My birthday is in August, so it fell during the summer holidays - I always wanted a birthday party like the other children had in my school, everyone singing happy birthday and blowing out candles on a cake, but I never once had a birthday party. I left primary school aged ten. I was the youngest in the class. I spent my school holidays and weekends with them, I would even stay during the week. I sometimes got to go home with them after Brownies on a Tuesday evening if Gabrielle asked my mum. I think Gabrielle may have noticed that things weren't easy for me at home. Art, Jane and George would be dressed nicely for school and Mum would put me in something quite raggy. At school I would be bullied and called names like 'fleabag'. If anyone accidentally swiped against me, they would wipe themselves down and blow off the pretend fleas, like I was dirty and full of germs.

I loved going to Brownies with Ruth. Brownies was a big part of my first spiritual experience, here I felt a different kind of love. There was also this one summer, I attended a Christian summer camp for children; it was held at Fulham Methodist Church on the Lillie Road, just down the road from my school. The feeling of God's presence was very tangible there and the love of all the people involved. I won a prize and was given an award for being the best-behaved child! I just remember it as very beautiful. We learned the song 'Jesus Love' and it made such an impact on me.

The lyrics went a little like this: Jesus Love Is Very Wonderful, Oh, Wonderful Love!

So High, You Can't Get Over It, So Low, You Can't Get Under It, So Wide, You Can't Get Around It, Oh, Wonderful Love!

 When there, I could feel God's presence with me but then I would go home, and my nightmare continued. My heart would drop into my stomach, the queasy feelings of anxiety would begin. This was because he (the monster) was living with us at the time, he had moved from Birmingham to London and wasn't just visiting; at this point in my little life, the sexual abuse was happening daily. Life at home meant I was constantly looking over my shoulder. I was on hyper-alert all the time, not knowing whether I would get blamed and punished for something someone else had done, when to expect the random punishments from Mum or when the next sexual assault was coming. I tried to stay away from home as much as I possibly could, thank goodness I had some respite with beautiful friends and their families.

The next friend I spent a lot of time with was Stacey Guard, another friend from primary school. She was in my sister's class but was closer in age to me as she was one of the oldest in her class. I always remember her having lavish birthday parties and she also went to Brownies with us. Her mum, Lauren, was separated. I remember Lauren having several boyfriends. Stacey's dad was a part of the Hells Angels biker gang. I remember him having very long hair; he had a very scary side to him. A few times he would turn up at the house and if there was another man in the house, Lauren would panic. She would try and hide the men, but he would go crazy, to the point the police had to be called.

Lauren then started dating Stacey's stepfather. I liked him; he was a tattoo artist, and he was also in a biker gang called the Rats. The rival biker gang to the Hells Angels, which didn't sit well with Stacey's dad one bit! They lived a bit of a crazy life, but they were very lovely people. They loved and cared for me deeply. They took me on holidays, I got to share in lots of happy times and whatever Stacey got, I got too when I was with them. They were very generous people but also had a very strange dark side, they never involved me in this, but I seem to remember it all very clearly. They were very interested in witchcraft and the occult, tarot reading and other quite spooky stuff!

We went to Devon and Cornwall, visited old castles and estates. I remember going to the Gnome Reserve and Wildflower Garden in Devon, there were gnomes all over the place. Hundreds of them! I thought it was quite bizarre and found it scary, I've never liked gnomes since! In the evenings we would go back to the caravan and with the lights down low in the dark of night, they would get out the Ouija board and tell spooky stories to try to scare us. Stacey and I would spend hours and hours playing with her Barbie. She had it all: the Barbie house, car, motorhome, horse, Kens and so many outfits there were too many to count. Growing up and sharing family time with the Guards' family provided me with many happy memories. I think the fact I had such safety with my friends' families growing up has imprinted in me and is likely why I'm the way I am with my own children's friends. My home has and will always be an open home. I have made it my personal mission to pass on the many blessings that I received as a child from others. I want to be able to give what I was given as a child, a safe space with a place to feel like home with love and acceptance all around.

We lived at Musard Road until I was eleven years old. Divided into two; we lived downstairs, and an old man named Harry lived upstairs. I remember him as old, wrinkly and smelly but very sweet. When you looked at our house there was a beautiful balcony on the second floor. Harry would spend hours making it all look and smell amazing, hanging lots of beautiful flower baskets all the way around. All summer beautiful, colourful flowers would bloom and cascade down onto our windows. The smell would waft into our windows, and it was beautiful every year without fail, until Harry started to get weak and unwell. One year it was so pretty that the school opposite our house used our house as an art project, a class of children painted our home. Mum, being Mum, went out to see what they were all doing, and she started talking to two children. She gave them some orange juice and then the rest of the class too as they all came over and joined them.

It's funny how life works. One of the young girls who she had been talking to, her mum ended up becoming my mum's boss in the school kitchens she worked in, and we moved onto the very same street they lived on. Mum and the little girl Caroline became very close; they both had a common enemy, her mum. that little girl Mum gave a glass of juice to has been a friend of the family ever since. It hurts sometimes when I hear her say things to me like "Your mum was like a mum to me. She always had time for me." Mum knew her mother was a mean lady and I suppose she could see what Caroline was going through. How could she be so loving to her but not to me.

Mum quite clearly felt compassion for Caroline, they spent lots of time together doing things together. She would listen to her like a daughter, possibly because she saw herself in the little girl; maybe it reminded her of how she was treated by her mother. But how couldn't she see that she was doing the very same thing to me? What was so wrong with me that she hated me so much? Many thoughts went through my mind as a child, maybe I wasn't Mum's but only Dad's and there was a big secret that I didn't know about. Art would tease me and say I was adopted, what if this were true? I searched our home many times trying to find my birth certificate and never could. All the important papers were kept in a box, Art, Jane and George's birth certificates were all in there but mine wasn't. At seventeen I applied for a passport, and it wasn't till then I finally saw a copy of my birth certificate. As a child I would daydream, like in the film Annie. I would often think my real Mum would come and rescue me. Many times, I would dream of running away, but where would I run to?

Harry would knock on our door and give us sweets and as he got on in age, we would run to the corner shop to buy him milk or whatever else he needed. Mum would take meals up to him as his health was fading. Harry was the first person I remember going to be with God. That was what my dad told me. We would often go and check on him, I remember there being a beautiful handmade doll's house in his living room. It was stunning. I couldn't take my eyes off it; there were lights that worked in every room, and it was finished to look like a palace. It contained the most beautiful furniture, rugs, carpet and wallpaper, the tiny little dolls sitting at a table with tiny little knives and forks. It was a little girl's dream. Whenever I checked on Harry, I would just stare at it and take myself right there, imagining what my life would look like in a safe, loving, beautiful home. I also remember a plate of butter left out with a glass lid over it. During the summer months, the butter would melt in a pool on the dish; isn't it strange the things you remember from your childhood? Unfortunately, his home was dirty, dusty, cluttered, in a state of disrepair and it smelled. After Harry died, no one moved in due to the condition of the house; we also had to move out because it was in such a state. Plus, the problems my parents were having with the manhole in the boys' room.

Down Disbrowe Road, lived a famous Scottish comedian. He lived at number one-and-a-half; no other house on the road was a half number, only his. Our family was not a big fan of his because he was once rude to my brother George and made him cry. The comedian was in an advert at the time promoting eggs and the tagline was something like "Crack an egg on your nut" and he would smash the egg on his forehead (I have no idea how this sells eggs). One day, whilst we were playing outside, he came walking past. George was on his tricycle and Jane had on her white roller-skates. The comedian was passing our house and George started shouting, "Crack an egg on your nut, crack an egg on your nut!" The comedian wasn't amused; he turned around and said, "F**k off!"

George ran into the house crying and this angered Mum. One thing about Mum was how she would protect her pack; anyone she classed as a friend or family, she would say it how it was, she was not afraid of confrontation at all. Like a mother bear looking after her young she found a way to get back at the comedian. Mum's side of the family often looked to take revenge if someone hurt you or your family. She got her revenge on the comedian the night before Prince Charles and Lady Diana's wedding. His fancy car was parked right outside our window and my parents were having a social night with friends and family, drinks were flowing, and Mum told the story of what happened with the comedian and my brother. With everyone nice and tipsy they decided to go out and write in bright red lipstick what he had said to George; yes, the F-word all over his beautiful, shiny, clean car. The day before the wedding of Prince Charles and Lady Diana.

There was a time where Art had an issue with his teacher and she pulled him across a table in the classroom, leaving a bruise. When Mum collected us from the school Art told her what the teacher had done to him. The next day when she came to collect us from school, her sisters in tow, there was a big argument between them and the teacher. Somehow the teacher's shoes ended up being thrown into one of the giant school bins, a story which is often told to this day at family gatherings when drinking and talking of the old days.

My beautiful sister Jane, nine months younger than me, has always been my hero. Even to this day, she is such an inspiration to me, she is so brave. I always wish I was as brave as her, I've always thought of her as my big little sister, because I always felt safe and protected around her as a child. She is strong and courageous, which I never was growing up. I would crawl into her bed every night, even as a teenager. Despite having our own beds there were times we would push our beds together and make a double bed. I'm sure this must have gotten on her nerves at times, always having to speak up for me, even as adults when we would go out, Jane wouldn't take any nonsense, just like Mum.

A lot of people used to think Jane and I were twins; we look nothing alike but for three months of the year we were the same age. Jane has dark hair, olive skin that tans easily and beautiful eyes that change colour with her mood from green to grey with a hint of blue at times. I have blonde hair, fair skin that goes red as a lobster in the sun and blue eyes. I have Dad's complexion and Jane has Mum's. We're also different in other ways. Jane is sporty, more like a tomboy; I'm demure and a girly-girl. Like Art, Jane left home and joined the army as soon as she was of age. She lied about her age to get into the cadets at secondary school, so it was no surprise that she went into the army. She is fit, strong, very brave and courageous. She was one of the first female tank drivers on the frontline in Afghanistan and even received a commendation from the Queen. I could never do what she does; it would ruin my nails! After making the choice to go into ministry myself, I did consider becoming an Army Chaplain but when I looked into it, I was told I would have to do basic training and I could never have managed mud under my nails. I reconsidered and decided prison, drug rehabilitation, counselling and trauma- healing ministry was my calling.

When I was bullied at school, Jane would always speak out. Even now, she still speaks out. I think my timidness gets on her nerves. If I'm out with Jane and someone bumps into me (their fault, not mine) I will always apologise first. Jane will say, "Why are you apologising? You didn't do anything," and then have a go at the person, telling them to come back and apologise to me. She was always, always on guard because I hate confrontation. Before I understood somatic therapy and what trauma feels like in the body, If I heard shouting, I would feel like I was going to have a panic attack; I couldn't breathe, my chest would get tight, and my body would become rigid. I would feel dizzy and nauseous. I think Jane thought that she had to protect me because I couldn't protect myself. My beautiful sister, my hero, Jane - my big little sister.

Mum would say things to me and Jane and I am sure it was in an attempt to create a divide between us. She would tell stories of when we were babies, her favourite was how we used to share the pram as I was a small preemie baby and Jane a newborn. She told how when I was born people would look down into the pram and see an angelic baby with blonde Shirley temple-like curly hair, boasting of my beauty as a baby. This was met with the reminder she no longer felt that way as she would then say, "Beautiful in cradle, ugly at the table." She said people would gaze into the pram and say, "Oh what a beautiful baby" but nine months later Jane popped out and people said "Oh, she's nice."

I never thought about the impact such comments would have on my sister, but it finally hit home when I found a photo as an adult and showed Jane. It was a photo of me and Jane when we were children. She was a chubby little baby, just adorable, very cuddly, she was like a little bear. When I saw the photo, what struck with me was a remark she made. She told how mum used to say "Look at her! She looks like Sabina's afterbirth." I was crying inside for her, thinking about the lies she'd been living with all her life, believing that she is ugly. However, Mum would say the opposite when telling the story of Jane "Ugly in the cradle, beautiful at the table" meaning she had grown into her beauty. Despite this, Jane had held onto the ugly comments Mum made.

Like Jane, my older brother Art also left home the first chance he got and joined the Army. He was a part of the Irish Guards (the ones that serve the Queen and wear the big black bearskin hats outside of Buckingham Palace, tower of London and Windsor castle). They are supposed to be expressionless and not acknowledge anyone. But Art was playful by nature and would often wink or stick out his tongue at children when their parents weren't looking. He loved their reaction; jaws dropping, mouths open wide and eyes sparkling as they turned to their parents yelling, "He moved! He moved! Mummy, Mummy, did you see? He moved! I saw him!" Of course, by the time the parents would turn and look at Art, he had returned to his statue like state.

Art was the first-born and was a very handsome young boy with white-blonde hair, just like the Milky Bar Kid but without the glasses. Art was intelligent and well- liked. He was our big brother and loved being the boss, keeping us all in check. But he could also be a bully, he tormented us lots, as big brothers do but he saved his worst for little George. Art was about five years old when George came along and at the time, he wanted nothing to do with him. He didn't want to share a room with a baby.

I would describe Art as a Type-A personality, a man's man with old-fashioned values. He rarely shows his softer side, but he has a big heart. Put him in front of the cartoon movie 'All Dogs Go to Heaven' and he'll be sobbing like a baby. He loves animals more than people. He has great trust issues, and he can be paranoid to the point he will talk himself into believing things that are just not true. He holds onto all his anger and finds it hard to see things from another's perspective. He always has to be right; he must have the last word and gets very loud, talking over people to exert power and hold authority over others in situations. He has a very violent temper and will just switch when drinking alcohol; he even stabbed George in a drunken argument about a girl.

Art is also a wonderful storyteller with a great sense of humour. He will go to great lengths to prank people often getting himself into trouble when he's had a drink or two too many. Coming home drunk one night he thought he had lost his keys, so he tried to climb through the window of his flat to get in. He slipped and fell back on the iron railings, impaling his leg. The fire brigade and an ambulance had to be called - to cut the iron railing and then rush him to hospital. Whilst being prepped for surgery, a nurse explained she would have to cut his trousers and as she was doing so, she asked him where he would like her to put his keys. The keys - They were in his pocket the whole time! I could sit for hours listening to Art's funny stories, he would have me in fits of laughter, to the point of nearly peeing your pants laughing. He got this from Mum, who also had the ability to make people laugh with her stories; they both had the knack of turning a bad story into a funny story.

I spent a lot of time with Art, most weekends we would stay with our grandma Edie, my Jewish grandma. We weren't blood-related to her; she was Grandad Reggie's new wife after his divorce from Mum's Mum. Nanny Edie was the only real Grandma I felt I ever had. Mum's Mum was a mean and cruel woman, and I never really knew Dad's Mother. I do remember my Dad's Mum, Nanny Lilly stayed with us in London for a couple of weeks after a fire had destroyed her flat in Birmingham. I think she was suffering from dementia and the only thing I remember of her stay is her wetting herself on our sofa in the living room. We were all in the front room. She got up to go to the other room and we noticed this dark round stain where she had been sitting. Mum was not pleased, her precious peacock-patterned blue and green sofa. She loved that sofa and was very house proud, she also may have had OCD as everything had to be just so. We were so lucky when Nanny Edie came into our lives, she would take Art and I everywhere at the weekends. Museums and galleries, the park to feed the ducks and we played boardgames – I loved playing the game 'Operation' with Art and Nanny. Art and I loved the time we spent going to stay with Grandad and Nanny Edie in Brixton.

Art was quite cheeky; he had a way of making you do things that he didn't want to do himself. I remember a time when myself, Jane, Art and Simon White, one of my Mum's best friend's sons and the same age as my brother Art, went to North End Road on an adventure. We went to Woolworths, a massive department store. As you walked into the store, there was a big carousel counter of pick n' mix sweets, every kid's idea of heaven. As kids rarely got sweets or treats, and this huge display was overwhelming.

Temptation was everywhere and we wanted it all. I was about seven years old; Art and Simon White were about nine, and Jane was probably six years old. Art gathered us together and whispered, "Let's take some sweeties home." So, we all started to fill our pockets with sweeties. My heart was racing! Art was look- out, looking around to see if anyone was watching as we all stuffed our pockets with as many sweets as we could. Then Art said, "Let's go" and as we were leaving the store, a security guard grabbed me by the scruff of my neck pulling me back inside the store. They others ran as fast as they could; they just left me.

The security guards took me into a dark, dingy back room with nothing but a desk and chair. I was all alone and terrified as they peppered me with questions; "Where's your Mum?" "What's your name?" "Where do you live?" "How old are you?" I was being interrogated like a real criminal. I didn't know what to do, I was sobbing, and I had no idea what I was supposed to say. Would I get beaten for my answers like I was at home? Are they going to lock me in a call and throw away the key like people often said? Or worse, are they going to tell Mum? I was terrified what she would do if she found out. I was released a short while later with no idea what to do next. I turned left at the McDonald's and as I went up the street, I noticed Wrigley's gum wrappers on the ground. So, I followed them, first a silver wrapper, then a Double Mint wrapper then another silver wrapper, one after another, just like in the story of Hansel and Gretel. McDonald's was a ten-minute walk from home. I had been following the sweet wrappers and when I got to Norman Park, I could see the three of them hiding in the bushes! The sweet wrappers had been Art's idea. Jane was bleeding from a cut on her stomach as she climbed over a fence and tried to hide. Needless to say, I never shoplifted again! We also made a pact never to tell our parents of what happened on that day. I knew for sure if Mum ever found out I would get a beating like no other.

****

On my eighth Christmas we had both the best and worst Christmas ever. That year Dad got a very big Christmas bonus (money tips from the people whose bins he would empty) from his wealthy clients. Being a dustman in Knightsbridge, came with very generous thanks at Christmas time. Every year, on Christmas Eve, Dad and his crew would finish early and go for a drink. Mum never complained as she knew he'd be bringing home extra cash. The Christmas money would be divided up between all the boys on the bin round, each bringing home a couple of hundred pounds, which was a lot of money back then. Mum knew the betting shops would be closed early on Christmas Eve and they wouldn't reopen again until Boxing Day. So, she didn't have to worry about that either. Dad was never a big drinker; he never really went drinking the rest of the year. He may have had the odd one or two drinks in the house if friends were over, but not very often. He had a very low tolerance to alcohol, he only needed to smell alcohol and he was tipsy. He came home that evening on Christmas Eve, quite jolly and a little tipsy; he had lots of twenty-pound notes that he just threw up into the air. Mum was overjoyed to see all the money; she was always happy when there was money, which meant a lot less for her to worry and stress about.

The next morning, we woke up to so many presents – they were everywhere. I remember I got a hairdressing doll, just a doll's head where I could play, brush and plait the hair. It really was such a happy Christmas, the best. I also got a design wheel to design outfits for paper dolls. We were very lucky that year. Dad still had money left over burning a hole in his pocket but there was no gambling on Christmas Day.

Boxing Day was when the gambling started again. which was a big tradition in England - Horse-racing, football games, you name it. So, Dad decided we would go as a family to the Wimbledon dog racing track. He lost the first race and was chasing the money he had lost from that point on. He lost it all. Mum was not happy at all, which made for a very sad and quiet ride home. The arguing didn't start until the following day and when he had no money left. He left the house and was out all day. We couldn't find him or any of our presents. He sold the bike brought for Art, as well as most of our presents. That is when Christmas changed for me and not just Christmas but the receiving of gifts. Nothing good ever seemed to last and from that point I learnt not to get attached to anything. It was given and taken away, nothing would be sacred to me, and material things meant nothing anymore. If it wasn't Dad selling everything for a bet, it was George taking things apart to try and put them back together again.

Almost every Sunday my parents would ransack the house to work out what could be sold. Dad would find stuff in the bins at work that had been thrown away by the wealthy homeowners; all the good stuff that was in good condition would be placed in bags and put down in the basement until Sunday, when they would take it all to the car boot sale. We would have nice things for a little while, only for them then to be sold the next week to feed Dad's addiction or to pay overdue bills and pawn tickets.

****

When I was about nine, we went on our first family holiday, which was both the best and worst holiday ever. It was rare for us to have a family holiday, which was always paid for by Social Services, once by Nanny Mog, who wasn't our real Nanny. I think she was somehow related to Grandad Rubens. One summer I helped look after her as she was very poorly, and one year she paid for us to go to Great Yarmouth. Mum's sister, Aunt Trudy, came with us. We had no money, but we had a family allowance book that could be cashed, but Dad had quickly gambled it all away. Luckily, the foresight of nanny Mog paid for our family holiday, also paid for half- board. So, breakfast and evening meals were paid for. We had to sneak a lot of food from breakfast to eat for lunch before we could go for dinner.

I remember Trudy stepped on a jelly fish on the beach, Mum was always playing the fool, making people laugh on the donkey rides; it was the holiday camp Donkey Derby race. Mum liked to get involved in everything. Mum got involved in activity and Dad would enter every competition possible. My parents were very competitive. For the first three days we had no money and Dad was getting us all to pick up cigarette butts as they had no money to buy any. Dad then won a table tennis competition, which won him a family holiday for four for free. Dad sold the family holiday to somebody for cash so that he could have more money for a bet. He then won a horse race. Dad also won on the fruit machines, while Jane was standing watching him playing on the machines. Jane got so excited with Dad winning and so excited by the sound of the machine paying out all the cash in coins that she wet herself, overwhelmed at seeing all the money flooding out of the machine. It was almost like going to Las Vegas, but it was a holiday camp in Great Yarmouth. We all scrambled to help to grab the money from the fruit machine.

We won the best father and daughter competition. Probably because Jane and I are so close in age and we looked cute together, Mum had made us matching dresses specially. I wonder if people felt sorry for us, for the lack of sleep that my parents were getting, having four children so close in age. With very little money to raise us, it must have been hard for Mum and very stressful, living in limbo and never knowing if you would be on an up with a win or a down with a loss with Dad's gambling addiction.

The holiday changed at that point. Dad won a lot of money, and we then had the best holiday ever! Mum was so pleased on the way home, most of the time Dad was losing not winning! It's so sad thinking about it, that people like my parents were not afforded the opportunities as kids that everyone should be afforded. No therapy as such to help people like Mum and Dad, who had been through so much trauma and rejection as children. I think that is why I am a giver more than a receiver. All our family would give you the shirt off their backs or last pennies they had because of our upbringing. We had come from nothing so we could live with nothing.

****

George is the baby of the family. He was a Mama's boy by no fault of his own. Mum babied him which was unusual because she didn't baby any of us and she just wasn't a naturally nurturing Mother. I think she was exhausted with child-rearing by the time George came along. She had four children by the time she was twenty-five, all under the age of five. I had three children over nine years from the age of nineteen, two with disabilities, which at times felt almost impossible.

As a child George was a bit tubby and his ears stuck out, so he got the nickname Dumbo. He eventually grew into his ears and filled out into a tall, handsome man with a bright smile and big heart. As a boy though, George was always getting into mischief. He was always dirty, messy and misbehaving. But he was Mummy's little baby boy and by far the noticeable favourite, he could do no wrong. He was overprotected when he was young; Mum wouldn't even let him go outside to play with the rest of us. He really wasn't allowed to grow up and it got increasingly hard to get him to school and keep him there. Especially when he started secondary school, it was a uniformed school, and my parents didn't have the money to get him the new uniform so on his first day Mum sent him in his normal clothes; you can just imagine being the only boy on the first day of secondary school not wearing a uniform. The bullying started from that moment on, and it really is no wonder he didn't want to go.

Bullying has a huge psychological impact on us which we can often bring into adulthood, I'll talk a little more about this later. George had dropped out of school by the time he was eleven years old, he would earn pocket money helping on the market stalls and it led to a job on the fish stall. Our family knew most of the people on the market, North End Road was very much like an episode of EastEnders, as gossip was rife, and everyone knew about everyone's business.

Unlike the rest of us, George didn't leave home at the first chance he had, in fact George lived with Mum and Dad on and off until my mother passed away. At the age of fourteen he tried heroin for the first time and became hooked. After Mum's passing, Dad firmly put boundaries in place, telling George he was not welcome at the house until he had been sober for at least two years. George had stolen from Mum on her deathbed; he took her purse from the hospice the day before she died and off, he went to buy his drugs. He came back after getting his fix, we were together as she took her last breath. At this time George was homeless, family were allowed to stay at the hospice and for the last week he did so. George became a shoplifter, a burglar and was in and out of prisons - he stole anything he could to feed his addiction.

Mum was diagnosed with CUP 'cancer of unknown primary' and the doctors said that the worst-case scenario was she possibly had months to live. Mum was a fighter, and she was hanging on for dear life. It was like she was holding onto something and wasn't ready to let go. She fought for almost eighteen months and was buried in a dress for an eight-year-old as she'd lost so much weight! The last two weeks of Mum's life were horrid, and I didn't leave her side. Jane was stationed away at the time, and I think Mum just couldn't let go with one of her children absent. As soon as Jane could, she got to the hospice and just like that, a few hours later, Mum was promoted.

Now I know it has been said, but little George was always getting into something, always dirty. I was about four and a half, it was one of the hottest days of the year and we had left nursery early that day. It is one of my earliest memories of him as a baby, seeing him come crawling towards me covered in either mud or poo - maybe both. Everyone thought it was hilarious, I thought it was disgusting but we did get to go and play in the pool at the park whilst George got cleaned up.

George was a boy who loved nature; when he was allowed outside, he made the most of it! He would stick his fingers in snails, catch bugs and examine them intently, pulling their legs off one by one. He was a very inquisitive boy. No toy in the house was safe from George and a screwdriver. His obsession with taking things apart mostly without success meant many parts left over, but he'd always try again. Nearly every toy in our home was useless through George's determination. If we let him touch anything of ours, we knew it wouldn't come back the way he found it.

George's best friend was called Nicky Sunderland. Nicky was about five years older than George and lived just down the road from us on the Lily Road. Nicky had cancer from a young age, and it was heart-breaking to watch him deteriorate. He was sick for so many years; he had huge growths and abscesses all over his body and this caused him to have a putrid smell about him. One of his treatments at Cromwell Hospital was placing maggots in his wounds to eat away the bacteria. George would be by his side throughout all of his treatments; he couldn't have been much older than about nine or ten. George was about fourteen or fifteen by the time Nicky was finally promoted to meet his maker, which broke my baby brother's heart, and he has never the same since. I believe this trauma is a big factor into his lifelong heroin addiction, trying to numb his pain.

Nicky's family life was also troubled. His brother went to prison for setting a homeless man on fire. Nicky's family lived near the Normand Park. One night, Nicky's brother and a friend of his, set some boxes on fire that a homeless man was living in. It was all over the news. People were angry and gossiping and avoiding Nicky's family at all costs. But George never left Nicky's side throughout his illness or all the trouble that he was going through with his brother. He was a true friend to Nicky right to the end. It's not easy to be around someone dying of cancer and Nicky suffered greatly for many years, undergoing all kinds of treatments. He was constantly in and out of hospital, but George would be there. I think losing Nicky really messed George up; he lost his best friend at a very early age and watched him go through such horrible sickness and pain. It pains me to know he has carried such grief for so long.

After Nicky died George turned to drugs. He was introduced to heroin and has struggled ever since. You name it, George has done it, but heroin has had a hold on him for nearly two-thirds of his life. He would snowball from crack to heroin. George's addiction has impacted the family in many ways. He's been in and out of rehabs for treatment and prison because of crimes commitment.

****

After moving to our new home because of the manhole, Mine and Jane's new bedroom was just at the top of up the stairs as you came up from the front door, just down the hall from the living room, just past our parents' bedroom. Our room was always clean and tidy. It had to be, or Mum would flip her lid. We had bunk beds but also had the room to take them down and still have space to play. Jane and I would change our room around often. Even though we were living in a new house, life didn't change much for me. I don't know why, but there seemed to be a different set of rules in our house. Whenever Art, Jane or George did something naughty, I would get the blame. I would get the blame for pretty much everything and with it lots of slaps and smacks with belts, wooden spoons, shoes, or whatever was nearby.

I felt like Cinderella sometimes. I wondered if Mum was really a wicked stepmother who had to take me on. Art teasing me all the time saying I was adopted, and my birth certificate was never to be found. I always felt like the unwanted stepdaughter forced to be a servant in my own home.

Mum even gave me a song growing up called "*Nobody's Child*". I overheard her talking to a friend's mum, saying "This is Sabina's song".

The song goes:

"I'm nobody's child, I'm nobody's child Just like a flower,

I'm growing wild

No mummy's kisses, and no daddy's smile Nobody wants

me, I'm nobody's child."

She would have a devilish smile spread across her face whilst singing along as she played it at full blast.

I had to do the washing- up, cleaning, ironing and keep the house tidy. Jane and the boys could go out with their friends and do whatever they wanted but I always had to meet certain expectations first. I needed to earn permission. I would have to have a fixed plan of who, where, when and what I wanted to be doing, to be able to answer the questions thrown at me when asking Mum if I could go out. I would also have to finish a very long list of chores, which would grow at my requests to go out.

On the weekend, I'd be all excited to meet up with friends and ask Mum if it was okay to leave. She'd ask if my room was tidy and then do an inspection, running her finger over everything to check for any dust and if anything was found out of place, she would fly into a rage. Pulling my dresser drawers out and dumping everything on the floor, she would scream, "You think this is f**king tidy?!" She'd toss the room upside down, until it was a massive heap, everything everywhere. "Now, f**king tidy it up!" she'd yell.

Mum had a song for the boys too, which was called "Two little boys had two little toys". I don't remember Jane ever having a song. I do remember at one time only ever having one record which was the Simon and Garfunkel album Bridge Over Troubled Water, Simon and Garfunkel were my parents' favourite singers and that's why Art is called Art. When we moved to Tamworth Street, I met my very good friend Diana Adams and her parents Paul and Jody. They lived just up the road. Diana's Aunt Zoe and Uncle Zack also lived by us Tamworth Street. One of the most beautiful families I have ever met and a family I have modelled myself on for years.

The Adams' loved me unconditionally. They showed me a parents love and treated me as one of their own. I learnt what family is and means through them; Love, kindness, laughter and joy surrounded me everywhere I went with them. Diana's Uncle Zack used to have a train set in his loft. Uncle Zack and Paul were very close brothers and good friends. They were both obsessed with trains; it was totally amazing how they had set it up in the loft, it was like a town with a train track, little trees and people with houses and ponds. It was truly a dream. It wasn't for little fingers; it was a big boy's' toy. They would spend hours up there. They were a very close family, and every member made me feel part of it. I went on trips with them to Devon and

71

Basingstoke to visit Diana's Nana and Papa. They were lovely too, just like the rest of their family.

On a holiday to Dartmouth, we took the steam train to Paignton Zoo and went crabbing where the River Dart meets the sea. We would go somewhere almost every day in the summer holidays. We always had so much fun. That was a truly wonderful time in my life.

My heart broke when they decided to immigrate to Australia. After Diana, her brother Dan and parents moved. I felt abandoned and alone again. I was around thirteen years old when they left; I still call them Mum and Dad to this day.

Aunt Zoe and Uncle Zack even kept me under their wing after they left. Once they took Jane and I with them on another holiday to Dartmouth not long after Diana and her family had left for Australia. They gave me a job cleaning their house.

The Adams' were such a beautiful family, inspiring me to be like them. To sit round the dinner table together, to talk and share stories of their days over a meal, to be joyful, thankful, to just love one another and be kind to each other, unlike my own family. Dad went on to work with Zack doing deliveries for them as they owned the Aussie shop in Covent Garden. A shop full of Australian sweets and goodies. Australians living in London could go there to get their Vegemite and chocolate Tim Tam fix.

Prior to the Adams' leaving, when I started secondary school, another angel came into my life, one of my schoolteachers. His name was Mr Rust; he often noticed that I was lonely and often picked on by the other school kids. He knew my family because he was my brother's form tutor and he knew that my Mum was having treatment for cancer, so he would check in on us to see how we were doing. One time, he asked if I would be interested in coming along to join him for a Christian Union shared lunch held in the music department every Thursday afternoon. I had no idea what he was talking about, but I said yes anyway. I was lonely and someone had noticed me. So, I went along to this lunch on a Thursday, it was fun, everyone brought food and shared it. Then he asked if I would be interested in coming along to the Billy Graham revival conference in Earls Court the following Monday. Again, I said yes not knowing what I was saying yes to, and it was only a few minutes from where I lived. So, I went along.

Admission was free. At the end of the meeting there was a call to go forward if what you had heard touched your heart and if you wanted to give your life to Jesus. I went forward while the song 'Shine, Jesus, Shine' was playing loudly and tears ran down my face. That song will always remind me of giving my life to Jesus Christ. I've had it played at all my children's christenings. I just love it! It reminds me of His love, His mercy and grace and how brightly He shines in the darkest of places. It really spoke to me at that time in my life, and still does. The revival conference lasted a week. I loved it so much I went back every night. Every night I would go forward just like the first night and give my life to Christ all over again! I was only eleven years old; I didn't understand that I only had to go forward once. Every night, they would ask people to come forward and put their trust in Jesus and that's what I wanted to do. So, every night when they asked, I said yes. I went forward every time and it felt so good! so, in the space of a week I gave my life to Christ five times.

At one of the Billy Graham meetings, I met a woman named Lynn Sue who introduced me to the Chelsea Baptist Church and her daughter Amanda. We became very close, and I started attending Chelsea Baptist Church and Amanda and

I were both baptised on Easter Sunday 1986. None of my family attended. Lynn brought me a gift for my baptism, it was a cassette tape with a song on it sung by Cliff Richard and Van Morrison called Wherever God Shines His Light. That song has also been a big part of my life and has a great somatic response on my body when I hear it; music is a beautiful thing to use for healing trauma. Whenever I went to Chelsea Baptist Church, which was most Sundays as well as bible study in the week, house group meetings and days out, it always left me feeling good. It was so nice feeling like I now had another new family, a church family, I loved being a part of Chelsea Baptist Church growing up.

I was eleven years old when I gave my life to Christ and thirteen years old when I was baptised. It felt great! I had new friends, a church community that loved and cared for me. I was a new Christian! But the good feelings didn't last long. I knew nothing about spiritual warfare as a new and young Christian, even though I had been living through it all my life. All I knew at the time was that things in my life started to go bad and then worse after I was baptised. My Grandad disowned me and my lovely family, the Adams' had moved to what felt like a million miles away, the place that felt like a real home, a place of love and safety, was now gone. I felt abandoned, lonely and trapped returning to my parents' home where I didn't feel safe, not knowing that it was about to become even darker.

Chapter four

Uncle Rob

"Speak up for those who cannot speak for themselves, for the rights of all who are destitute. Speak up and judge fairly; defend the rights of the poor and needy."

Proverbs 31:8-9

I didn't know it at the time, but Uncle Rob was fleeing Birmingham. There was a warrant out for his arrest - He had set the fire that destroyed my Nan's home. He also slit his wrists in front of Nanny Lily and threw her two poodle dogs, which she carried around in a handbag, off the balcony in Birmingham. Rob went missing as the police tried to search for him. As an adult, I learned that he had made my cousins dress him up as a woman, shave his legs and paint his nails. Then, one evening, he decided he would take them home, on the bus, but not dressed as Uncle Rob. My aunt and uncle were so upset at what they saw, what started out as a big argument, quickly escalated into a physical attack. He strung my aunty by the neck and pinned her to the wall, my uncle desperately trying to free her. She was the sweetest soul, timid, like a little butterfly, how could you hurt someone like that? They both carry the scars from that incident to this day. After he had beat them both up, he left for London, to live with us.

Uncle Rob must have arrived during the night after Jane, and I, had fallen asleep. I must have climbed into Jane's bed at some point that evening, as I usually did, and when we woke in the morning, we found him sleeping in my bed. We were so excited to see him. We crawled out of Jane's bed and bounced into his, jumping on him, celebrating. He settled us down, sat us next to him, one on either side. We would do this most mornings.

Rob moved in with us September of that year. The morning after he arrived, he began telling a story, and would do so for the weeks that followed. Stories about a worm that wiggles up through the ground and finds its home in a beautiful garden. He would make up silly songs and started to sing: "There's a worm at the bottom of my garden, his name is Wiggly Woo. He wiggled and he wobbled; he wobbled, and he wiggled; he wiggled like me and you!".

It didn't take him long, as he sang the song, he would become aroused, and his worm would grow.

As he sang, he pulled out his penis and showed us his "worm". I remember it so vividly. He sang it like a nursery rhyme, he made it fit for a small child, like a game, his worm had a character and a name. He would do this every morning, sometimes when I woke, his worm had already gotten bigger and it was like a game of peek-a-boo to him, and me, at the time. It seemed harmless, he made it, fun. That is how I would start my day, at four years old. He had many names for it, and he would ask me to befriend it, telling me to talk to it, asking me to give it a kiss, to be its best friend. He would grab the end of his penis and squeeze it open and closed, as if it were a puppet, talking to me.

Jane has no memory of this happening. Maybe she has removed it from her memory bank, or she was just too young to even know that this was an invasion of our innocence - she never saw the dark side of Uncle Rob. Jane was more outspoken than me; maybe he knew he wouldn't get away with it as easily with her, as he did with me. He gave me such positive attention and came to my defence at times when Mum would be mean to me. Even though the stories had started with the both of us, there came a point, he would wake only me or even wait until Jane wasn't around, it was now just our story. That's how it started, the building trust and making me feel special, safe even.

It was about a week after Rob moved in that Ted came about. He lived in the mansions directly across the road from our house. They met as everyone played cricket down the road as they all loved to do and hit it off right away. I guess it takes one to know one. Ted was tall and skinny, and he lived alone. One evening that week, Mum and Dad went to Bingo and Rob was looking after us kids. Ted came over and we were all in the front room, they were teaching us how to exercise. Ted lay on his back, in the middle of the living room floor showing us how to do bicycle wheels, with his legs in the air. He held my siblings, so their face was held up above his, holding his hands in their hands, lifting them off the floor and making them fly. When it was my turn, he held my feet and told me to hold onto his, he had a rip in his trousers and no pants underneath. I had a full view, I was so little, I felt the fear wash over me, I was so deeply embarrassed. He knew exactly what he was doing, while I struggled to comprehend and understand what had interrupted my evening with my siblings. That was the first of many times Ted joined Uncle Rob when our parents went to Bingo.

Uncle Rob continued to tell me my special stories each morning and came to my defence when Mum was mean. He was, I thought, my protector. He would give me the attention I hadn't been getting otherwise and stuck up for me when Mum's moods would change. He made me feel safe, he was earning my trust more and more each day. Eventually, pairing what presented to me in my innocence as simple kindness and protection, Rob became bolder.

Just past my parents' bedroom, was a narrow hallway with a wooden door that led down to the basement. The weather was becoming increasingly colder, darker and wet, as we were now in the thick of winter. One day Dad decided to cut a little square shaped hole in the basement door, so that the cats could go in and out as they pleased, there was also a hole that it led out onto the street and meant a lot of the neighbours' cats would frequent the basement too. Dad didn't like the idea of any cat's being stuck out in the cold, wet, British winter and now they had a dry, safe space to seek refuge. There was a broken glass block tile one of six which formed a small window that let a little light into the basement, which also let a lot of water in when it poured down, making the basement damp and musty over time but it was better than being completely exposed. The last and only happy memory I have of that basement was finding a little ginger cat that had made itself at home. Overtime, we had become quite attached, we named him Ginger, and he would come up to the main house to spend time with us. We had to return him to his owners once we had spotted some missing posters around town, but Ginger would still visit us from time to time. By this point though, the basement absolutely reeked of cat pee, it was ridden with all sorts of creepy crawlies, spiders of varying sizes and there were often rats.

It was now early December and the build up to Christmas. Mum and Dad were at Bingo, and Ted had come over to help babysit. It was late evening, the other's had fallen asleep, and by this point, I was drifting off too. Uncle Rob gently shook my shoulder, stroking my hair out of my face, and told me he had a present for me, I was so excited to see what it could be, I was no longer sleepy. A present for me. I never got presents, especially before Christmas Day. He even said we could play a game; he explained the rules to me, he called it the 'hot and cold game', if I was close to finding it, he would say hotter, if I was far away, it was colder. I hadn't played it before that night, I wondered how quickly I would be able to find the present.

Okay, I thought to myself, where should I start and that's when he told me to follow him, he would give me one clue. I followed in anticipation as he lured me into the basement, the little light from the street shinning in through the small broken tile, as the door creaked open, Ted was stood there, a wide grin spread across his face. I looked up at Uncle Rob, who reminded me, I wouldn't get any 'hotter' if I didn't start looking. To my surprise I quite quickly found my present, I unwrapped it, I couldn't believe it, it was perfect, I had my very own Barbie Doll. As I said thank you, Uncle Rob told me to close my eyes, and then I heard him say, "You can open them now." He was holding up a cat that had made a home in the basement out of the elements, the expression on his face had changed, Ted still grinning, Uncle Rob now staring at me, soullessly. He snapped its neck and said, "If you tell anyone what is going to happen next, you will end up like this cat, do you understand."

I nodded, paralysed with fear, clenching onto my Barbie as tightly as my tiny hands would allow. Ted placed a cloth in my mouth as he whispered "Shhhh" with a finger pressed against his lips. He wrapped a rope around my little body so I couldn't move, they both stood over me for a minute, saying not a word. Uncle Rob broke the silence, as he took out his worm and urinated on me and zipped himself back up again. He then began to slice the cat with a small Swiss army knife, holding it above my head, the blood slowly dripping down me as I now laid restrained on the cold basement unfinished floor. He took the doll from my grasp, and I clenched my eyes shut, I felt his breath against my neck and his body now pressed against mine. I was helpless.

"Don't worry, it's just a toy, it's your doll." and I felt something push up inside me. It was sharp, it hurt, I squirmed and then I froze. I lay there, in urine, covered in cats' blood, as the barbie was pushed up inside me, over, and over again. I could see Ted, watching intensely as he played with himself. Uncle Rob then unbuttoned his trousers, he no longer needed the dolls help, as he forced himself inside of me. I lay there in the basement and focused on the broken window and the sliver of light it let in, as my life was changed forever.

That dark, dirty, foul-smelling space became my torture chamber.

When the sun came up the next day, Uncle Rob wasn't there, he didn't tell me a story, in fact, he never told me that story again. I was sore, I was tired, I was filled with a heavy, sad feeling. I looked out my bedroom window and staring back at me, was Ted's living room, he had a lamp that would sit on a table perfectly in view, I had never really noticed it before, but from that day, it was all I could see. As I turned back and sat on my bed, I noticed my knickers felt wet, I got up and pushed my body against my bedroom door, so to not let anybody in, staring down into my knickers, they were filled with blood. A wave of emotions flooded my mind, the only one that I was able to focus on, was the fear of my mum finding out. So, I hid the knickers, behind the big wardrobe in the room, just like I hid what at happened to me that previous evening.

I was only just five years old; I didn't have the vocabulary at the time to express to anyone in a way they could understand, what was now happening to me, when Uncle Rob would get me on my own. Had I have found the words; it is likely that nobody would have believed me anyway. The gifts kept coming, but after the first time, I knew not to get excited about them anymore, it just filled me with dread. They were always used on me in such dark, perverse ways, they weren't toys, they were tools for torture.

Mum was very wary of Rob; they fought many times. She was jealous of the bond that he had with my dad, and she didn't appreciate the way they both stuck up for me. Little did she know that the attention I got from Rob was by no means the same attention I got from my dad - it wasn't protective in any way. It was all an act, a mask he wore in front of people. Abusers have two faces, the one they show to the world, which is fake and the real one that only their chosen victims get to see - A real Jekyll and Hyde.

Mum would break the toys that Uncle Rob would bring me as gifts, she did it to spite me, she had no idea the sense of relief it would give me, knowing that he would no longer be able to use them, on me. It would only be a matter of time before he replaced the broken toys of course. Mum and Dad went to Bingo most evenings and there were points the abuse would be every night. Paedophiles are known to share their toys, but Ted wasn't always there, Uncle Rob liked knowing I was his. He would whisper things like, "If only you weren't my niece.", as I lay stiff, enduring the pain.

The little bit of refuge that school afforded me was taken away every time I had to go to the toilets, where I could see very clearly from there our house; reminding me the minutes were ticking away and bringing me closer to whatever fate I would find on my return from school, be it Mums temper or the monster.

Often when I got home, I would head straight into mine and Jane's room. We had a beautiful cartoon Donald Duck wallpaper. That wallpaper is ingrained in my mind; it was Donald and his three nephews, and I would stare into the images of the scenes on the wall and imagine I was right there with them.

Some nights, Uncle Rob wouldn't bother waking me before carrying me to his chamber. I would wake up in the basement, met with the unfinished dirt floor, brick walls and cobwebs. The stench of cat urine in the air. This particular evening, he gifted me a set of multi coloured plastic children's golf clubs and blindfolded me. What happened next is truly unspeakable, a memory I wish I could erase forever. That is where I learnt, without even realising it at the time, to disassociate, leave my body, focus on the light shining in through the glass. That little light brought some comfort to me; it drew me in so that I didn't have to fully be there whilst they were doing these things to me. It was like the light took me to a different place, a place of calmness, maybe it wasn't the light, maybe it was whatever they had added to the cherry cola they would watch me drink before taking it in turns.

It goes without saying that I didn't feel safe around Uncle Rob anymore. He was only nice when people were listening, otherwise, he was always intimidating me, telling me I was just a stupid girl, and no one would believe me, that it was my word against his. Him and Ted would be sure not to forget, before beginning their fun, to warn me, threaten to kill me if I even thought about saying anything to anyone. They told me so many times that it was my fault that I really did believe them. They would tell me how Mum would beat me black and blue for lying and causing drama. Later, when she found my bloodstained knickers, I felt she had confirmed what they had told me, she beat me all around my bedroom, calling me an endless list of names. Despite it all, I didn't want to be taken away from my family, so I kept quiet, I didn't want to be blamed; it would be all my fault.

I was five years old when he first stole my autonomy, treating this body — my body — as if it were not my own, but his, to do with as he pleased. I was five years old and carrying a secret heavier than me.

This went on for years, no two evenings the same, but they continued down the same sadistic path that they had set out on. Often, they would abuse me together. Sometimes they would watch each other and masturbate over what the other was doing to me. Sometimes Ted was there, sometimes he wasn't. Sometimes I was blindfolded, other times not. Sometimes he used the toys he had picked out for the occasion, sometimes he had me all to himself. I had become withdrawn from my friends and family; I didn't know how to be present anymore. That basement is etched into my mind, to this very day. It lives with me, the feelings of terror and helplessness from all that had happened down there with the monster and his accomplice.

Six years later – we moved from the house on Musard Road. Once we had settled into the new house on Tamworth Street, my parents threw a big housewarming party. That night, Mum and Uncle Rob got into a huge fight, after that, he wasn't welcome at the house for some time. My Mum was no stranger to starting an argument, she could stir up a fight effortlessly; it was no secret she didn't like Uncle Rob, and this was her new home, her new start, not his.

I thought this could have been a new start for me too, it turned out to be just a whole new set of abuse but with a very different format and now, multiple players willing to engage in such sordid activities.

Rob was still in London, living in different hostels, but he wasn't welcome at ours when Mum was home for a long time after their fight, so we didn't see him as often, but when we did, he was as vile and evil as ever, and he still had his hooks in me. I was older, I had given my life to Jesus and was gaining more understanding of the world around me. I was maturing and so was my body. If I resisted, he would remind me that he would kill me, tell me I was a slut, a whore. He would repeat, over, and over again whilst assaulting me, "No one will believe you." I was trapped. I thought he was probably right. I got blamed for everything already. Nobody ever believed me. I was grateful it wasn't happening as often as it did before, at least.

Fast forward a couple of years and I was now in my early teens, thirteen or fourteen, the same time the Adams' moved to Australia. We hadn't seen Uncle Rob anywhere near as much in the last year, and when he reappeared, he was announcing plans to travel to the Philippines for an arranged marriage. He had been paid to meet someone, marry her, and bring her back to the UK. I just counted my blessings that his stay this time was short lived, although of course he made sure to pay me a visit, he didn't stick around for long and now he was flying to the Philippines.

In my heart, I felt an immense amount of sorrow for a woman I had never met, I wondered what her life was like and what would become of it, marrying such a monster. I would feel guilty for wondering whether having her meant I would no longer be his toy. I would spend some evenings praying he would love the Philippines so much that he wouldn't return.

He married Lucy and somehow, they made it work. When they returned to the UK and were waiting to be housed, they stayed with us. It was difficult for me; it was always difficult when he was around. I was fourteen, I had a boyfriend, Simon. It was clear to me now, that being married wasn't enough to stop Uncle Rob thinking I was his toy, nor was the fact I had a boyfriend. He would often make comments about how Simon would never be able to protect me from him. I was counting down the days, probably more eager than Lucy was for the council to give them their new home. I felt so sorry for her, Lucy was so kind, so gentle, she had no idea the monster she had married.

About a year later, when I was fifteen, Lucy was in hospital having their first child, Rupert. This time was different, it was in his house; this time I couldn't focus on the soft light entering the basement, instead, I stared at piles of new baby clothes and gifts. I felt a different kind of dirty, I didn't think it was possible, but he was more aggressive than ever before. The pain was excruciating. He still used toys, just not the same kind. He opened a big bag and took his time choosing, these toys were designed for sex. I hadn't seen anything like it before, some were shaped like penis', others vibrated. It was a sordid, sleazy experience. He savoured every minute of the abuse this time, he knew what I did not, that very day, he abused me for the last time.

Lucy delivered Rupert that day, his first child. I have no idea how she lived and stayed with him, I always felt her love; she was always kind, he didn't treat her kindly at all, but she stayed. Shortly after the birth, there was another argument between Mum and Uncle Rob. This time it was more serious, he wasn't allowed near the house at all, whereas before, if Mum wasn't home, he would still pop over. I don't know if it was because she had somehow found out about what was going on, but he held her up against the wall by her throat, tried to strangle her and, they didn't speak to each other for many years. I might have been free from Uncle Rob physically, but mentally, he had his claws in me for forty years without me even realising it, and, just as he had left, Owen arrived.

Mum couldn't get over the way he had attacked her, not without getting her own back. My boyfriend Simon, worked at a paint shop and Dad didn't do much except from support the decision he wasn't welcome at the house so, she took it into her own hands. She asked Simon to bring home some paint stripper from the shop he worked at; and then poured it all over Uncle Rob's new car.

Somehow, Uncle Rob made the marriage work, and it became a real marriage; Lucy had a son who was still in the Philippine's, he ended up coming to London and living with them. They also now had two beautiful children together, Rupert, as you know and a daughter. He gave her the middle name Harmony, the same middle name that my father had given to me. I was extremely disturbed knowing he had named his innocent child after me, his victim; like a trophy.

For many years, I didn't have much to do with Uncle Rob at all. He had a family of his own, and I couldn't wait to leave Fulham, I had begun my own journey in the big wide world.

Four years after marrying Bob, the priest, my third husband, I began to relive the abuse all over again, I was suffering with night terrors, flashbacks, of what Rob had done to me for all those years. I would wake up with a shriek, in a pool of sweat and frantic.

The night terrors were relentless, so vivid, a unique form of torture. They took me straight back, to the basement. I was completely paralysed by the flashbacks, stuck there, back with Rob. Every detail, every sensation, every inch of my being, back in the abuse. There was no getting away from it, I couldn't physically wake up until the nightmare had replayed the full extent of what I had endured all those years ago, start to finish. I was, yet again, five years old and scared and violated, except this time, it was my subconscious, holding my forty-year-old body prisoner. The night I seemed to revisit over, and over again, was the first time Uncle Rob hurt me, the night he had given me the barbie. The night he stole my innocence and that changed my life forever. It was unforgiving, witnessing again, after all this time, the sordid and satanic ways in which I had been used and treated like his toy.

By this point, I was an ordained minister and had done a lot of work on myself through therapy and other means of healing, I believe forgiveness is freeing, and I couldn't go on with these night terrors. I decided, one morning as we stood in Bob's kitchen, my heart racing, to send Uncle Rob a Facebook message, it read;

"Good afternoon. Rob, today I was doing my prayers and the Lord rested you on my heart, he wants you to know He loves you and your forgiven and I want you to know you're in my prayers."

In that moment, it didn't matter whether he saw the message, or not, it wasn't for him, I did it for me. It brought a sense of freedom and release.

The last time I saw Rob in person was Boxing Day, 2015. Just a few months after Mum passed away. Bob was with me, and we had just celebrated our first Christmas together in the UK. We had taken Dad to Birmingham, to spend the holiday with his sister Monica, brother-in-law Tom, and their family. This was Dad's first Christmas without Mum, so I wanted to try and make it as special as possible without her.

As we were returning to London, Dad was driving, and he asked if we could pop in to see Rob, Lucy and the kids. Rob looked nothing like the monster that haunted me for all those years. He was in failing health, on oxygen in a hospital bed in his living room, bed-bound with various illnesses. Mountains of medication cluttered his bedside. One of the last things he said that day in front of us all was that my cousin was always his favourite, Bob my husband was sickened by this comment as he knew what he had done to me as a child.

I was still living in fear of what would happen to my dad or my brothers if they found out? Would they even believe me? Would I be rejected again or blamed? I decided a long time ago that if, if I was to tell anyone, I would wait until Uncle Rob had died, before sharing my truth.

Uncle Rob died a few years later.

I summoned the courage to tell my dad what had happened to me all those years ago. I made a choice to start with him, even though it was his brother and his best friend, my dad was my biggest supporter. If anyone would believe me, it was him, even if he didn't want to believe it, he had never doubted me.

I invited Dad over and after some pleasantries, we all sat down with a cuppa in our back garden. Me, Bob and Dad - I was nervous, so with sweaty palms and a shaky voice, I told my dad that I had been sexually abused for ten years by his brother, his closest companion.

He sat and listened, and I had braced myself for his reaction. But really, he had none. There was a pause a silence, I'm sure it was a lot to take in. He wasn't angry, sad or even startled. He might have been stunned, he may have felt all of those things, but he didn't show emotion at all. I waited and as he finally acknowledged what I had said, his reply was something like, "That's a shame, love," and "I didn't see none of it." Then, with a resigned shrug, a sort of "it is what it is," he moved on, changing the subject.

If I am honest, I don't know what I had expected him to say, Rob was dead, Dad was sick. I had basically just told him, the time he spent protecting his little brother came with a price of not being able to protect his princess.

I now knew I wasn't the only one Rob terrorised. He had victims of other sorts. My aunty Monica and her husband Tom told me tales of abuse they had endured over the years, not of a sexual nature but the violent and emotional torment that he had subjected them too. We all knew what he had put Nanny Lilly through all those years ago. Mum and Rob had many run ins, and God only knows what Lucy and the kids had to put up with.

We gained a psychopath when I was only five years old. I don't know for certain why my uncle targeted me. At my young age I had a soft, gentle, and trusting nature. I was naive and susceptible to his manipulation and control. Jane said to me many years later when discussing the incident in the bedroom with her in preparation for this book, that it was my beauty, and soft nature, that saved her from the monster. For a split second, as she said that to me, for the first time in my life, I felt like her big sister, her hero, rather than her being mine.

To this day, despite knowing what they now know, my siblings are not able to understand why I am so different to them having grown up in the same family.

Having had very different childhood experiences and now understanding how abuse affects us all in different ways, I have reached an understanding; I have been able to forgive and release my uncle and myself from the chains that bound us together for so many years. I came to see my uncle as a frightened young boy that was also abused, controlled and threatened by monsters, Paedophiles, and I was able to separate the monster from the man. The abuse he had suffered ignited something dark and sinister within him.

It happened to him first. Maybe, if he had not been molested as a young boy, I wouldn't have been a victim. Maybe my whole life would have been, completely, different. Maybe.

My uncle had a monstrous and ugly side to him, but he was a victim first. And his perpetrator was a priest.

Chapter five

Traumatised parts, IFS and TA therapy.

I was trapped for years in a traumatised body. Part of me was stuck in a place and time; a part of me frozen, still scared and afraid. The part of me that didn't know what safety felt like, a part that was always on constant alert, hypervigilant, untrusting, needing to control. I was stuck with a part of me that longed to be held, loved and accepted, but I didn't know how to get her needs met. The poor little broken traumatised girl still stuck inside me.

There isn't a person on this planet that doesn't have parts, giving a voice to all parts of self, witnessing to them, loving every part of you; even the broken parts. This is where healing happens. Using internal family systems (IFS) therapy, you can begin to develop an embodied self. Using mindfulness, engaging in exercise, healthy eating and ensuring you are getting enough sleep will all aid with holding both the vulnerable parts and inner strength. As a trauma therapist, internal conflicts are to be expected. I steer away from labelling clients "therapy-resistant" or "difficult to treat" when conflict arises. Rather we shift, to noticing the parts that are standing in the way. Most often there are worries, fears or insecurities that need to be reassured, honoured and given space before ploughing through with the treatment and processing of trauma. This is relevant in Cognitive Therapy, Somatic Therapy and Psychodynamic Therapy. All components need to feel safe, in order to trust, and one of the most known terms is "inner child". This refers to a younger version of yourself that has experienced life from birth. There may be one specific inner child part that you'll be working with or sometimes there are different "child parts" – a baby part, a toddler part, a school-age part, a teenager and evolving adult part. These parts hold onto happy moments as well as challenging, scary or traumatic events that were unresolved; parts hold them until you're ready to process and resolve them as an adult. This is why sometimes emotions and/or memories resurface when you're an adult – your inner parts system combined with your internalised family system.

You may also develop an IFS of those whom you were surrounded by as you grew up. It's almost like a copy-and-paste version of those closest to you, where you internalise their personality traits and characteristics. You might see this clearly when you have developed a part that mimics a member from your family or someone who played a large role in your developing years. We also all have three ego states: child, adult and self. This is called Transactional Analysis (TA).

Everyone has an "internal system" that has learned to protect you. Beginning therapy or diving into something that is raw and fragile may kick up a worry that you're jeopardising your current safety and sense of self. Parts can include managers, firefighters and exiles.

Exiles: the younger parts of self that hold emotions, vulnerabilities, needs and memories that went ignored, unresolved and went to "exile" or put them away because there was no space to process the needs, or the trauma experienced.

Firefighters: the managers, the ones that keep the person "going". They help put the exiles aside so that the functioning part of self can go on with life. Managers can be healthy or unhealthy. Being able to compartmentalise is a good manager skill, but constant pressure or perfectionism is a burdened form of managing that adds stress.

Firefighters are extreme versions of "managers"; they act more impulsively and engage from a desperation to make any pain or hurt go away. They might present with addictive behaviours, completely shutting down (dissociating and disconnecting from self and others) or self-destruct. All of this is to keep "exiles" away, fearful of what will emerge if they arise.

Sometimes there can be an Inner Rebellion – a hint that something needs attention.

When there is an inner conflict, it can feel like there are parts rebelling against each other. As uncomfortable as this may be, it is often the best way to know something is needing your help, which can be addressed and resolved in therapy.

You will feel signs of inner conflict, like internalised aggression. You feel anger, but possibly you're lashing out at yourself. You're being super- hard on yourself, you're have thoughts of self-harm, suicidal fantasies or severe self-criticism. It feels like there's a seething anger beneath your skin. Usually, anger turned inwards is a sign that you didn't have permission to be angry as a child. It wasn't safe enough to express anger when you were younger, because the adults around you could not tolerate the intensity of the experience and therefore it's been turned inward instead of expressed.

To work with these parts, you may want to first give that part a space to be heard and witnessed to. Bring the emotional bully into the room, give it an empty chair and invite it to a conversation known as (Gestalt Therapy).

You may feel it using words that were told to you by a caregiver, someone who was abusive or absent (and the message could be anything from "You're not worthy of my time" to "You're a bad boy/girl", or "You made me hurt you/yell at you".)

You'll notice that the self-blame may be misplaced as it wasn't feasible to expect your own, often, younger, self, to protect yourself in that specific incident. That part often needs to be told, "It wasn't your fault".

Sometimes this isn't about a person, but rather, sadness that God, society or the world didn't protect or defend you. Your healing will be about slowly rebuilding trust in the universe as you heal. Your disappointment or anger may be outward with some other form of construct that "should have" protected you and you're wondering, "How was this allowed to happen?" and "Why was I not protected?" In your healing, you'll slowly reconstruct a sense of safety and trust with personalised experiences.

Most often after being abused, you are left with an unshakable shame.

Shame makes you truly believe that you're bad at your core. It's an emotion that distorts your entire identity, making you believe you're damaged, no good and unworthy of love and kindness. Often, if you were ignored, hurt or shamed as a child you will carry shame as an adult. Shame expresses itself in many ways; the way you interact with others, the kinds of relationships you believe you're deserving of, how you speak up in the workplace, ask for that promotion and how you parent your kids and set boundaries.

Shame has a way of digging itself deep on the mind and body; it impacts how we carry our bodies, our muscle tone and the stability in our voice.

Notice if you hunch over when you're asking for that promotion, if your voice quivers when telling a child to stop hurting yours or if you doubt yourself when presenting your work at a conference. You may also carry shame about your body, and this impacts how confident and forward you are regarding expressing and asking for intimacy, physical contact and how present you are when you have sex.

One of the ways to unravel the shambles of shame is catching yourself when your mind starts spewing negative, shame- filled thoughts and replace them with more positive ones.

You can also do this by expanding your body's bandwidth for emotions and changing how you interact. If you notice that somatically you lean over, lower your voice or hesitate when engaging with others, you can teach your body to keep going, speak up and stand tall. You will notice how empowering it is to make a conscious approach and try a new way of being. I call this shifting the atmosphere from negative to positive.

Regression is also a symptom of PTSD.

Ever feel like a little kid in a grown-up's body? Ever had a full-blown tantrum that would seem more appropriate for a five-year- old than a forty-year- old? Ever find yourself back in an old power struggle you had years ago when interacting with someone who reminds you of a family member, or when visiting family, you haven't seen in a while? There are times where you might regress back to a younger self-state than your chronological age. You may also notice that you're suddenly craving certain foods, are not sticking to your regular schedule and are getting into a dynamic with your loved ones that are not aligned with who you are as an adult.

Often when there is a regression there's something that brought it on. It could be a time of year that is reminding you of something that happened, maybe there was a trigger, to a loss or trauma or maybe there was something related to an event that shifted you back to a younger emotional experience.

When this happens, take out a piece of paper and literally draw an adult part gently holding or sitting next to the younger part that's been activated. Younger emotional parts need to be reminded they are not alone. They need to be reminded that there is an adult who can guide the way and offer compassion.

Younger emotional parts need to be reminded they are not alone. They need to be reminded that there is now an adult who can guide the way and offer compassion.

The inner child may set the bar high. Then moves it higher and higher. A perfectionist pressure. You want that perfect meal-plan, the "just right" parenting intervention, the latest business technique and impeccable meditation or prayer to your morning routine. Of course, you want to see yourself as put-together, capable and strong and you probably want others to see you in that light as well. However, when you start feeling like a car running on no gas, that's a sign of too much pressure.

It's OK to allow the imperfect, the humane, the messy parts of yourself to come out. When we stop hiding, we allow our creativity and individuality to come out and shine. And your young inner self will be happy to enjoy life and have childlike fun without the need to always protect yourself.

Try doing one thing today on purpose that is imperfect. Watch to see what that's like. You may not love what you see but it may not be as scary as you had imagined; you may even uncover a new lovely part of yourself. That part may not have some golden skill, but it may be a more comfortable, less judgmental part of self that makes life a little sweeter.

Warmly welcome the richness your life has to offer. To build a successful life you'll need to iron out the creases along the way. Real growth and transformation can be frightening and bring the unknown and it's normal to be hesitant.

However, by working through conflict you untangle the webs of sabotage and allow new opportunities to unfold. You need to be ready to do the work, to show up to love, life and possibilities with more clarity, strength and confidence, Therapy can help. Therapists who are skilled in using trauma-informed methods and utilise parts-focused work can help you lots.

The first time I had truly witnessed trauma being exposed was after moving to Tamworth Street. There were two sisters that lived just up the street from me; a big scandal broke out because one of the girls spoke out about her own sexual abuse. Little did anyone know that I, too, was a victim. The pain the family suffered because of her speaking out frightened me so much. Seeing what they went through as a family, it convinced me that I would never be able to speak out. Mainly through fear of what might happen to my family if I did. What would Dad do? My brothers? I already carried enough shame and living with the responsibility of causing a response that would put them in prison, well the thought was unbearable. I didn't want to be responsible for anything like that, I couldn't watch anyone else suffer because of what had happened to me, so I kept quiet.

There was also my best friend Alice. Who was, along with her sister, being sexually abused by their mum's boyfriend. She had no idea that I was being abused too and I couldn't find the courage at the time to tell her. It broke my heart to watch her, and her sister go through the ordeal of speaking out when it came to giving evidence in court; them having to relive it and give evidence at such a young age - they were so brave. I wish I could have been as brave as they were.

I saw the pain, the anguish that my friend's family went through. I saw first-hand the hurt and devastation when someone had spoken out. It was difficult to witness let alone do for myself. Would my family even believe me? Would I be rejected again or blamed? In both cases, my neighbours and my best friends, the perpetrators were convicted and imprisoned. I learnt later it doesn't end there, I saw the fear in my friend when her perpetrator was being released; she lived in fear. Fear that he would return and either do it again or want some type of revenge.

I had now seen abuse through the eyes of so many others. Personally, and now professionally. The one time that had the most profound impact on my personal healing was around the time of my Uncle Rob's death. I was a safeguarding officer and pastoral support worker and counsellor in a church. I will tell you a little more about that later.

Elle Ministries categorically bought me a sense of healing, be it I had been working on myself for a long time at this point. I undertook a couple of inner healing courses here and ultimately; I was able to let go of a lot of what I had been carrying for so many years. This led to me being becoming Chaplain in Brixton Prison for Men. I loved working in the prison, helping the men deal with their own issues of trauma, which most of the time was the reason why they had ended up in the prison in the first place. So many people who carry their trauma into adult life are misunderstood but I had a way of being able to connect with them. They didn't see me like the rest of the Chaplains, they said I was "not like the other glossy-haired Christians". Maybe it was my tattoos or just my openness to share some of my own experiences with them. My stories of overcoming, which in turn gave them a little hope to continue with the time they had left to serve.

Once when working in the prison a young man was suicidal, he was on G Wing the wing for vulnerable prisoners, to keep them safe, he was just sentenced for being a Paedophile, I had to sit with him for hours, and he started to share his story with me. Which, I am certain, he was sharing with me in an attempt to both shock and intimidate me. After he had stopped sharing his story, something came over me and, in that moment, I decided to share with him a piece of my own testimony. I expressed the impact it had on my life, to which his response, a tear came to his eye. It was followed by more tears as he began to sob. He had, in front of my eyes, turned into a helpless little boy.

I found myself full of pity for him. I explained to him about my near-death experience and not being able to get into heaven with unforgiveness in your heart. He needed to forgive himself, just like Jesus did – there and then he gave his life to Jesus in a four- by- six cell. This has been one of the most enlightening experiences of my life; the power of forgiveness and the prophetic act of sharing one's testimony and how it can bring healing to others.

No one is born a Rapist, Paedophile or Murderer. Throughout my healing journey, I have learned and employed skills and techniques that are invaluable, but forgiveness truly sets us free. True forgiveness can lead us to compassion and understanding, not to justify wicked behaviour but to understand where it came from. I was finally able to separate the monster from the man. The old saying "monkey see, monkey do" comes to mind. It's learnt behaviour, they learn it from somewhere! As a therapist it's not always easy but we must try to put aside the behaviour and ask the reasons as to why people behave in such ways. Explore the contributing factors that led them down the dark road they have travelled - the causes of their behaviour. Love the sinner not the sin!

Unfortunately, you can be born into a life subjecting you to victimisation, typically our abusers are abused. The difference is what you do with it. Throughout my exposure to other people's struggles with abuse I often compared my situation to theirs, like why wasn't I brave like Alice and her sister. The truth is, no two situations are alike, and we will all have our own individual factors to navigate throughout the long road called recovery.

Most of my symptoms subsided when I started trauma therapy.

It is important to note that didn't happen overnight. I tried everything: DBT, CBT, CAT talking therapy, then EMDR. As well as specialist psychodynamic trauma psychotherapy. Vigorously learning to feel safe in my body again, learning grounding tools as well as starting mindfulness meditation, morning and evening to relax as I worked out to getting my body moving every day becoming unstuck from the trauma left behind. That is when my life truly changed for the better. I then trained to become a psychodynamic psychotherapist in the trauma field myself. Now I can finally say "I'm a proud adult survivor, now thriving, an overcomer of childhood sexual abuse, enjoying my life to the fullest."

There are a lot of things people often say to a loved one who has suffered abuse. These things are intended to be helpful but can actually, result in the individual feeling worse.

For example:

- "This will make you stronger. Find the silver lining!"

- "You won't heal until you forgive him."

- "Be flattered. They wanted you that bad."

- "Talk to me. You won't get better until you talk about it."

These statements tend to put the pressure on. They may seem like good things to say, but to us, for the most part they are hard to hear. Some of us can find a silver lining and some of us can't. Whether we do or not, we need to get there on our own. We all heal at our own pace. There's no set timeline.

I know most of you have good intentions, but these statements can make us feel bad. I also understand that without guidance, finding the words to comfort someone in their time of need can be tricky.

So, with that being said, here are some things I recommend saying:

- "It's not your fault."

- "I believe you."

- "I'm here for you."

- "What do you need?"

- "You can talk to me if you want, but if you're not ready, that's OK too."

Overall, please know nothing you say can take away our pain. There's no magic fix. Just let the individual know you're there. Being honest about that is also a great response.

- "I don't know what to say but I do know how to listen. I hear you."

Whatever you decide, in the situation you may be facing, just please don't put pressure on them. Offer your support and love, let them heal at their own pace. Please don't make it about your anger or how uncomfortable you are. However awful you feel about it, know the individual that experienced such a horrific act is feeling much worse. Don't try to pretend you understand, we are glad that you don't.

If you have been a victim and are on your own path of healing, I really found writing a letter to my five-year-old me helped so much.

Here is a part of that letter;

First of all, I need you to know how proud I am of you that you survived. I have been angry with you at times but that stops today. You were only five years old; you did not know what rape was, never mind how to stop it. When I really think about everything you had to do to survive, I am nothing but proud that you fought so I could have the life I do today. Although the flashbacks and the memories have made me at times feel terrible, I am alive and that is because of you.

I have finally come to realise how hard I fought at five years old just to survive. Did I run out of the room screaming and tell someone I was being raped? No, I did not. Did I continue to be raped for the next ten years until I was fifteen years old? Yes, I did. These are two things I used to blame myself for, holding onto this incredible guilt, leading me to hate my childhood self. I blamed myself for not saying anything.

I am writing this today because I have come to forgive myself and I am starting to be compassionate towards my childhood self. I am sharing my story because I have come to realise, I did not survive childhood sexual abuse to not say anything. I did not survive to not share my story. I want to break the silence about childhood sexual abuse and hopefully offer support to those healing. Most of all, I did not survive to hate myself—that is why I have decided to love myself. That does not mean I 100% love myself fully today (I wish it was that easy) but I'm getting there one day at a time; it does mean that I have begun to forgive myself and I am finally working toward loving myself instead of hating everything about me.

****

If you were abused as a child, no matter how old you were, you did nothing wrong before, during or after you were raped. However, you acted before the rape and however you reacted during the rape and however you coped with this trauma is OK. None of your actions led to your rape. The only thing that led to your rape is at the fault of the perpetrator.

You did everything you could to survive, and you should be proud of yourself. You are here today to live a meaningful life; you are not here today to criticise yourself for something that was out of your control. For anyone who survived childhood sexual abuse, no matter where you are in the healing process, I want you to know I am proud of you. You survived. I know how much it takes to keep fighting when living seems impossible some days yet here you are. I could not be more grateful you have decided to stay. Although I do not know you, that does not mean you are alone. You're not fighting this alone — I am here with you and so are millions of other survivors.

Telling my story is one of the hardest things I have ever done. As I am preparing to share this with the world, I go through a compass of emotion: I am scared, I am anxious and embarrassed. I still wonder if anyone will believe me as I prepare and anticipate for those who won't. I wonder, am I talking about my past too much and being selfish? Am I making people uncomfortable with the weight of my truth? Does anyone even care? Feelings that were hardwired a part of me and despite intensive therapy I still must face. But I am committed to sharing my story - I am speaking up.

My, Why?

It is empowering.

Sharing empowering, it is liberating, and I believe, necessary. There is absolutely no way to describe the weight of carrying trauma or the anxiety and fear that come with the journey to recovery. My innocence was stolen from me. I lost all control over the sovereignty of my body. When I share my story and un-tell the lies of my past, I take back control over my life. I take back control over my body. I take back control over my feelings. Now I can focus on healing from the abuse. Believe me, I became zealous in the need to release myself from the past.

It is OK to feel it?

I needed to teach myself that feeling it was OK, especially when it is on my terms. As a survivor, I learned early on the importance of a protective shield. It is a hard defence mechanism to rewire. I started learning how to feel all of it, rather than pushing it away, which is not easy. I realised I was often emotionally detached and physically cut off from the neck down. As I reconnect to myself and my emotions, it was uncomfortable and intensely painful at times, but I keep hearing that amazing growth comes from the deepest of pain, so I trudge on.

I needed support, help and compassion.

I needed the support of others, plain and simple. I couldn't do it on my own. Support is crucial to the recovery process and can be found in many different places. My support system consisted of my best friends, my therapists, Bob, my husband, my children and a few close friends who are also survivors. I cannot stress enough the benefits of having understood loved ones and their help with coping. The support from others makes you feel less isolated. It helped me accept that my feelings were important and that others do care. Connecting with other survivors also helped me not feel alone. Courage is contagious. I want other survivors who are not yet sharing their stories to know they are not alone. Together, we can all hold each other up.

I hope I am shedding light on the real recovery process for trauma survivors. Trauma recovery and healing can be messy, chaotic and not for the faint of heart. My trauma is not a flash point in my life, it is a part of who I am. It has influenced how I perceive things and how I respond. Through therapy, I learned to respond more appropriately to high- stress situations and I also developed coping skills for anxiety, nightmares and flashbacks. However, it will always take a little extra effort on my part. As a survivor, I can view obstacles in life as challenges to overcome and get past. I do not get past my trauma — I learned to integrate it into my life and live with it. Healing is cyclical, not linear.

I hope my sharing helps loved ones and friends of trauma survivors better understand the complexity of recovery. I don't think trauma ever goes away and triggers can be everywhere. People who have never experienced a traumatic event usually have no point of reference for understanding. That is OK. In fact, I would often tell my husband that I didn't need him to understand. I just needed him to be with me in the space, so I knew I was not alone when things got heavy. Through recovery, survivors learn how to better cope and navigate the chaos when the past comes knocking.

It is my right! This is my life, my experiences, my pain — I can talk about it all I want. I am done protecting the people who did not protect me. For me, that means sharing, even when my voice shakes.

It is your right, too!

Chapter six

Sexual abuse and traumatised parts.

My whole life has been affected by the sexual abuse I suffered as a child. Hyper-perfectionist. Master over-thinker. Fear of trusting others. Anorexia and bulimia because food was the first thing that gave me what felt like control over what had happened to my body. Attachment anxiety. Difficulty having/enjoying sex without being triggered. Feeling dirty and uncomfortable in my own skin. My childhood was so messed up from the abuse, it took my innocence, but I used to get into these moods that would make me almost childlike at times. It's embarrassing really thinking about it now, to tell you the truth. I used to have horrible nightmares, so vivid to the point I was almost stuck back in the abuse. I would either find myself too scared to fall asleep or waking myself up in a pool of sweat. I felt unlovable. I had no real idea how I should be treated or what to look for in a partner. I would stay in the most toxic and abusive relationships because, well, in a way it was all I knew and all I felt I deserved. I would always stay; I had no self-worth, and I had a difficult time saying no or putting in safe boundaries. Sometimes, I would have this feeling of unimaginable disgust when a significant other would touch me sexually; an overwhelming repulsion because my abuser used to touch me there. I've never told anyone that, in fear I would hurt or offend them. Sometimes, when I would get really triggered or upset, I would try to hide away. I would go into my closet in the dark and hide behind my clothes in a little ball and muffle my own cries with a pillow while I rocked. Just like I did all those years ago in the wardrobe or attic. I used to find it difficult for me to speak up for myself or what I wanted. I was the ultimate people-pleaser. This also led to me being gaslighted by partners when I was an adult, which I didn't see until after I was out of the relationship. The list is long and there was this childlike belief, the next partner would be different. This need to always look for my forever soul mate, the longing to not be alone and to be loved. To be very honest with you and very much the opposite to a lot of my struggles above, I think I also became addicted to sex at one point in my life, in a way to try and heal myself, to regain my power back. It probably did more damage than good, rather than heal me, yeah, it was my coping mechanism. I had the overwhelming urge to be in control of my own sex life, to enjoy lovemaking and for it not always to be a trigger, so I tried my best to do exactly that. I wanted to take back the power, my power, the power that Rob, Ted and Owen had stolen from me as a child. I wanted to enjoy intimacy, I wanted to have a healthy relationship and a good sex life in my marriage. But, in kicked the people pleaser in me and I would just be back, doing certain things that made me uncomfortable or simply not feeling good or sexy enough. No matter the approach I had taken, it always seemed to be me that suffered.

The effects of sexual abuse in childhood can be both debilitating and far-reaching, often extending out of childhood, into adolescence and adulthood. For some, this looks like being unable to trust anyone, because intimacy can feel a lot like giving someone access and a license to hurt you. For others, trauma manifests physically in nightmares, panic attacks or dissociative episodes. As I started to educate myself, I wanted to know more about the kinds of effects childhood sexual abuse can have on adulthood, so I started doing my homework!

Sadly, there is considerable evidence to suggest that those who have experienced CSA are also likely to be re-victimised. A recent study involving 12,252 survivors found that 47.5% were sexually victimised again later in life. Similarly, there is also evidence to suggest that the children of CSA survivors are also more likely to be abused themselves, suggesting that the cycle of abuse may continue into the next generation.

The process of healing was not an easy one or a quick one, but it was well worth the hard work in the long run. Going through the pain of processing helped me to live freely and happy in my adult self, and I wish I had started at a much earlier age. I would love to have it made a law, that every child at the age of eighteen when leaving school takes the ACE score test (adverse childhood experiences) and anyone above a four on the test be put straight onto a waiting list for therapy. I think this will not just help victims of abuse heal quicker, and have better relationships and be better parents themselves, but I also think it would save the government a lot of money—saving the healthcare system money in the long- term—as symptoms would be seen sooner rather than later. I wish I had learnt the tools I know now, back when I was eighteen years old! My life would have been a whole lot easier.

No matter how childhood sexual abuse affects you now in adulthood, I want you to know that you never deserved what happened to you, IT WASN'T YOUR FAULT. If you are struggling with shame and self-blame, I want you to know, you are worthy, you are important, you are deserving of love. I hope these words can be a small reminder and bring a little comfort when the darkness of past abuse feels thick and overwhelming. Tell yourself, IT WASN'T MY FAULT!

Chapter seven

School Days

"If anyone causes one of these little ones—those who believe in me—to stumble, it would be better for them to have a large millstone hung around their neck and to be drowned in the depths of the sea."

Matthew 18:6

School should have been a place of refuge for me; somewhere safe to escape the abuse at home. It should have been a place to learn and grow, make forever friends, to be free and childlike. But school wasn't really any of that for me. I struggled a lot as I found it hard to focus; often my days spent daydreaming. I loved creative learning; I loved to make things, paint and draw. Give me a pencil and a piece of paper and I would be content for hours.

I had learning difficulties and was diagnosed as dyslexic at an early age. I had to attend a special support class a few hours each week with a one-on-one to help me with my English, reading and spelling. Reading was especially hard because of my dyslexia, especially reading aloud. I was so nervous when asked to read aloud in class. My anxiety would rocket and magnify my dyslexia. Inevitably I would stumble in fits and starts, get laughed at by the class and sit down feeling embarrassed, ashamed. My reading difficulties in class only added fodder to the bullying that I was already receiving.

My Mum was a good seamstress and she used to make some beautiful clothes, for herself, our family and even for some of our friends. But me, I was sent to school in old and tattered clothes and met with the taunts of 'fleabag' as a result. Even the one or two friends I had would be bullied because they were friends with me. The other kids would scrunch their faces and say to them "Eeww, why are you talking to her?" Besides the name- calling, the kids would put drawing pins on my seat and chewing gum in my hair. I was bullied for the duration of primary and secondary school.

There was this one girl in particular that found great satisfaction in both my humiliation and physical pain. Her go to taunt and at one point it was nearing daily, would be to come up behind me, pull down my skirt and as I bent over to pull it up, BAM, she would knee me in the tailbone. Oh boy, did that hurt! It even had a name, 'the bunny hop kick'. It felt like an electric shock that started from my coccyx and shuddered through my whole body. Typically happening in the lunch queue with most of the school around, the shrieks of laughter rumbled throughout the hall. I couldn't leave the queue, or I'd lose my spot, so I fought back the tears. People I thought were my friends would eventually join in at my expense. To fit in with the group even though it was cruel.

In the end, the nerves in my coccyx had to be cauterised to stop the continuous chronic pain that ran through my legs daily affecting my mobility.

When I was around twelve or thirteen, there was a young boy called Graham Bell; he was a bit of a loner like me, and we would often sit talking together in the lunch hour. He lived just across the road from the school. We soon became friends, and he would invite me back to his house at lunch time to watch movies. He was crazy about the film The Terminator and goodness knows how many times we watched it together during our lunch hours. I think he had a little crush on me. I suppose you could call him my first sort of boyfriend, although we only ever pecked each other on the lips, once. Both of us were very shy, we had a great bond, he was a lifeline at school for the time I had him in my life. Whilst we were sort of boyfriend and girlfriend, he had an accident on a motorbike, and it killed him. It was the first funeral I ever attended. After Graham died, lunchtime again became hard to face, I was alone. That was until Alice, and I became best friends.

When I was around fourteen years old, I started dating Simon, a boy in my year at school. At first, I went out with Simon as a dare. Everyone at school was pairing up. Both Simon and I, possibly would have been classed in school as misfits as; we weren't in the cool group, a part of the emo or hippy or tech group. I will add that I tried to fit in to most of the groups at some point, even dying my hair black and wearing tie dye for a short time. Needless to say, it wasn't a success. Simon was a great football player and had try-outs for a big team, because of this he fitted in more. We were in some option classes together – classes you choose to do your exams in. Two of the classes we had taken were "Design and Realisation". We'd design to scale and make things out of wood or plastic, learning to use all different types of DIY hand and power tools. Then there was "Design and Communication", which was mostly prospective drawing and designing. These lessons were taken by my form tutor, the wonderful Mr Lipot. He was a wonderful teacher, very talented. I remember he was building his own boat, and he would often share updates by showing us photos of his progress. Physical prints of course, there were no mobile phones back then. Gosh, now I'm showing my age! He was very proud of his boat, I was always happy to hear the excitement in his voice when he was explaining how it was developing; how he used dovetail joints, carved by hand. As well as being my form tutor, he was passionate about his job. He was always kind to me.

Simon had a best friend Mark. He was a Kiwi and had a cute accent, very good looking and could always make you laugh. Not long after Simon and I started dating, Simon's best friend and Alice got together. Best friends dating best friends, we became inseparable and did everything together. They all sat behind me in the next row in both classes; we often didn't get much work done as I would be leaning over the table behind me chatting to them. One of the only times I spent in my school days laughing and joking.

Simon had a younger brother, and they were living with his Nan at the time. His Mum had left them when they were very young and his Father raised him as a single Dad - By the time I knew the boys their Father had met someone, then married her and went on to have a few more children. They decided to move out of London to Leicester. I have many happy memories of visiting his Father and new family in Leicester.

We were a crazy, strange bunch. Simon was my first real boyfriend. We were together until I was almost eighteen; we had planned to get married on my eighteenth birthday. I was desperate to start my own life, to get away from my family and away from all the abuse. The idea of getting married was the best and only option that entered my head.

By the age of fourteen I was working four jobs. One of them was taking care of our neighbour's children, baby Oliver and his sister Jessica. I loved children and babies. I was always very motherly; I so wanted a child to love and protect and call my own. To become the Mum that I never had.

During the latter part of our school years, we had entered the rebellious stage. We would sneak a cigarette, we tried cannabis, we would binge- drink alcohol during our lunch hour. I remember one lunch hour we got so drunk and had to return to class. Lucky for us it was with Mr Lipot in woodworking class. We were finishing up our final piece for our final GCSE exam. I was making a desk with a lift-up drawing board and storage unit. I was painting the drawing board, but I was so drunk I could hardly stand up. Simon, who was working in a paint store at the time, brought me in some white gloss paint from work to complete my drawing board ready to submit. I was pouring the paint on, not just a little bit, lots of it and then just smearing it with the brush. Then I leaned against it, tipsy as I was, I slipped. The paint went everywhere, all over the drawing board, the floor, my clothes and in my hair! It was a mess. I was a mess! Mr Lipot was more concerned about me going home stinking of alcohol and being drunk. How would the school explain that one of their students was stinking drunk and covered from head to toe in white gloss paint?

My parents loved a night out; a few laughs and a few drinks with friends. Almost every night after dinner they would be off to Bingo and wouldn't return home until late. If they won, they would stay for the late session. There would be promotions and special events quite often. I was about thirteen years old when Mum and Dad won a contest and had the chance to be on a TV game show. The contest held in the bingo hall was a mock version of the popular TV show "Mr and Mrs". My parents took part and they won! Winning meant they were invited to be on a taping of the real show at the ITV studios in Carlisle. "Mr and Mrs" was a popular TV game show that involved couples attempting to match each other's answers to six questions about their married life. There were cash prizes and a special commemorative carriage clock given to the winning couple.

All us kids were so excited that our Mum and Dad were going to be on TV. They had an all-expenses paid trip to Carlisle, including transport and hotel accommodation for two nights. Nannie Barbara – Mum's Mum – stayed with us.

We sat around the TV in the living room as a family waiting for the show to start. One of their questions was, "What part of a roasted chicken is your spouse's favourite?" that was an easy question for them both. Dad only eats the breast and Mum's favourite was the crispy skin. The final question was, "Of the following three choices, which album would your spouse choose?" One of the options was Simon and Garfunkel's Greatest Hits, which was my parent's' favourite album. In fact, it might have been the only album they owned. They even named my big brother, their first-born son, Art, they loved the band so much. They won! It was that music question that won them the big prize, I think it was approximately £1200, a lot of money, especially in those days as well as the commemorative carriage clock. That clock was so proudly displayed in my parents' front room on top of the telly for many years, and now is with my beautiful sister.

Nannie Barbara left us kids to fend for ourselves for a few hours. I heard the phone ring, so I picked it up, it was my Auntie Monica, Dad's sister. She asked to speak to Dad, so I told her that they were on their way back from Carlisle. She then said, "When they get back, tell your Dad his Mum has died."

The day I had to tell Dad his Mum had died is etched in my mind to this day. I had school the next day, business as usual. It wasn't just any day either it was a big day, the first of two whole days doing a mock art exam. I was stuck in my head, I was upset, wondering why I had to be the one to give my Dad the update. Had I delivered the news as well as I could?

Why me? My art teacher was so understanding. She could see that I was hurting, so when the mock exam was over, she asked me if I would like to be a model for the A level and GCSE still life art class. An absolute blessing as it excused me from all my other classes for the rest of the week and it gave me the time and space to process what had happened. She even let me have lunch with them in the staff room where we spoke and celebrated my parents recent win on the tv game show.

Around the end of that school year, after taking my mock exams and breaking up for summer, I was spending lots of time with Simon; in hindsight, God saved me from what could have been. An Arabic man came into the paint store where Simon worked; he bought some paint and then started asking advice and recommendations for a decorator as he wanted to repaint something. He went on to say it first needed to be stripped to the bare wood. So, Simon got me a little side job stripping paint to earn a little extra money. We were just young teenagers and this man seemed kind of sleazy. He would go on about wealth, power and money. He told us he was getting a car and that he would teach us both to drive. It was all pretty creepy; we didn't even know this man, but we overlooked the creepiness so that we could earn the extra money. Simon would be at work, and I'd be at this guy's house by myself stripping paint off the woodwork.

My job was done when the man decided he wanted the wood to be painted gold and rubbed with gold leaf. I agreed. It was an exciting job, a few weeks' work and a good little earner. I still felt uneasy with this guy when Simon wasn't around. The job took about two weeks to complete. Simon was great and would collect me after he finished work. Luckily, what could have been, wasn't. I was so used to be in these types of high risk and vulnerable situations, not that it made it any easier, but I didn't like saying no to people no matter the potential risk to myself.

As I worked on finishing the gold leafing one day, the man begun to make conversation. Asking me what I wanted to do with my life, so I responded "I want to be an airline hostess'. He jumped up, announcing he has something for me and off he went, returning with a hostess uniform. It was a real one, it was made beautifully, the quality undeniable, it looked just like the ones I had seen on TV.

I didn't stop to ask myself why this single, creepy old guy had kept an air hostess costume in his house. He said to me "Go on, try it on." So, I did. I loved it! It fitted perfectly. In that moment, I looked at myself in the mirror for the first time wearing this beautiful uniform and I thought to myself, I could really do this. Next there was a knock on the door, it was his friend. They went off to the kitchen and I spent a moment admiring how I looked. Suddenly, there was this smell. Innocently I went to check what it was and there they stood, passing a pipe between them and then he passed it to me. My stomach in knots, I didn't know what it was at the time, but I knew I didn't want any. I panicked, I started crying and intense response to not knowing if they would force me to as that is where saying no usually got me. "I'm still wearing the uniform." I said, as he began shouting at me to shut up, "You're ruining my buzz!" I ran out of the house; I called Simon who met me immediately. Crack cocaine. That's what they had just tried to get me to try. I never went back to his house after that. What were they doing offering it to me, a child? Was it simply to take advantage of me there and then? or was it darker? did they want me hooked on drugs to make money from my body? The air hostess uniform, the gesture of giving it to me, followed by offering me the pipe makes me think I had a lucky escape that day.

I was about fourteen when we got a little white dog; I named him Tequila. I would walk the dog before leaving for school. My route of choice was through the market and each morning I would pass Owen's stall. He knew my parents, was friendly with the whole family, he'd known me from a very young age. His family had run the stall for over sixty years. George had worked on almost every stall the market had. Owen was good looking, always had a nice tan and would stop to make small talk most mornings. He would smile and tell me that I was beautiful. At the time this made me feel grown up, special. Sometimes he would wolf-whistle at me and give me a piece of fruit to take to school. I won't lie, I enjoyed the attention; I felt good about myself. Of course, I was a young teenage girl enjoying the attention from an older guy. I'd never really received this type of attention, at school, I was bullied, and Uncle Rob was horrid towards me. So, Owen was a breath of fresh air and I felt desirable.

Next to his stall would be his fruit and veg van and the smelly little beat-up car that he drove. It wasn't long before he asked to take me out. Most of the time he would take me to Dukes Meadow Park. He would drive down to the end of the footpath along the River Thames, park the car and then start kissing me. He would then make me give him oral sex. I was young and naive, and Owen knew what he was doing. This happened about twice a week for about a year; more often in the summer months during the school holidays. He never drove me all the way home, he would drop me at the end of the street. I didn't realise that I was again being groomed. Later I learnt the park he had been taking me too was a dogging site. I would also find out he was in his early thirties and married with two children. I think his children were just a few years younger than me.

I had got a job at a hair salon, on Kings Road as a Saturday girl washing hair at about the age of fourteen, Owen would sometimes turn as the salon was closing. Everything he did felt kind. This wasn't like Uncle Rob and Ted, Owen was different. He would buy me hot chocolate in the winter mornings before school or ice cream in the summer. He was older, with a job and a car. I felt like I was finally making a choice, like I was in control. Owen wanted me, maybe he even loved me? I was so, so wrong. I was being used and lied to by another man and I was only fourteen. I was confused, searching for my ticket, my escape - ready to start a life of my own and desperate to find a person to do that with. I worked at the salon for a few years first as a Saturday girl washing hair, then full time once I finished my GCSE at age fifteen. Just before I left home, Owen and I had full intercourse in a small, dingy apartment near his fruit and veg stall. When we had finished, we spoke a little, I asked if this was his flat and he laughed, explaining that the apartment belonged to a friend of his that worked on the market. He told me he lived in Wimbledon and that he was married with two kids, a daughter and a son. He spared no thought for my feelings when revealing the news. I was disgusted. The thought of dating a married man and being his bit on the side – his toy!

I wanted as far away from Fulham as possible knowing what I now did. I ended things with Owen - I now had another secret to keep. Another thing I couldn't tell anyone. So, a few months before my sixteenth birthday, in the May of 1990 and just before my exams, I moved into Simon's Nans with him. I was fifteen when I left school due to be the youngest in the year with an August birthday. On our last day of school Simon proposed to me; we were engaged.

We quickly moved into a place of our own in Hounslow. It was his Mum's house but since she now lived in the pub her husband owned, she rented it to us. I had a real chance, to create my own life with Simon. He remained working at the paint shop, he was earning good money there and I went full time at the hairdressers - apprentice hairdresser to the stars. We were teenagers out on our own for the first time, we had bills to pay, a holiday to book and a wedding to save for. It started out a dream.

As Simon and I were building our life together, my childhood friend Stacey contacted me. She was in trouble, and she asked if she could stay with us for a while. So, that was that I moved Stacey in with us without hesitation. We had some crazy, fun times in that house. We would play video games on an Amiga console for hours, which was at first a novelty and for the first time in our lives there was nobody to tell us to stop doing anything. We would get stoned and have loads of people around. We were teenagers doing teenage stuff. It felt good. I was free. I could do what I wanted.

There were times when I would go to work, Simon would have a day off and of course Stacey would be there. They would play video games together and hang out, which honestly made me feel uneasy. It reached a point; I would go to bed, and they would stay up playing video games. The next morning, I would come out of mine and Simon's room to find they had both fallen asleep in the living room on the sofa bed together. Stacey had her own room. The sofa bed was for when our friends needed to crash.

One very hot summers day, Stacey and Simon were having a water fight in the bathroom. Every window was open in the house, but we were all still sweating from the heat. I was busy playing Tetris in the living room. I was in deep concentration trying to fit all the blocks together at super - speed so I could beat my last personal best score. All of a sudden, I heard screaming coming from the bathroom. I got up to see what all the noise was about. I tried to open the bathroom door, but it was locked. Simon and Stacey were in the bathroom. I called out to them to let me in. When they finally opened the door, they were both standing there with a guilt look spread across their faces. They told me they were having a water fight, which didn't sit right with me. Stacey looked like she had just won first prize in a wet tee shirt competition. I started to get suspicious.

A few nights later, they were playing video games again; I went to bed because I had to be up early for work the next morning. I woke up during the night and Simon was in the living room. I noticed that he had moved the alarm clock from our bedroom and set it thirty 30-minutes earlier than usual. Likely so he could wake up and get back into bed with me in the morning before I woke up. I left for work that morning, but I wasn't feeling that well. I left work early that day. That's when I found Simon, my fiancé, in bed with my best friend! Just a month before our wedding!

My Mum had done a nice thing and paid for everything. She had just been made redundant from her dinner lady position in the school in Chelsea and she had received a small pay-out. With the money she had bought me a wedding dress, paid all the deposits to save the dates hiring the hall for the reception and booked a lovely vintage Rolls Royce. It was all planned out and it would have been a beautiful event.

I ended it with Simon. He tried to make up for it, but how could he? I was being rejected again, betrayed by another man; and, by my best friend, someone that I had grown up with. Was there anyone I could trust? After leaving Simon, I moved into a flat with my sister Jane in Fulham just before my eighteenth birthday. Someone had moved out of their council house and sold us the keys, so we moved in and became squatters. It was a beautiful little flat; we both made it a home, until we were evicted, about seven or eight months later. At least I felt safe with Jane, and I was still working at the hairdressers.

My experience at Smile Hairdressers was amazing. Being situated on King's Road, lots of famous people would regularly get their hair done at the salon. I wasn't an apprentice anymore but a hairdresser to the stars! I met Kylie Minogue, Bryan Adams, Rod Stewart, Cilla Black, Michael Aspel, Michael Parkinson and the members of Guns and Roses to name a few. We'd do fashion shots for Vivienne Westwood and runway shows. It was all so glamorous and as you know, my life before Smile was far from it. Anita, my mentor, had taught me everything I knew about hairdressing. She took me under her wing and for that I loved her dearly. We were like sisters; we'd hang together outside of work too. I spent some time wanting to be just like her.

Anita went away for a month-long vacation to see her family and many of her client's rescheduled appointments awaiting her return. Those that hadn't asked for me when they came into the salon as I became familiar working so closely with Anita. When she came back from her holiday, some of these clients had continued to work with me. Whilst she'd been away the salon's owners didn't want to see clients turned away. It was never my intention to take away from my friend and mentor any of her clients. After this, everything changed, Anita would belittle me in front of the others and generally made my days a misery. I began to dread going to work, I couldn't stomach anymore rejection, the bullying and bitching was too much for me to take. I eventually decided I couldn't take it anymore and I quit. I'd been forced to leave a place I loved; a career I had become passionate about.

Time ran out where me and Jane were staying, and I moved back home to Mum and Dad's. It was a very short stay, a few nights even. I don't think Mum had fully forgiven me for the disappointment of calling off the wedding, although she wouldn't admit it. It wasn't easy knowing Owen was just around the corner, if I went to the shops, I'd have no choice but to bump into him. Mum started where she had left off, verbally abusing me and taking my kindness for weakness. One of my aunts had told my mum "One day Sabina will hit you back". I quickly found myself another place to live; as I was packing my things, Mum got upset because I wanted to take a rug that I had bought. She liked it and wanted to keep it. She took out a large bread knife and tried to cut up the rug, to stop me from taking it. We were arguing and suddenly she came at me with the knife. I heard my aunt's voice in my head and what she had told Mum. For the first and only time in my life, I defended myself against her, I pushed her away.

I left. I had survived my Mother, Uncle Rob and Ted, Owen, Simon and Stacey's affair, losing a career I loved and so much more. it seemed my luck was turning. I was looking forward to a bright future! Little did I know that as I was growing up, so were my problems, they were just morphing into new and bigger disasters.

Chapter eight

My first husband Dick

"Lord, confuse the wicked, confound their words, for I see violence and strife in the city."

Psalm 55:9

Valentines' day, - I was seventeen and still working as a hairdresser at Smile on Kings Road. That was the day I met my first husband, Dick. He came into the salon, selling single long-stemmed roses and was ready for the hard sell. Dick didn't waste any time and despite making me pay for my own rose that day he had immediately made it clear he fancied me as he flirted away.

My family knew him despite it being the first time we had met. Mum and Aunt Lisa were working in the salon selling coffee and sandwiches at the time, sometimes putting on a nice homemade meal and listing it a special. Aunt Lisa was a bit of a ladette, or tomboy so to speak. She knew Dick well, they ran in the same circles and were both members of the 'Monday Club' at the local pub, The Jolly Brewers; Drinking their way out of their hangovers acquired over the weekend, a kind of hair of the dog thing.

Dick was dating someone when we had met. Months later, I was in Charing Cross Hospital having my wisdom teeth pulled out under a general anaesthetic. I was supposed to be in and out the same day but had an allergic reaction to the anaesthesia. I woke up in intensive care with tubes in my nose and I had to be kept in for three days.

One day I was getting some fresh air by the little fishpond at the front of the hospital, and I noticed Dick outside having a smoke. He was in hospital being treated for a skin infection after getting into a fight and being bitten. Since we had first met on Valentine's Day, Dick had split up with his girlfriend. He had gotten into a fight with her new boyfriend in the pub after a few drinks and was glassed in the face. He needed stitches, which had left a visible scar. It turned out that Dick knew the new boyfriend's brother who had a stall on the North End market selling fruit and veg. He knew most of the 'barrow boys'; he was well known, a hard- man, gangster- type figure and he had connections. An occupational hazard so to speak, given he was selling them all weed, pills, hash or dodgy goods. Like a real-life Del Boy!

After his break-up, often Dick had to pass by this guy's stall on North End Road and even though he was only the brother of the new boyfriend, seeing him would make Dick see red. He would curse at him, get angry and spit on him as he passed his stall. Eventually, they came to blows. Dick attacked him with a claw hammer and during the fight, the guy bit him on his finger! The bite became infected, that's why Dick was at Charing Cross Hospital. He had to have IV antibiotics to clear the infection. A human bite is worse than a dog bite. Dick had returned to the hospital for treatment so drunk one day that when the nurses tried to change his dressing and lowered his bed, his arm wouldn't reach the sling. Maybe I should have seen the red flags then, all the times I met him he was drinking.

Aunt Lisa was always talking Dick up to me, she thought I should go on a date with him. It took a little persuading, but she said that it would help cheer him up after the break-up with his former girlfriend.

Despite not really being one for drinking in Pubs, one night aunt Lisa invited me down to the Atlas around the corner from my parents. It was probably the third or fourth time I had been to a pub; drinking in pubs wasn't my thing. Maybe because Uncle Rob was often drunk and would spike my cheery cola as a child.

Anyway, that night, we were drinking a lot faster than I was used to; I wasn't a drinker whereas Lisa could keep up with anyone. Drinks kept showing up faster than I could drink them. Little did I know that Lisa had called Dick to join us; I was very tipsy by the time he entered the pub. Lisa had invited him to try and cheer him up. Looking back now, he was clearly depressed after the glassing in the face, his recent break- up and the bite to his finger. He was spending a lot of time at home drinking and smoking weed; he was still living with his parents on Bramber Road, just off the North End Road. Dick was really down; I tried to cheer him up and he took to my ability to listen. We talked for a couple of hours.

A few months later, Jane and I had a joint birthday and housewarming party at the squat house that we were sharing. Dick was there, along with lots of other people that he brought along with him (I wouldn't mind, but he had gate-crashed; he wasn't even invited). I think Aunt Lisa probably told him to come along. It turned out to be a huge party; friends and friends of friends came, even old friends from my primary school turned up and there was lots of loud music and dancing which went on until the early hours of the morning. I remember the police turned up due to the noise disturbance.

I was really drunk that night; it was a great party. This was the first time that Dick and I kissed, in the kitchen.

After that night, Lisa was relentless in trying to get me to go out with Dick. She was living at my parents' house in Tamworth Street and working at Smile Hairdressers, I saw her every day at work, and she was constantly badgering me. She kept telling me that he really fancied me and that we would make a good couple. I felt sorry for him, so I agreed to go on a date.

We went to a club in Hammersmith, where the security was patting everyone down at the door. Dick was found with four wraps of paper containing some sort of white powder; the bouncer opened them up and whatever it was just blew away in the wind. Dick was furious and got into an altercation with the bouncers, I just froze as I watched all this unfold. My heart was pounding. I was scared and quite naive, I didn't know anything about the drug scene. I'd never done any hard drugs. I had only smoked Weed so, we left that club and went to the Hammersmith Palais, which was the first "Palais de Danse" or dance hall built in Britain and could hold over 2,000 people. It was also where Mum and Dad had met on their first date. I didn't know what else Dick might have on him that could get us into trouble; I was still shaking from the previous altercation and decided I didn't want to go in; So, instead, we went back to his parents' and talked for hours. It was clear he wasn't over his ex-girlfriend; he went on and on about her and this wasn't his recent ex - this was the girlfriend before her. I knew who he was talking about as she used to live on Tamworth Street. I told him he needed to find out if it was over with his ex before we could go any further. He spoke of his undying love for her and was crying, feeling sorry for himself.

Valentine's Day, 1994 - the first anniversary of our initial meeting the year before at Smile Hairdressers. We had now been talking for a while and it is safe to say feelings had begun to establish their roots. I again urged Dick to see his ex-girlfriend to make sure things were over between the two of them. I also had slight feelings at the time for a guy named Lorenzo, a short Italian guy that I'd been out with a few times, and I was honest with Dick about this. So that's what we did, Dick went and saw his Ex and I went out with Lorenzo.

Lorenzo and I went on a date to Chinatown, Soho. He was outgoing and a had a friendly personality, he was in fact the owner of the place where Owen had taken me to get ice-cream before school. One of the first things Lorenzo asked me on our date was how do I knew Owen, I quickly shut him down as it was embarrassing to talk about. I told Lorenzo that he was not a nice person and not at all who he made himself out to be. I said no more, leaving it to his own interpretation. We had a lovely time and after finishing up in Chinatown we went back to his place. After a wonderful night together, I slept with Lorenzo, leaving me even more conflicted. I really liked Lorenzo, but I was open with him, I told him about Dick. He knew Dick, I could see the fear on his face when I mentioned his name. Lorenzo quite quickly decided he didn't want to commit to a relationship and we both left it there. We remained good friends, our birthdays were only days apart. Dick didn't like that we were friends.

Jane and I were served the eviction notice and that's when Jane decided she was going to join the Army; I wasn't sure what I was going to do.

The night of our first date, I shared with Dick that we were getting kicked out of the flat. Of course, I could go home to my parents but that seemed like a step backwards and I did not want to be stuck there. Dick said there was room at his parents' house if I wanted to stay there with him. So, after two nights at Mum's, I moved in with Dick and his family and he declared that it was truly over with his ex, that she had moved on and that's what he wanted to. He said he wanted to be in a relationship with me. So, we started dating and became a couple. he also admitted he had slept with her that Valentine's night.

A few months later, I found out I was pregnant. I wasn't sure if it was Dick's or Lorenzo's. It had only been one night with Lorenzo – on Valentine's Day – but I still didn't know for sure who the father was. I was so confused. Dick and his parents were so excited with the news of me being pregnant and them becoming grandparents for the first time. So, I went with it.

Dick was going to be a dad, but in the back of my mind I wasn't sure the baby was his. Later that year, my son was born. Dick came to visit me at the hospital, paralytic drunk after having been out with all his friends celebrating the birth of his son – "wetting the baby's head". He staggered into the room and in a loud drunken voice he said, "By the way, his name is Gabriel."

This took me by complete surprise - three generations of his family all had the same name: Dick, his Dad and his Grandad. Dick was changing the play. That Christmas Eve, Dick proposed to me outside the church at the end of the North End Road. It looked very festive as he went down on one knee and popped the question. He gave me a beautiful topaz ring. The ring came about Del Boy style, using a stolen credit card that he found on a boat whilst the local boat show was being held down the road. After stealing the bag off the boat, he went home, got all dressed up in a suit and then took me to Harrods to buy it with the stolen card.

I was shaking like a leaf. Dick was very confident – some would say cocky – I was unable to back out. I just stood there and played the role, feeling like a gangster's moll.

Once I found out I was expecting, I put my name down on the housing list and it wasn't long after that I was given my first home on Walham Grove, a couple of streets away from where my parents lived. It was a Victorian-style house on a beautiful street in Fulham. Like most of them, it was divided into two and I lived in the flat in the basement below. It had a sweet little back garden that Gabriel could play in, but the flat needed a lot of work done to it before we could move in.

Dick was a painter and decorator but also a perfectionist. He had a vision and he wanted to do the work himself. He stripped the flat bare, so the house became more like a construction site than a home. He would sometimes go to the flat to do some work on it, but it was all dependent on his drinking, which began to stress me out as it dragged on and on. The remodelling project wasn't urgent to Dick. I think he loved living with his parents, as his Mum would do everything for him without question, at the drop of a hat. She called Dick her "little soldier boy". She would even get out of bed when he would return home drunk in the early hours of the morning and ask if he was hungry. If he was, she would make him bacon sandwiches, which could be at four or five o'clock in the morning.

Dick's mum was very well known for being the village gossip. She loved getting the latest scoop from Dick on all the antics that went on in the pubs so she had more gossip to share on her next visit to the donut shop, where she would go for her daily cuppa and gossip with anyone willing to listen.

Dick was just too drunk or hung-over to do any work on the flat despite having the opportunity of a first home together with our son as a family. I was still living at his parents with a new-born baby. Yes, it was a great support and they loved

Gabriel so much, but I just wanted to get out and move into my new home. The first time Dick hit me; we were still living in his parents' house. Dick's sister Tracey and her boyfriend had moved out of the big spacious upstairs bedroom to move into a new flat together. The room was beautifully redecorated for us.

One of Dick's friends was a taxi driver, one of his customers had no cash and had paid him with Cocaine. He didn't particularly want the Coke, so he came to Dick and exchanged it for the equivalent in Hashish. Dick and the taxi driver went upstairs to complete their transaction while I stayed downstairs with Gabriel and Dick's parents. After Dick's friend left, I took Gabriel upstairs to breast-feed. As I rocked Gabriel in the rocking chair, watching my beautiful baby boy nurse, I heard sniffing and snorting noises. I looked up and asked, "What are you doing?"

Dick explained the transaction with his friend and said he was just trying the coke out. I suddenly felt afraid and protective over my infant son and yelled, "I don't want you doing that around Gabriel!" I was still feeding; Gabriel was getting restless. Dick tried to take Gabriel out of my arms, I resisted. It was almost like a tug-of-war with a baby in the middle.

I yelled back, "I'm not upsetting him! You're upsetting him!"; then Dick smacked me across the face hard enough to leave a bright red mark and eventually a bruise around my eye. Dick stormed out of the house, probably to the pub, as he was a high from the line of cocaine he had just taken., I was left holding the baby and crying.

I went downstairs and Dick's mum said, "What on earth is going on?"

I said, "Look at me, Cathy! Look at me! He hit me!"

"What did you do?" she asked.

I said 'how would you feel if Tracey was given a black eye'

She replied, "My Tracey wouldn't give anyone a reason to hit her in the face."

I was astounded, I felt unsafe. So, right then and there I decided to move into my unfinished home on Walham Grove. My cousin Sue from Birmingham, who was staying with my parents, helped me. Gabriel's room and our bedroom were finished. I had painted a beautiful mural in Gabriel's room but there wasn't any carpeting; the front room was still gutted and the wall between the kitchen and living room had been removed, making it open plan. The toilet and bathroom weren't finished. The house was still a shell, really.

Dick was nowhere to be found. He had gone missing, as he often did, "on the piss" as they say. He finally surfaced three days later pleading and crying, apologising and saying he would never do it again. I needed to hear this as I did not want my son to grow up without a father and having Dick in my life was an opportunity for me to create my own real family.

We used to visit Devon a lot to stay with his family when they were having any celebrations. Trips to Dick's family in Devon reminded me of happy memories in my own childhood with my best friend Diana and her family. I so wanted to believe that it had been a one-off, that Dick had just behaved in a way that was out of character, not him but due to the cocaine and if it was just the cocaine that changed his personality, then I could help him to stop.

We made up. To make amends, Dick finished the remodelling project in the house. Before long there was new paint, new carpeting, a new boiler, all the finishing touches.

He paid out thousands to prove that he wouldn't hit me again. He moved in, although I think he missed living with his parents. Sometimes it was like looking after another child, being in a relationship with Dick. I would have to run his baths, iron and put out his clothes, everything had to be done for him just so, before I could even attend to Gabriel's needs. Hindsight really is a beautiful thing; I can see so clearly now what I didn't then.

This is the cycle of domestic abuse. First, tensions building., With Dick it was always fuelled by alcohol or drugs. Then the tension builds up and explodes into a violent incident, which is followed by the remorse and honeymoon phase. Then it starts all over again. Perpetrators become very skilled at manipulating, trapping their victim using a myriad of manipulation techniques unbeknownst to the victim. If I got too upset and tried to leave, he would beg me not to and try desperately to make up for what he had done. I wanted to help him with this "problem" that he had; however, it became more difficult to leave the longer the abuse continued because I was becoming increasingly more isolated from friends and family.

During his violent outbursts I would often run to friends or family, who would of course tell me not to go back to him. They did not understand the manipulation and control that Dick was capable of. Every time I kept going back, they all started stepping away. As they did, Dick gained more power with an opportunity to ramp up the abuse. During the times that things were going well, it would never last. Dick was becoming increasingly more obsessive with me and sought to control pretty much every aspect of my life. He was always so scared that I was going to leave him. He had very bad separation anxiety when I wasn't with him at home.

When he went out, he would lock me and Gabriel in the house. Every time I tried to leave; he overwhelmed me with promises that he would change. Lavish gifts and holidays to prove to me that I would see a new Dick, but it never lasted. I wanted so badly to believe the changed character that I saw in front of me. I felt it was my duty to help him with his problem, but I could never pinpoint what the problem was.

Sometimes he was perfectly charming but as things became tense, or when he would open his first beer of the day, I would feel like I was walking on eggshells. The first thing that he would do was to smash the telephone so that I was not able to call for help. During his violent outbursts, which were usually drug or alcohol induced, there would be nothing I could do or say to calm him down. Dick couldn't control his anger. His anger was always there, just below the surface. He would get into arguments all the time with anyone; I was always aware of his temper and sometimes it reminded me of being back at home with Mum, never knowing when the next beating would come or why. He could be having fun, laughing and drinking, then someone would say something or look at him a certain way and BAM, he would turn. It was like flipping a switch; he would turn into a mad man; a real monster at times. He would not remember a thing afterwards.

He was like that with everybody. If he didn't get his way, he would get angrier, louder. If the bar tender didn't make his drink the way he liked it, he would return it along with some pointed insults. He didn't show kindness or grace to anyone unless there was something in it for him. Instead, it was f**king this and f**king that until he was happy with the result. He had an overinflated sense of self-importance and was completely entitled. He would often say, "Do you know who I am?" A big trigger of his was that he always felt belittled if anyone would endearingly refer to him as

"Son". It was like a red flag to a bull. He would often say to them, "Who the f**k do you think you're calling son?"

He spoke to his mum the same way; very rude and demeaning, which he had learned from his Dad. Dick's father Dick was also known as Timmy as it was confusing him and his son having the same name. Timmy could be a very nice person but was extremely verbally abusive to his wife Cathy. Even more so if he was drinking. He would hiss at her through clenched teeth, "Look at you, hiss… you fat f**king cow! Get out of my face!" Dick hated hearing his Dad talk like that to his Mum, ironic really considering he would go on to do the same.

Often people who use threatening behaviours have learnt this behaviour emulating from the behaviour of their role models, even though the outcome is uncomfortable for them. In Dick's case it cost him a fortune in apologies. To be able to understand if a behaviour is truly ours or that of the fleas that we pick up from others, we must develop an "observer" view of that behaviour, be able to recognise if this belief that lies behind it is in line with that of our own.

I made the mistake of telling Dick about Owen, who was still working on the fruit stall in the market at the end of our street. I told him about all that he had done to me, him grooming me when I was a young fourteen-year-old girl. Taking advantage of me in the flat above the flower shop which was at the end of the very road we lived on. It was so very hard at times living on the same street as that flat; walking past the door almost every day turned my stomach.

Dick knew Owen because he knew all the barrow boys. Every time we walked down the North End Road, Dick would curse, spit or physically attack Owen. It got to the point where, if Dick and I had a fight, he would walk down the North End Road and give Owen a beating. There would be no stopping him. I was so worried. My Dad and brothers would start asking why Dick kept beating him up. Dick's best friend, Billy Smith, also knew what Owen had done to me as Dick blurted it out one night when he was drunk in our living room. I think Dick was highly triggered by Owen, possibly because it may have brought up bad memories for him, his first girlfriend was sexually abused, and Dick was there to support her during the investigations. If I'm not mistaken, the man who did it to her was shot in his privates on his release from prison. I have no idea by whom.

Finally, the house on Walham Grove was beginning to feel like a home, except Dick would come and go as he pleased, and often be gone for two or three days. He would bring people back to our home – friends and punters who would buy and use drugs from him – sometimes they would stay and have a smoke and a chat. One night he came home so drunk and so high he couldn't sleep. He wanted me to stay up with him and listen to whatever he was rambling on about. As he talked, he started shouting and became more agitated and aggressive. He suddenly grabbed me around my neck and slammed me up against the wall. I was terrified. I was able to wriggle away out of his tight grip; I ran into Gabriel's room barricading myself in. Gabriel was about eighteen months old. He had a little red plastic car bed. I crawled into his bed with him and just held him tightly. Dick was yelling, pounding and kicking the door. "Open this f**king door!" Bang! Bang! Bang! He broke through the bedroom door; pieces of wood were flying everywhere. I don't think we had a door in our home that didn't have a punch hole in it.

The next day, you could almost see the shape of his silhouette in the broken door, where he had smashed his way through the night before. He was in such a rage and completely out of control. He stood over me, screaming and cursing. I pleaded with him to stop. I kept saying, "Please leave me alone! Stop! Stop! Just leave me alone, please!"

Then, "I'm sorry, I'm sorry," to get him to stop and go away. I woke up the next morning in the foetal position, still clinging to Gabriel, my beautiful innocent baby boy, in his little red car bed. I was terrified of what was to become of me and my son.

To make things better this time, we went to the "Ideal Home Show Exhibition" where Dick bought us a waterbed. He also paid for two new sofas. The sofa wouldn't fit through our front door because we lived in the basement flat. We had to carry it through the flat upstairs, taking out windows, bringing it into the flat through the back garden. It was a real palaver. In the process of trying to move the sofas in, Dick slipped a disc in his back. He was in tremendous pain all the time, which made things so much worse, he was drinking as if he wasn't on strong medication. only making matters much worse for me.

Finally, I'd had enough. I kicked him out of the house and double- locked the door from the inside! He was enraged, screaming, cursing and banging, trying to kick the door in. He then picked up a large heavy stone and threw it, smashing my bedroom window. The waterbed situated right by the bedroom window and Gabriel happened to be lying asleep right there on the bed! Broken glass came crashing down on my baby. He started screaming and crying. The broken glass pierced the waterbed and there was water everywhere. Goodness knows what the neighbours must have thought. I lost count of the times the police were called.

Dick only left in fear of getting arrested again. He went back to his parents and was gone for days, leaving me to sort out a broken waterbed and smashed bedroom window. Not knowing what to do, I called Lorenzo. Yes, that Lorenzo, because we had remained good friends. Dick didn't like the fact we were friends, but I needed help. At this point, I still didn't know if Gabriel was Dick's or if he was Lorenzo's. Lorenzo popped by, he fixed the waterbed, he also brought with him a beautiful white orchid plant as a gift for me. Which later died as Dick poisoned it with bleach!

The police were notified because the council had to send someone around to board up and replace the window, which couldn't be done without an incident report. Dick wasn't arrested because I chose not to press charges. Pressing charges would have meant that I was a grass. Dick had drummed it into me that "snitches get stitches". Dick hated the police. The report was filed regardless and later helped me when building my case to get a restraining order against him.

Dick, of course, apologised and pleaded for me to forgive him again and as usual he promised he would never do it again. He said, "Let's go away on holiday. Let's get married." So, foolish me, that's what we did. We booked a trip, and we took Mum along to help with Gabriel. You couldn't separate those two. Mum was like a second Mum to Gabriel and a bloody good one at that. She would do anything for him, she was always asking to have him over night. She took him everywhere with her; she loved being his silly Nanny and she was so proud of her Grandson.

We got married in Negril, Jamaica. I had conflicting thoughts about marrying Dick, for lots of reasons but the main one being; I didn't know for sure whether he was Gabriel's actual father. Back then there was no DNA testing, so I just went with it. Hoping for something to change, I genuinely believed that as he was now going to be my husband, he would somehow turn into the man that we needed him to be. My earlier abuse had trained me to accept unacceptable behaviour and I was not able to see the displays of abuse from Dick as being outside of the norm.

Not long after we returned, our house was raided by the police for drugs. Not exactly the honeymoon period most newlyweds experience. It was about 6am. All of a sudden, I was woken by an almighty crashing, it sounded like there were hundreds of police rushing into my house. I had no idea how many there actually were, I was in shock, I'd just woken up. They were all shouting, "Police, Police, stay where you are! Don't move!" They allowed me to get Gabriel from his room so he could sit with me. In their search they found weighing scales, the ones that drug dealers use, lots of cash that was all in one- hundred- pound bundles along with a tick list, a list of money owed to him by punters as well as half of a nine- bar of hash, which was approximately 4.5 ounces of cannabis resin.

Dick was arrested and taken into custody. He was released that evening, but gossip spread and news on the street was that Dick could be a grass, as they hadn't charged him with anything. He even got all the money and scales back. Dick decided he needed to lay low for a while. But laying low affected his mood, he felt caged but wouldn't leave the house. He was drinking lots, feeling depressed. Still, our house was very busy. A constant flow of people popping in to buy their hash or weed. I was feeling increasingly unsafe, more so for little Gabriel. The flat was in my name. I didn't know what to do.

Not long after, Dick started selling Cocaine. Coke was easier to handle, the profit margins were larger, and he could support his own growing habit. Dick also partnered up with a guy who was a heroin addict and dealer; coincidentally, he was the same person who introduced my brother George to injecting heroin for the first time, showing him how it was done so he could later do it himself.

This wasn't what I signed up for, it was just spiralling out of control at this point The drugs were harder so were the beatings and although feeling unsafe was something I was used to, that was before I had a baby to protect. Dick's dealing and the crowd it attracted, his constant drinking, partying, the drunken rants and violent attacks lit up the fight, flight, freeze response of my central nervous system. I was now constantly on hyper alert, like an animal in the jungle not wanting to be shot down by the hunter.

Sometimes I would run to survive. Never would I fight back – only in extreme situations when my life was at risk would I push him away, where I would try to fend him off just trying to protect myself. Mainly, I would freeze and appease. My earlier dynamics between my parents and my abuser sadly taught me to appease the abuser. Nobody understood when I kept going back to him, they all started to avoid me, but I did not know how to make it stop.

I took so many beatings from Dick, but once he took a beating that I'll never forget. It was the night before Jane's wedding at Fulham Town Hall. Dick and I left little Gabriel with my Mum and joined other family and friends at The Wee House, a tiny pub near West Brompton Bridge. The pub was so small; a bar with two doors at the end leading to single cubicle toilets and chairs set along a narrow pub not much wider than a hallway. Capacity couldn't have been more than twenty people. So, the pub was filled with family and Jane's friends. Drinks were flowing, everyone was having a good time. As the evening progressed, I was getting very tired, I was ready to go home. The next day I would be busy doing everyone's hair for the wedding. Of course, Dick wasn't ready to go and was trying to get me to stay, getting more and more belligerent. I finally announced loudly, "I'm going home," Dick looked up at me and then hit me in the face. In the bar! In front of everyone! I was hurt physically but probably more so emotionally, we were in public, in front of my family and friends. I left the pub and walked home alone; I fell asleep before Dick got home.

I woke up the next morning and started getting ready to go and do everyone's hair for the wedding. I was also one of Jane's bridesmaids. I walked into my living room where I found Dick on the sofa. I thought he simply he had too much to drink and was sleeping it off on the sofa. But when he turned and looked up at me, I was stunned. His face was swollen, so misshapen, he looked like the Elephant Man! His lip was split, and both eyes were almost swollen shut.

Dick mumbled through puffy lips, "Your brothers did this to me." I didn't know what to say to him, I didn't want to say anything that would trigger him to get angry with me. I turned and finished getting ready, doing my hair and make-up ready to go to Mum and Dad's. Dick obviously didn't want to show his disfigured face at the wedding, so he stayed home on his own. I walked the two streets to my parents' house where friends and family were milling about, photos were being taken, there was a real buzz in the room. As soon as I walked in, there was an uncomfortable silence. No one said a word about the previous night, about what happened at the pub. Nobody asked about Dick or where he was. Neither of my brothers – who Dick claimed had beaten him up – said anything to me. It was as if nothing had happened, but the silence spoke volumes. No discussion, no questions, no concern. Nothing. I went to the wedding by myself but skipped the reception. After the wedding, I just went home to be with Dick.

Abusers like to control the people in their lives. Control is another form of abuse. One way Dick tried to control me, was by taking my car; he didn't even have a driving licence. By taking my car it limited my options if I wanted to run away to family or a friend. Sometimes I would take the car, Gabriel and my emergency bag, which was always hidden ready to get away quickly. I also thought he might worry not knowing where I was, which might finally result in some display of genuine love or affection. But most of the time that wasn't the case. Usually, I would return home a few days later to a party in my own house. All these people drinking, smoking and partying in my home, I guess I wasn't missed that much after all.

Dick hadn't passed his driving test and didn't have a licence. He just didn't care for the law. It was registered in my name, so I was always worried when he took it. It was late in the day and all the barrow boys had packed up their stalls. Dick had parked the car illegally on North End Road where the stalls were normally set up just opposite the pub, The Jolly Brewers. He had been missing for three days; "another three-day bender". Then he only resurfaced because he needed to do some more 'business'. I put Gabriel in the pram and walked to the pub, I was fuming. I walked in, Dick saw me and called out, drunk, "Alright, love, you wanna drink?" I said yes, "I would like a tomato juice". Then I walked to the table, confronted Dick and demanded the keys back to my car back. He refused so I poured the whole glass of tomato juice over his head. Dick was fuming, screaming and yelling obscenities, the argument spilled outside the pub as I tried to get the keys from him. He wouldn't give me the keys back, so I picked up a big stone and threw it through my car window screen. I thought to myself, well, if I can't have or drive my car, then you can't either. Plus, I was worried that he could hurt someone driving under the influence of drink and drugs.

Most weekends, as Dick sold more cocaine, his own habit

grew. The parties at our house lasted for days, then so did the comedown, leaving him even more moody. That's the nature of Cocaine bingeing. When Mum had Gabriel, which was nearly every weekend, our house was party central. If I didn't have Gabriel, I started to dabble, but coke had a strange effect on me, my jaw would lock, and I became unable to talk and unable to sleep. I was so tired of resisting; I just went along with everyone else. People would be drinking, smoking, Dick would be selling and sniffing. Dick and his friends Billy and Tim would be up all hours partying with us. I would overhear Billy sometimes say to Dick, "You need to respect Sabina." I think that's when I first started to begin to have feelings for Billy. It felt like he cared – it wasn't often someone spoke up for me, especially against Dick. I first met Billy at my housewarming party before me and Dick became an item.

After one of these three-day coke binges, Dick, Billy and Tim were drinking at a restaurant/nightclub in Fulham at the end of our road and a big fight broke out. One of them had punched a woman during the fight. When the police arrived, both Billy and Tim fled but Dick couldn't get away fast enough, so he was pulled in for questioning. During questioning, Dick refused to rat out his friends or give any information, he was then arrested and charged with GBH for hitting a female. He was released on bail, whilst waiting for his court case to come up, which took months. Dick became more and more paranoid and continued to consume huge quantities of alcohol, cocaine and smoke lots of pot. The realisation and limbo feeling that he may have to go to prison, filled him with fear, making him even harder to live with.

Dick made a spontaneous decision to drive to Devon for a family party on the final bank holiday weekend of the summer. He had so much nervous energy as he waited for his court case to be decided, he just needed to be doing something, go somewhere. Dick's uncle worked at the Darlington Crystal Factory in Devon, they lived in a beautiful area not far from the coast. We left Gabriel with Mum, who was a reliable "silly Nanny". All the love she withheld from me, she poured into Gabriel. They were thick as thieves; she spoiled him rotten.

On our way back from Devon, both Dick and I were feeling terrible. I had been vomiting, we were both dreading the drive back to London from Devon. In the back of my mind, I thought I might be pregnant, we quarrelled all the way home. Tensions were high, we decided it best to go straight home and pick up Gabriel the next day. The arguing continued at home, my emotions all over the place I reached a breaking point with Dick. I just couldn't take any more. I was tired of it all. I had no fight left in me. I was in the kitchen doing the washing up, Dick was behind me shouting in my ear. I couldn't face yet another beating, so as I was washing up I grabbed a knife out of the sink, and I turned around to face Dick. Putting the knife to my wrist and looking Dick right in the eyes, I screamed with tears streaming from my eyes "I can't take this anymore! Living with you is hardly worth living at all! I hate it! I don't want to be here anymore!"

Dick tried to stop me from hurting myself and reached out with his hand and grabbed the sharp end of the blade of the knife. It pressed into his hand just by the thumb as he tried to wrestle the knife away from me. Blood was gushing out running all over us both, dripping on the floor. I let go and all I could see was the enormous gash in his hand. We rushed to the hospital.

Tendons and nerves had been severed and it looked like he might lose his thumb. He didn't but he was left with a nasty scar as well as needing surgery and six months of physical therapy to regain the strength and use of his thumb. Later that evening, after I returned from the hospital, I took a pregnancy test, it was positive. The date, 31 August 1997, always stands out in my mind because that was the day Princess Diana died. Who doesn't remember what they were doing that dreadful day?

Mary was a difficult pregnancy. Dick was in a very bad way, the control had heightened, I wasn't allowed to dress nicely or go out without him. He would call me horrid names, maybe it was because I was pregnant that the physical abuse lessened, but he was sure to top it up with verbal abuse. While bruises go away, the verbal and mental abuse is embedded. He was still disappearing for days, locking us in the house whilst he was gone. He was possessive, paranoid and insecure. I was also in and out of hospital with complications. I would have to attend these appointments with no make-up on, couldn't do my hair nicely and in baggy clothing. He knew I was getting injections to stop me from going into early labour but that didn't stop him obsessively questioning me; "What are you doing? Where are you going? Who are you going to see?"

Once I found myself in the hospital in the next bed to my Aunt Lisa, who was also pregnant and about to deliver her son; she was the aunt that ended up having a baby with my best friend from my primary school's brother. I was released from the hospital and sent home on total bed rest, but Dick had disappeared again. He was gone again, for days, leaving me alone with three-year-old Gabriel so much for having complete rest. Thank goodness for Mum.

It was past midnight; I was fast asleep when Dick burst into our bedroom. He was totally off his face, high and drunk. He turned on the light and started screaming and shouting,

"Get up, get up! I wanna talk to you!" He was stumbling around, wobbling, drooling and jabbering incoherently.

I tried to wipe the sleep out of my eyes and whispered, "Shhh, Gabriel's asleep," but he just carried on. "Please, I need to rest.," The next thing I knew, he had me by the hair. He yanked me out of bed and pulled me, by my hair out of our room, dragging me, heavily pregnant, down the hall, kicking at me all the while. I pleaded over and over, "Stop! Stop! Please stop!" He finally did. I was in so much pain but managed to crawl to the bathroom and lock the door. I had been spotting blood throughout my pregnancy, as well as having false labour pains because of stress and the domestic violence, but this was different. I was haemorrhaging badly, I was terrified.

Dick yelled through the bathroom door, "Haven't you lost that fucking baby yet?!" I'll never forget those words. They are burned into my heart, my soul.

I was rushed to hospital where my only daughter, Mary, was born on 27 March 1998, six-weeks premature with a hole in her heart. Ultimately, she didn't need surgery, but in just a few years it was discovered that she also had autism, epilepsy, ADHD, PICA, borderline severe learning disabilities and PDA. There was no conclusive evidence that Mary's disabilities were a direct result of the stress and beatings that I took from Dick while pregnant. But there is no doubt in my mind. I have often asked myself the question, would Mary have lifelong disabilities if Dick hadn't have done what he did? Or if I had left sooner? I wish I had left him sooner as I have often blamed myself for Mary's disabilities, I live with the question, would it be different for her?

Mary was kept in hospital for tests to confirm whether she needed an operation to close the hole in her heart. She was also tube- fed for days and needed to be in an incubator under special lights. She was always a very sick baby with reflux, projectile vomiting; she was a crying baby and was hard to settle, she hardly slept and when she did it was only for an hour or so. We had to attend a sleep clinic to try to seek help. She didn't walk until she was almost three, she didn't talk until almost six. Getting answers to help her wasn't easy, it took years.

Dick was useless; he was too busy doing his own thing, in and out the pubs, going on his benders and coming home drunk. Nothing had changed. After yet another fight, Dick again apologised profusely and again pleaded with me to take him back. This time, to make amends, he paid for a holiday to the Dominican Republic. We took both Gabriel and Mary with us. While we were away, we got a phone call that Dick's Mum had suffered a stroke and had bleeding on the brain. She was in hospital having immediate surgery. There was nothing we could do; our flight home was not for a few days and changing our flights was impossible; so, we finished our holiday, although the last few days were hard. Dick was drinking even more than usual as he was worried about his mum. It didn't help that it was an all-inclusive holiday, it made it even easier for him to drink all day, every day.

As soon as we landed home, we went straight to the hospital. Cathy looked horrible! Her head was swollen to three times its regular size. There were tubes and wires everywhere and the staples holding her head together were impossible to ignore. When we had left for our holiday, she seemed fine, it was difficult to see. Cathy was in hospital for months. Eventually she was transferred to a rehabilitation facility for three months. She hated it there; the whole family were consumed with how best to care for her and how to adapt the house, as so many changes had to be made. She lost movement down one side of her body, her speech was affected, and she would need to use a wheelchair.

Amidst the life changes, to try and cheer Cathy up a little, Dick decided to treat his Mum and Dad to a holiday to Florida. Dick loved Florida; he had been twice already, once with his first girlfriend and once with me. He loved the parks and the rides, but this time, with his Mum being in a wheelchair, it was different, we didn't have to spend so much time queuing for rides. Dick was very good at saving money, stashing away rolls of cash from his drug deals. But he was also quite a schemer. He always did the suitcase scam whenever we went on holiday, which would ultimately pay for our holiday. In the "suitcase scam" he would claim that one of our suitcases had gone missing. He didn't use the same name twice. First, he did it saying it was his case, the next holiday he said it was my case. He then paid for my Mum to come with us to Jamaica and her case would be missing on our return; but this time it was his parents' turn to lose a suitcase. The way it worked was by checking in the hand luggage into the hold with the main case, that way you are given two bag receipts. While on holiday, Dick would shop for all the latest, branded clothing. Dick loved shopping; he loved clothes! He had to have all the designer labels, all top shelf, no knockoffs. He would save and collect all the receipts from whatever he brought, saving them up to use in the "suitcase scam", turning them in saying that these were the clothes in the case when the airline lost his bag. The airline would then reimburse Dick for everything that was "lost". He ran this scam on every holiday we had together.

On the trip to Florida, we took Gabriel with us but left Mary with my Mum. That was not easy for her as Mary was very fussy. She was about a year-old; she didn't sleep through the night, and was still being breastfed, so while I was away

Mum had the hard job of getting Mary to take a bottle. Mum tried everything she could, but nothing worked. When we returned, she moaned that it was the worst ten days of her life! Mary was always hard work to look after.

After returning from Florida, just weeks before Christmas, the Police raided our house again, as well as Dick's drug partner's flat, simultaneously. This time the police found a tick list, some money and a tiny amount of weed and hash. I think most of the cocaine had been stashed at his partner's house, so again, Police didn't have much on Dick. The embarrassment of being raided for a second time, not knowing whether he would be charged and locked up, made him more suspicious of everyone, including me. We were back to square one, he was locking me in the house again, drinking more and doing more and more Cocaine, the result? More fights.

I was running out of options. On different occasions, I had run to my Mum's house to escape the violence, to Aunt Trudy, Aunt Lisa, my friend Alice and many others I'd met along the way. At this point I felt like I couldn't ask for help from anyone whose advice I hadn't taken. Because I didn't take their advice to leave him, I couldn't run to them anymore; but leaving him was a scary option. Where would I go? It would mean starting from scratch with two children, being a single mum.

It was Christmas 1999, and I really wanted a computer. It seemed like everyone had a computer except us. Dick's dad had a desktop computer and a printer and a completely decked- out video room. Whenever we needed to use a computer, we had to ask to use his. Oh, how I remember the dial- up tone trying to connect to the internet back in those days. We did end up getting our own computer for Christmas that year.

It was the Millennium New Year's Eve and we decided to celebrate by watching the fireworks with a huge crowd of our friends on the Embankment near Lambeth Bridge. It sure was a night to remember. We took lots of drink with us to party with and we wrapped up warm. My Dad was there; although not typically the drinker, that night he had been drinking lots and was very drunk. That same night, whilst he was drunk, he confessed to me that he had been having an affair with a woman named Katherine, his business partner in an antiques shop. I was shocked, angry and devastated.

The next day, New Year's Day 2000, I went looking for Katherine. I'm not normally a confrontational person at all, but when I found her, I poured out all my pent-up anger and fury on her. Everything came spilling out: my anger and frustration with Dick, feeling trapped in a violent marriage, fears over my parent's relationship, I unleashed it all on Katherine. I yelled and screamed! How dare she, she was always going to my parents' house. Mum would cook for her as they socialised together. How dare she go to my Mum's house to eat her food and look my Mum in the eye, knowing she was having an affair with my Dad? It took me back to what Stacey had done. Why are these women so brazen? How can they look you in the eye and smile, even laugh, knowing what they are doing?

I felt so alone, so fearful in my marriage. I didn't know what Dick would do next. My babies, they deserved so much more. I needed something; someone to talk to, a friend who would listen. I was so lonely, I spent so much time a prisoner in my own home. So, I logged on to my new computer and found the chat rooms online. That's where I first met Nicholas, who would change my world for the better... and worse.

Chapter nine

My second husband, Nicholas

"A false witness will not go unpunished, and whoever pours out lies will perish."

Proverbs 19:9

It was peaceful with Dick gone all the time, I didn't miss the arguments or the drinking when he was gone. I had stopped caring if he was 'missing' for days on end. I was quite literally, a prisoner in my own home, locked in with no way out, but I was also a prisoner when he was home, beaten black and blue and called every name under the sun. Mixed feelings I guess, and I was lonely. The isolation, although physically quiet is psychologically loud. Confined to your own thoughts and suppressed by the anticipation of his return. I had to distract myself, I needed to have a conversation with somebody other than myself. I used my new computer and started to make friends in online chat rooms.

February 2000 - The first time I spoke to Nicholas online. To begin with he had told me his name was Richard and I didn't find out his real name until I met his family some months later. He explained he worked in computers, a high security position and needed to protect his identity online. Made sense, right? Convinced me, besides, what do I know about tech? I had only gotten my first computer a few months earlier. We were getting to know each other, he seemed intelligent and had great confidence. He spoke of his professional kickboxing days in Thailand. He was tall

(6'4"), handsome, drove a silver sports car, had his own place in Crystal Palace; it seemed like he had it so together. He was the complete opposite of Dick and before I knew it, I was hooked.

After a few online conversations, Nicholas and I decided to meet in-person. I was going out with my best friend Diana Adams, who had now moved back to London from Australia. Dick didn't want me going out, even if it was with Diana. We argued, yelling obscenities at each other. I was so over his control and jealousy. He took my purse so I wouldn't have any money, but I went anyway. I had told Nicholas that he could meet me at a pub in Shepherd's Bush called The Walkabout. Diana and I went to Pizza Express for dinner first then onto The Walkabout, an Australian-themed pub. It was packed because it was the Aussie Football League's trophy night. One of the best cocktails in there was called "a cock- sucking cowboy" – they were very moreish, a shot of Baileys and a shot of toffee vodka. I needed a few to calm my nerves.

Diana and I sat down, ordered drinks and took in the atmosphere; TVs all around blaring Aussie football matches and folks dressed casually in tee shirts, Bermuda shorts and flip-flops. It had a real feeling of being down under, a real surfing style. I was wearing a little black dress with a Native American style fringed bottom; my hair was in two plaits and I looked a little like Pocahontas. Nicholas walked in, looking sharp but completely out of place in a grey three-piece suit, white shirt and a tie. He had sent me some photos, so I knew it was him. I didn't tell Diana that I was meeting anyone that night. After all, I was still married to Dick. I wanted it to look like I'd just met him; I think I told Diana I knew him from back in the days at school, there are several years between me and Diana and we never went to the same schools, so there was no way of knowing this wasn't true. I honestly didn't want to meet a complete stranger, I had just met off the internet, on my own, he could have been a mass murderer!

He stood at the bar and ordered a drink; this was my queue to excuse myself. I told Diana I needed to use the dunny, Ausie slang for the toilet. Nicholas followed me outside; we had arranged to talk away from the noise of the pub. The attraction felt online was only multiplied in person, before he left, we shared our first kiss.

Then I went dark; I cut off all communication for about three months. I didn't reply to any of his emails, I didn't log into any of the chat rooms because you can see who was in the chatroom when you log in. I knew in my heart my marriage was over. I didn't want to be with Dick anymore, but I was still legally married to a lunatic, a violent alcoholic. I didn't want Nicholas pulled into our mess and the drama that always followed Dick. I had to tread very carefully. I knew the trouble it would cause if Dick found out I was seeing someone. It was time to make some very big decisions.

We had 'the chat', it didn't go down well at all. It ended in another beating, this time he threw the phone at me, it hit me, cutting my face, landing me with another black eye. It didn't change a thing, I knew it was over, his attack just confirmed to me what I already knew. I told him it was over, for good this time and that I wanted a divorce. Dick went back to stay with his parents, which he often did after we fought.

I just knew I had to do something, I couldn't take any more beatings and my two children were getting older. I needed to keep them safe. I was done, but he didn't take me seriously. Just like so many times before, he thought he could cry, apologise and I would take him back. When he realised, I wasn't budging, he started crying on everyone else's shoulders – everyone we knew – one by one, they all called me, to inform me how much he had changed, how much he still loved me, how much he missed me and to give him another chance. The pressure was on, and he knew exactly how to play me. He threatened to take his own life if I wouldn't take him back.

When that didn't work, his tactics took a turn. He bad-mouthed me, calling me "a horrible bitch" and worse. Then he would shift back, promising me the world if I got back with him. His behaviour hadn't changed; he was still selling drugs from his parent's' house and going to all the pubs, seeing all the people we knew and either crying about me or cursing me.

He would call me at all hours, often inebriated, crying, screaming, shouting down the phone. He would then say he wanted to see the kids. I would agree he could, then when he came over, paying no attention to the kids at all, he would plead his case to me, begging me to take him back. The more I stuck to my guns the more aggressive he would become; he hated to be rejected, it was his biggest trigger. The next couple of weeks took a lot out of me, focusing on not giving in to his manipulation.

He knew about Owen on the market and threatened to tell my family, if we didn't get back together, he said he would tell them everything. I didn't know what to do, this was one of my weaknesses and he used it against me. Knowing I had carried the shame for so long and chosen to protect my brothers, my dad, from what might happen if they found out, he was playing me.

Dick was relentless. He tried everything he could to maintain his control over me. I was scared and tired of fighting. I was so exhausted at times; I let him wear me down to the point that when I allowed him to visit the children, rather than go through the arguing and beatings whilst asking him to leave, I would just let him stay the night.

Three months passed and I finally replied to one of Nicholas's emails. I thought there had been enough separation and Dick had finally gotten the message; I thought it was safe to start dating. I was so wrong.

We arranged to meet; he took me for a drive in the country in his beautiful silver sports car. I liked his company. He asked why I hadn't replied to any of his emails in three months. I had to tell him about Dick. I had to warn him that I was still married to a drug-dealer; a violent alcoholic gangster. Nicholas took it in his stride. Maybe he wasn't threatened, with all the kickboxing training he did to become a professional. He said, "Tell him I'm a police officer." Of course, he wasn't, but I was scared, and I knew Nicholas was trying to make me feel safe, so I went along with it. In hindsight, I now realise that Nicholas was engaging me in the first of many lies. Just like he told me to tell Diana he was an old school friend. It seemed harmless but it turned out to be one of the biggest mistakes of my life.

A few months later I discovered I was pregnant. I was stunned! I was in denial, but with all the stress I had going on, I didn't even realise I had missed two periods. Then great fear set in, I didn't know who the father was. Nicholas, who I was now seeing regularly but, on the down-low, or Dick from one of the few times he had worn me down and I let him stay the night. One thing I did know, if I had another baby with Dick, I would be tied to him even deeper, trapped in an abusive and violent relationship. I was so frightened of having another child with Dick. I was in so much fear of a door being opened for Dick to walk straight back into my life. I froze. I didn't know what to do. Then I panicked and took an overdose. The baby would surely die even if I didn't.

I was found and taken to Charing Cross Hospital where I was put on a heavy dose of Lorazepam to calm me down. I was completely out of it, like a zombie, yet still being interviewed by the nursing staff as if nothing was wrong. Every moment that passed I felt I was being pushed, closer and closer to the edge. I screamed, "Get this baby out of me! Get this baby out of me, now!" I was having a complete breakdown; the hospital staff rightly didn't think I was capable of making such a decision in that frame of mind. So, they continued sedating me, but every time I came back around and remembered I was pregnant, I wanted it out of me. Nobody was listening, I again took it into my own hands, I made another attempt to self-abort whilst in the hospital.

When they finally released at the hospital, they had scheduled me for a planned abortion at Queen Charlotte's Hospital.

As I was sedated, I remember clearly seeing the scans before the surgery. I pleaded with the nurses to tell me if it was a boy or a girl. They finally told me that it was a boy, that's the last thing I remember before losing consciousness. I named him Harry. I had to give him a name to honour him. Every year on 28 April – Harry's due date – I feel such sadness, I struggle with the heaviness, the guilt and shame of knowing that I aborted my son.

Through it all, I was open and honest with Nicholas, who was a great support and he stayed by my side. He didn't like the hospital drugging me. He seemed to understand what I was going through, and he got me out of Charing Cross Hospital, where they were giving me such highly sedative drugs. He was like a hero, my rescuer. I needed to get away and start feeling like myself again. So, we booked a trip to the Dominican Republic. It was autumn 2000, and we had a wonderful time together. It was so good to get away from everything. It was there that we decided to have a commitment ceremony.

I am not proud to admit I had an abortion. It was a horrific experience, something I've tried to blot out of my mind. In my mind at the time, I had to look after the children I had and that meant getting away. I just couldn't bring another child into the world with Dick and let his hooks get that much deeper into my life. He was already insanely, violently obsessed with me. I needed to break free from him, not be tied to him even further. So, I did what I did. No one else is responsible. It was my decision. It's part of my story and I'm not running from it any longer.

I think every woman who has aborted a child will understand the agony of that decision. The heart-breaking burden of guilt, shame, loss as well as the grief and unforgiveness that we try to mask. I think of Harry every day. What he would have looked like, what he would be doing with his life. It tears me up inside. I think God was saddened and disappointed in the choice I made, but I also know that through my remorse and tearful confession, I am forgiven and have been welcomed back into my Father's embrace.

The commitment ceremony. The 5th of November was a beautiful day and after we made the commitment, we both jumped into the pool, fully clothed in our special outfits. It was a bit like a wedding, but we couldn't get married; my divorce from Dick wasn't official. We returned from our holiday renewed in our commitment to each other.

****

Things were changing for me and Nicholas after our holiday, but upon arriving home, I realised nothing else had. Dick was relentless in harassing me, stopping by unannounced, yelling and banging on the door, phone calls at all hours, either pleading with me or threatening to kill me. In one of the arguments with Dick, I blurted out that I was dating someone else, a 6'4" police officer who was also a kickboxing champion in Thailand! Dick didn't care. This just made him madder. I was his and nobody else could have me. I was his wife. He didn't stop.

Nicholas kind of turned into the police officer that he had asked me to tell Dick that he was. In hindsight, Nicholas possibly suffered from narcissistic personality disorder, unbeknownst to me then. He got me to agree that we needed to build a case against Dick to get a restraining order from the court. Every time Dick called, I had to record him. Even though I had quietly started dating Nicholas, I was still a single mum at home with Gabriel and Mary. Meaning Dick could still harass me freely, which, he did almost every night and day. He would call, drunk out of his mind, yell obscenities over the phone and threaten to kill me. He would often be waiting at the school gate at collection time. Gabriel's teacher had to be told, I needed them know that only I could collect him. I would be so fearful of bumping into him whilst popping to the shops.

One time Dick called, completely off his head, drunk and angry, screaming, yelling and threatening me. Finally, he said, "I'm coming around… I'm on my way!" I immediately called Nicholas, who was driving back from work in Guildford; about a forty-five-minute drive on a good day, but this was a Friday, so traffic on the A3 was bumper-to-bumper moving at a snail's pace. We hung up the phone; Nicholas called the police, and I ran to lock all the doors.

Dick arrived and the first thing he did was slip something through the letterbox. Then he started banging, kicking and stomping on the door. I was terrified! I called Nicholas again; he was still stuck in traffic. I called the police, all the while Gabriel was crying, Mary was screaming, Dick was yelling and kicking the door. I stood on the other side pushing against it (as if I could hold it back if it was kicked in). I had a different feeling that day, it felt like if he got through the door this time, I would be in pieces after he had finished with me.

Finally, the police rolled up, sirens blaring, they arrested Dick at the door. They dusted for fingerprints and investigated like it was a crime scene. The police were lovely, very caring and understanding. As they were taking my statement, my five-year-old son walked up to one of the police officers in his Superman costume, cape and all. One of the officers said, "Oh, I really like your Superman outfit."

Gabriel replied, "Yes, I'm wearing it because I have to save my Mummy." My heart sank hearing him say that and I started to cry, knowing he was getting to an age where he was understanding so much more. The police used that in the statements that were later presented in court.

They also took into evidence what Dick had slipped through the letterbox; a videotape rental of the film "You've Got Mail". It was a movie about finding and dating someone online. Somehow, through the Fulham grapevine, Dick had found out that I had met someone online. We had a joint account at a video rental store at the top of the road. This was Dick's way of letting me know that he knew.

Following the incident, I no longer felt safe alone in the house with the kids. So, despite it being just a few months after Nicholas and I started dating, I asked him to move in with me and the kids, after all we had made a commitment to one another whilst we were away. Nicholas stayed with us at Walham Grove during the week and at the weekends we would take the kids to his house in Penge. I just wanted to feel safe but having Nicholas move in just incensed Dick even more. The harassment got even worse. Every time we left the house it felt like everyone was looking at us, whispering. By this point I was pregnant with Nicholas's baby, I didn't need any more stress, we had to get out of Fulham.

I had the domestic violence advocacy group working with me after opening my case against Dick. They helped through the court process and sorted for all our stuff in the flat to be put into storage. They wanted to put us in a refuge for battered women, but this would mean Nicholas wouldn't be able to visit or stay. So, Nicholas' family let us move into their home with them in Bromley. After all, I was carrying their first grandchild. His family were all nice to me. I loved his Dad especially, we seemed to have a connection; he had the ability to always make me laugh. He was a functioning alcoholic, he would finish work and immediately pour himself a glass of red wine or possibly a brandy, but he was a happy drunk. Nicholas's Mum and sister were both young at heart and so much fun to be around, I felt accepted into their family. They all had such beautiful hearts and made room for me and my children without hesitation. My son was very blessed to have them as a family.

We were all squeezed into a small house, perfect for two or three people, but now there were four adults and two children. Nicholas and his dad didn't seem to get on too well; there was a discord between them, I didn't know why.

I thought he was lovely; he also took a special liking to Mary. He loved her character and her mischievous ways; they would play and laugh for hours. It was beautiful to see because at this point Mary had no verbal skills, but somehow, they were both able to communicate so well together, often watching cartoons in the living room before it was time for bed. Mary loved the "bear in the big blue house" and so did Ben, Nicholas's Dad. I finally felt safe. I was miles away from Dick, he didn't know where we were living.

After marrying Dick, he was legally added to the tenancy for the house in Walham Grove and without finalising the divorce, I couldn't take him off the tenancy. Instead, I had to give my beautiful flat in Fulham back to the council and I had to promise them that when they rehoused me, I wouldn't stay in the area. I would have to independently exchange homes, moving to a different area for my own safety. So, we stayed in Bromley until Hammersmith and Fulham Council found me a flat somewhere else.

We painted the flat in Fulham white, a blank canvas ready for someone to move into and as soon as I was given somewhere else to live, we listed it on a house swap website. Finding a match in terms of the desired location and the number of rooms, wasn't easy but for me, the toughest part of leaving Fulham was giving up my beautiful flat in Walham Grove. I loved that flat so much, it was my first real home and we had done so much work to make it ours. It was truly a bittersweet moment, but I knew it was right by my babies.

Once the court case had begun, I had to relive the stress of seeing Dick regularly. There were so many hearings; after the "You've got mail" incident at the house, we went to court for his violation of the restraining order and new charges from that night. We were also fighting over visitation rights in Family Court and there was also my divorce from Dick which also required court appearances. All I could think is thank goodness he doesn't know where we live.

It was a lot to process. It felt like we were appearing in one of the courts at least once a week. One time at Croydon Family Court, Nicholas and I walked into the lift, turned to push the button and as the doors were closing, a police officer stuck his hand in, opening the lift doors. He walked in with a handcuffed prisoner, it was Dick! Just seeing him so close, in a confined space, made me shudder. The four of us went up in the lift to the courtroom and I was shaking, even though Dick was in handcuffs. He made some snarky comments as we rode the lift, "Magpies steal nests!" he said. Implying that Nicholas had stolen his family.

Dick had a new girlfriend who just so happened to work at Chelsea and Westminster Hospital in the admin department. She was known as "Big Bird" because, well, she was; big, tall and gangly. She was able to access all our medical records and that meant, our new address. I had to update my details as Mary was still on the system awaiting tests for her delayed learning. When Dick asked her to find out where we were staying, she was happy to oblige.

We had agreed that Dick could give Gabriel a cheap mobile phone so that he could keep in touch with the children and call them at set times. It started out as every other evening at 7pm but that agreement was quickly violated. Dick would sometimes call after having been drinking, but he didn't really want to talk to Gabriel. He'd ring up drunk telling Gabriel to "put his Mummy on the phone". It was never really about the kids with Dick. He was completely obsessed with me and didn't want anyone else to have me.

We changed the agreement to once a week on Friday night, but that just caused more grief with Dick, more arguments, more tension, more stress. Nicholas bought the latest recording device and just like before, we decided to record Dick's abusive phone calls to build a case for a tighter order, to prove his violation of the restrictions that were already in place.

As we anticipated, he called in an angry drunken stupor, spewing out venom and cursing at me and Nicholas. Then he blurted out, "I know you're living in Bromley! I know you live in Whitefoot Lane!" Then he threatened to put a bullet in our heads! It was a complete surprise that he knew exactly where we were living and with his connection in the criminal world, I didn't take his threats lightly. No time was wasted in turning the recordings into the police and Dick was arrested. An investigation began into how he'd discovered our address. Eventually, he was sent to prison for violating the court order, the restraining order, as well as his bail terms. His sentence was brief – however, we were granted a lifetime restraining order against him. Not that it meant much to Dick, he didn't care about the law and being told what to do was the thing he hated the most, to him they were just pieces of paper with words on.

****

Summer 2001 - I was roughly twenty-six weeks pregnant and I had a hospital appointment for a regular check-up. When they began an internal examination, I started bleeding, it was decided that I should stay in hospital so they could keep an eye on me. Before I knew it, they were quickly prepping me for an early labour, I had an injection to build

163

Abel's lungs as they anticipated he could be born right there, right then. After a while the staff concluded it was pre-labour contractions and discharged me. Once again, the stress of dealing with Dick was taking its toll on me.

Two weeks later it was Father's Day. Nicholas had found a guitar online that he wanted, so off he went to get his Father's Day gift. While he was gone, my waters broke. I called Nicholas and he immediately turned around, he was in such a rush to get back, he got two speeding tickets. I was in labour and taken to Lewisham Hospital. I had already received a round of injections two weeks earlier to build Abel's lungs, but the midwife watching over me kept saying, "She's not in labour." It sure felt like I was in labour! I was bleeding and having very strong contractions all night!

10 o'clock the next morning, the doctor making his rounds looked at me, took a scan of my stomach with a portable scanner and suddenly everyone was rushing about frantically. I was quickly prepped for emergency surgery and at 10.15am. Just ten minutes after the doctor had entered my room, little Abel was born by emergency C-section. Later, Nicholas overheard the doctor raise his voice to the midwife saying, "Why the f*** did you leave her this long!? Why?"

I was distressed, my baby was distressed and suffering in the womb, yet the hospital staff simply did not respond in time. It was nearly twenty-four hours after my waters broke that Abel was born by emergency C-section. He was 3lbs, 4oz, born twelve weeks premature. For such a long time I blamed myself for not being able to carry him to term. I questioned whether it was my fault because of the abortion I had just months before I fell pregnant again. I was all over the place not knowing if he was going to live or die!

We weren't sure if this tiny baby that you could hold in the palm of your hand, was going to make it. Two days later, little Abel's lung collapsed. The delicate surgery on his lungs saved his life and we breathed a sigh of relief. He was returned to the Neonatal Intensive Care Unit (NICU) and kept fully ventilated for about a month, then he was transferred onto a CPAP breathing machine for about a month before he went onto using oxygen via a tube in his nose. They kept me in for five days, and every day a porter would wheel me to the NICU so I could see my baby. I would stay with him all day expressing milk so he could be tube fed. I had put a little Walkman in his incubator with speakers that played the song "Stay another day" by East 17 on repeat, which reminds me of him still when I listen to it. To this day it still brings a tear to my eyes listening to it; it's amazing the way the body experiences somatic responses when listening to music. It can be a great tool to use for healing.

Abel stayed in hospital for three months, and those three months were horrible. I was expressing milk and visiting him in the hospital every day. Every day I would come home to an empty crib next to our bed. Every day, for three months. It was agonising. In-fact, it was a strange time in the world, the same time as Twin Towers coming down and my sister going off to war.

September 2001 - Finally, Abel came home. He was released just after his due date and weighed close to six pounds. We had to bring him home on oxygen as his lungs were still very weak; he had to have a special monitor in his crib that would bleep if he stopped breathing. We also had to have oxygen tubing put throughout the whole house, as well as a portable saturation monitor and nebulisers – the house almost became like a hospital. He was on lots of medication, and it took a lot to take care of his needs, twenty-four hours a day. It wasn't easy, but I was so happy to have my little baby boy home, I would have done just about anything. Soon I began to feel like we were intruding on Nicholas's family. A year earlier, it was just the two of them in a cosy three-up, two-down house. Now there were four adults, two children and a new-born baby. Ben and Karol were great, but it was time for us to have our own place, our own home again.

So, I started hounding Hammersmith and Fulham Council. I called them every day. "Have you found me a place yet? Have you found me a place yet? How much longer?" We were still waiting to be given a flat that I promised we would put on the house-swap website to do a mutual exchange. All my stuff was still boxed up and in storage. So, I was on a mission, I called them relentlessly every day. I'm sure they got tired of me, and finally a house became available.

We were able to swap with a five-storey, four-bedroom townhouse in Streatham with a bigger garden which also had a driveway. It was at the top of a hill, it had beautiful views of London, especially at night with all the lights.

It was hard work moving into the house. Abel was still on oxygen twenty-four hours a day; his lungs were still weak, so it had to be clean and free from any dust. There was so much to do as it was a complete mess; bugs everywhere, grease nearly an inch thick in the kitchen – it was just disgusting. The woman we swapped houses with was a single mum with several kids, it was probably very difficult to keep it neat and tidy, and it showed. It took us months to get it in shape so we could move from Bromley to Streatham.

Well Close in Streatham, our new home. It was at the end of the road and at the top of our driveway there were steps leading into the house. The first floor consisted of a toilet and living room, the middle of the house was a staircase leading to the second floor and a large kitchen with a door providing access to the back garden. The house was semi-detached, so the garden wrapped right around to the front of the house with a gate on the side; the third floor was a big master bedroom and to one side there was a large storage cupboard. Another five steps led up to the fourth floor, which included a Jacuzzi bathroom and another bedroom, which was Abel's room. Five more steps to the fifth floor were two more bedrooms. To the left was Gabriel's room, to the right was Mary's. I painted murals for them all: Mary had a Disney room; Gabriel had a Pokémon room and little Abel had an underwater room with lots of fish.

Gabriel was six and Mary was three years old when we moved to Well Close in Streatham. Gabriel went to Sunnyhill Primary School, which was at the bottom of the hill just across the road. It was so close he could walk it on his own. This was now his third school, and he was only six; he had experienced bullying at the school in Bromley, so his self-esteem was very low. I was hoping it would be a smooth transition into his new school and it was. However, Mary was struggling. She was not getting along with others, having meltdowns, she still had no verbal skills. She had been in a special need's nursery at the Ladywell Centre in Lewisham, but she hadn't yet been diagnosed with anything. When we moved to Lambeth, Mary was given a place at the Sophie Centre, which included a pre-school for children with disabilities. It was at the Sophie Centre in 2003 that Mary, now aged five, first received a diagnosis of autism. Of course, I knew something was not right with Mary, but it took years to get her diagnosis so we could get the right support in place.

We needed three medical assessors to agree on a diagnosis, and each used a battery of tests to assess Mary. Finally, she received her diagnosis, and each subsequent year, as her

Statement of Educational Needs was being developed, she was diagnosed with additional disabilities, including Pica, Pathological Demand Avoidance (PDA), epilepsy and borderline severe learning disabilities. Mary's behaviour was much harder to handle than Abel's medical conditions. I often said I would rather have 1000 Abel's over one Mary, as I just didn't know how best to help her. She had very little means of communicating with us. So, most of the time I was second- guessing all her needs, which would cause her even more frustration and then more meltdowns. It was Mary's way or the highway. A bit like her Dad. You could see Abel needed extra support, but Mary's disabilities were invisible. She looked like butter wouldn't melt in her mouth, but then she would have massive meltdowns that lasted for days, lashing out, self-harming and screaming all the time.

When she was old enough, just after her autism diagnosis, Mary was placed in the nursery at Sunnyhill School. She couldn't handle the large classroom settings. Without any verbal skills, Mary was disruptive, throwing tantrums, biting, kicking, getting into fights and hurting the other children. We had hired a carer to help with Mary because she was such a handful and having two other children, we needed to ensure each one's needs were met. Linda, Mary's carer, was simply walking her around the school grounds because she could not adapt to the classroom. She was getting no education at all, so we had to pull her out for her own good. I had to start home schooling her, which also became almost impossible.

A few months later, we were given an appointment to see the doctor who had given Mary her Autism diagnosis, because I was worried about Abel. He was about eighteen months old and wasn't walking. He seemed delayed in his development, so I was concerned. I walked right up to the doctor and bluntly asked, "Can you tell me, is Abel autistic like Mary? Because I'd rather know now and know what we're dealing with."

The doctor tilted her head and looked at me oddly before answering, "No, he's not autistic. But you do know he has cerebral palsy, don't you?" I immediately thought, Cerebral palsy… what's that? I had never heard of it, but I'm told my precious child has it. Whatever it is. I was in a daze, totally shocked. When I got home and told Nicholas. he immediately got on the computer and started researching. Tech was his thing and a lot faster than books; he would tell me what he had found, but it was all very clinical. Nicholas never told me what he was feeling. He just clammed up. He went completely silent. Sometimes for days and then weeks! It felt like forever. I was getting the silent treatment, and I didn't understand why.

I should have realised that Nicholas was dealing silently with his own grief. He had to come to the realisation that he wouldn't be able to play football with his only son or teach him how to kick-box. At the same time, I was processing Mary's diagnosis of autism and wondering what kind of life she would have. Would they ever marry or have children? Would they finish school? How would they be as adults? How could we plan for their future?

I was all over the place emotionally; two of my three children were disabled. What kind of life would they have? Would Mary ever talk, would Abel ever walk? Was it my fault? Was my body defective? I was feeling a lot of shame and guilt and not getting the support I needed from my partner because he had completely shut down and checked out emotionally. Nicholas withdrew and wouldn't talk to me. He refused to open up, and finally I had had enough. I picked an argument just to get a reaction from him.

I walked into the room where Nicholas was on the computer, and I started an argument with him. It escalated, I was sobbing, crying and yelling, then sobbing some more. I was so upset with his lack of response, like he didn't care, that I slapped him across the face. Nicholas was stunned. He stood up, turned around, and punched the back of his computer chair so hard that he broke the middle knuckle on his hand. It was a mess and he eventually had to have surgery to repair the damage. This was our first fight.

Because Nicholas wasn't communicating with me, I felt very lonely. I was used to over-communication. I was used to men spilling their emotions, becoming violent and shouting their needs. But at least I knew, to some degree, the demons they were facing. This time was so different. It was me that lifted a hand. I didn't understand. Our relationship was teetering on the edge for months.

5th of November - the anniversary of our commitment ceremony in the Dominican Republic. Nicholas asked his sister Kelly, who was so great with the kids, to babysit. I loved his sister; we got on very well. Nicholas had booked a table at an Indian restaurant called The Three Monkeys in Dulwich. When we got back home, I walked up to our bedroom and was greeted by a room full of lit candles. There were candles everywhere! The heat in the room from the candles was almost overwhelming. There must have been 250 to 300 separately lit candles! Then I turned around and Nicholas was down on one knee. He opened a ring box and asked me to marry him. How could I not?! Of course, I said yes! It was the most romantic thing anyone had ever done for me.

****

I immediately threw myself into the planning. It was going to be an extravaganza. The wedding of the year! I took out a bank loan to make sure it would be everything I wanted. I handmade all the invitations as well as wedding favours. I ordered all the dresses for the wedding party; I made all the flower arrangements with help from my Mum. Kelly and Jane were bridesmaids, Diana my maid of honour. Jane had just finished a tour in Afghanistan and was based back in Germany, so she was able to bring lots of cheap booze for the free bar at the reception. I was friends with Gabriel's best friend's Mum, Christine, so her daughter Anna and Mary were flower girls. Anna and Gabriel are still best friends to this day, she is GodMother to my Grandchildren. My brothers Art and George were ushers, Gabriel and Abel were page boys, Nicholas's best man was Toby, an odd choice since they had just met about a month before the wedding. How could someone you just recently met be the best man at your wedding? It appeared Nicholas didn't have any close friends. No mates from his childhood, no work colleagues.

The wedding was planned for 12 June 2004, the day after my Mum's fiftieth birthday, and just a few days before Abel's third birthday. Both Nicholas and I were planning our bachelor and bachelorette parties. Nicholas decided on a golf outing with his mates and even bought some second-hand, custom-made Ping golf clubs that would fit his height. Being six-foot-four, Nicholas needed longer clubs. He had played on his own just a couple of times during our relationship, but this time he had such fun with his friends.

The very next day after his party he said he really wanted me to learn how to play, and he persuaded me to go with him. So, we went to a golf course near Tooting. I hired some clubs for me and then we headed out to the first tee. It was a beautiful day; the sun was shining, and the course was busy with golfers.

On the fourth tee, I was standing a safe distance behind Nicholas as he prepared to hit his drive. I heard the whack of the club striking the ball, but the next thing I remember I was waking up on the ground with Nicholas kneeling over me. I noticed another person kneeling over me, I could feel the wetness of blood all over my face. I heard voices shouting, "Call an ambulance! Get an ambulance, quickly!"

The two men that were playing ahead of us rushed back and with Nicholas they tried to cradle my head, I was carried like I was a battlefield victim. Then more voices shouting, "No, no! Put her down. Don't move her!" The ambulance finally arrived, siren blaring, lights flashing, they pulled right up onto the tee. I was rushed to the Moorfields London Eye Hospital at St George's Hospital for emergency maxillofacial surgery to close a cut over my left eye and on the bridge of my nose. In total I needed about twenty stitches in my face just days before my big day!

After closing the wounds, an ophthalmologist began testing my sight. Dye was put in my eyes and lots of other tests were performed. After he examined the back of my left eye, he gave me the bad news.

He said, "Your eye is like a planet, but the back of your left eye has a crack from top to bottom, like an earthquake fault line. You'll never see out of that eye again. I'm so sorry."

What? How could this be? I was now blind in one eye because I played golf, for the first time ever, with my soon-to-be-husband? What happened?

Nicholas returned the following day to retrieve the clubs

that he had left behind, and to fill out and write an accident report for the golf course. When Nicholas returned home, his 7-iron club, was in two pieces. He said the shaft of the club just snapped in half. Nicholas said it was a complete freak accident. But hold on a minute! I'm now blind in one eye and I'm angry! Golf clubs aren't supposed to snap in half and fly around like missiles. I'm outraged and want to sue! I contacted a "no win, no fee" attorney to sue Ping, the golf club manufacturer. We were told that the snapped club first needed to be tested by a metallurgist. The lab would forensically test the metal in the shaft of the club to determine how it snapped.

So, what really happened? Unfortunately, I don't know. Nicholas said it was a freak accident, that the club snapped in half at the force of his swing, then came flying back towards me, the shaft striking me across my nose and above my eye, while the butt of the club hit me flush in my left eye.

Is that really what happened? Another possibility is that Nicholas snapped the club purposely when he went back to the golf course to retrieve his clubs and write the accident report. When I think back, I remember that Nicholas wasn't hitting the ball well on the first three holes we played. He wanted to impress me with his golf playing but was struggling and getting more frustrated. I think maybe, Nicholas was upset with his shot, slammed his club on the ground, and it ricocheted backwards towards me. I don't know if the club had snapped or was still in one piece because the impact had knocked me out and put me on the ground bleeding profusely from my face. I may never know for certain what exactly happened. But I did know the outcome, I was now completely blind in one eye less than a few weeks before my wedding.

****

As I tried to recover from my wounds and adjusted to sight in only one eye, I pressed on with the wedding preparations. The wedding of my life still needed planning and organising. The men were going to be in classic tuxedos with top hats and tails. Nicholas even had a cane to accompany his outfit. We had a stretch limousine for the wedding party, the reception was in the church hall, so we didn't have to go far; included was buffet-style food and an open free bar. Just a couple of weeks before the wedding, I got a call from my sister Jane, who said, "You'll never guess who I ran into: Lorenzo. I told him that you had split up from Dick, that you are with someone new, and getting married. He wanted your phone number, so I gave it to him."

It was a couple days later when Lorenzo called. At this point, I hadn't told Nicholas about that situation. I would always say to myself that Nicholas didn't need to know. I didn't want him thinking less of me. Deep down I felt shame at the idea of having possibly three children from three different fathers. If left to me, I wanted it to remain a secret. The less said, the better. Besides, I really wasn't sure myself. I didn't have confirmation and I wasn't seeking it, but Gabriel certainly resembled Lorenzo much more than Dick.

The guilt ate away at me since Jane had bumped into Lorenzo, so, I sat Nicholas down and I told him. Whilst I was explaining, he just began to smirk and as the details unfolded, Nicholas absolutely loved the idea that this could seriously hurt Dick. His now nemesis. He began to investigate DNA testing and couldn't wait to invite Lorenzo over to get to know him better. He befriended him, because he relished in the idea of having something over Dick.

174

Nicholas encouraged Lorenzo to get a DNA test and get an answer once and for all. Lorenzo first paid for a test from the internet, but we then found out that it was a fake website giving out fake reports, but he didn't give up. He then went through his GP for testing... then we waited... and waited. Lorenzo called and confirmed what I had suspected; that Lorenzo was Gabriel's biological father.

Lorenzo became a regular fixture at our house, spending time with Gabriel and taking him out. Him also stepped in and offered to help with organising and preparing all the catering for our wedding. He did an amazing job; it looked and tasted great.

As the Big Day approached, I got a call from Ben, Nicholas's dad. I had a wonderful relationship with Ben, but usually it was Karol that called. Ben watched a lot of shopping channel TV and he wanted to tell me that had bought me some expensive stage make-up that would hide scars and bruises from the golf club accident. He wanted me to be confident and look my best on my wedding day. It was such a sweet gesture.

Just days before the wedding, I found myself at Anna's house. Christine had been a good friend ever since Gabriel and Anna were in the same class in school. I would often pop by Christine's to drop stuff off for the wedding as she lived just next to the church where we were getting married – St Peter's on Leigham Court Road in Streatham. After a couple of glasses of wine, I began to open up to Christine about something weighing on my mind. That something was Lorenzo.

I had always been drawn to Lorenzo; I'd always had a crush on him. Having him back in my life so frequently was bringing those feelings back up. Nicholas had befriended him; he was helping with the reception food; he was spending time with Gabriel. I had avoided started things with Lorenzo because Dick was in the picture and the fear of what might have happened meant it was easier to choose Dick over him. Suddenly, I burst into tears, sobbing to Christine that I was so confused. Feelings for Lorenzo were bubbling up inside. I was just days from my wedding, I was an emotional wreck! Should I carry on and marry Nicholas, or should I call it off? What was I supposed to do with these feelings?

Fast forward a few days, I went through with the wedding, it was a beautiful day. The ceremony was perfect, we had a full choir and the reception was great fun; dancing, food and an open bar.

As the day reached its end, family and friends stayed around to help clean up the hall. We married on a Saturday and with Sunday fast approaching, St Peter's church needed to be cleaned and returned to its previous condition ready for the Sunday service. It was the only way to get the deposit back, so we did what we needed to do.

It was nearly 2am when we finished and luckily only a short distance from the house; Nicholas and I walked home from the church. Gabriel was staying with my parents, Mary had gone to stay with her carer and Abel was with his grandparents, Karol and Ben. It was our first night as a married couple and we were looking forward to some time alone.

As soon as we got through the door, I went to the bedroom to get out of my dress. Suddenly a loud banging on the front door; BANG, BANG, BANG. Then shouting, "Hey Sab, open the door. We need to call a taxi, C'mon, open the door." It was my brothers, one of Art's friends Billy Jones-also Dick's best friend.

I hadn't seen Billy since I had split up with Dick. Turned out they were all hoping to carry the party on at our house, on my wedding night. Nicholas went down and reminded them of the taxi office at the top of the road and quickly sent them on their way.

****

Although life was often a struggle, having three children, two with disabilities was a daily challenge, I was feeling a little better about myself. I must admit that Nicholas helped with that. He helped me find myself again. He treated me so differently to Dick who had been imprisoning me, punishing me for wearing nice things or making an effort with my appearance. Nicholas, on the other hand, loved shopping and picking out clothes for me to try on. He encouraged me, he complimented me and gave me the freedom to explore. He wanted me to look attractive and maybe a bit risqué and suggestive. Nicholas brought out a part of me that had been dormant. It wasn't that I grew out of an ugly stage; but now someone was encouraging me to show of my beauty.

When we were in the Dominican Republic, where we had our commitment ceremony, we read a book called "Think Sex" together. It came free with a magazine I brought at the airport. It was a very sensual book. As we were reading it by the pool, Nicholas suddenly asked if I found women attractive and sexy. I hadn't really thought about it until he had asked me, but I admitted that, yes, I did find some women attractive. We left it there because it wasn't something that we could ever explore while we lived together at his parent's' house in Bromley, but when we moved to Well Close, we finally had freedom. Nicholas had an addiction to porn; he was watching it more often and would frequently steer the conversation to threesomes. He said he wanted to see where my interest in finding women attractive might take us.

He spent a lot of time and finally had convinced me to try "soft swinging", which we defined as girl-on-girl play only, with another couple. The more we talked about it, the more excited and interested he became, and he was very persuasive. When I had finished breast-feeding, Nicholas encouraged me to get breast enhancement surgery. So, I did, and I loved the results, my confidence soared! Nicholas invested in a very good professional camera and took some sexy photos, then he created a profile on a swinger's' website. He then worked the chat rooms and exchanged photos with prospective couples. If both couples agreed, we would arrange to meet at one of the swinger's' parties posted on the website. That's where we met Toby and Michaela for the first time, about a month before our wedding. Toby quickly became Nicholas's best friend and his best man at our wedding.

Nicholas really admired Toby. Toby was a big guy, very well- built, he was completely ripped and had a bit of a gangster, bad-boy vibe. He was also a cage fighter and, he was always working out at the gym; it wasn't long before Nicholas wanted to body build with him. He started going to the gym and Toby eventually introduced Nicholas to steroids. Toby also liked to party, and when he did, he took Cocaine.

We had dived in, headfirst, without really thinking too much about it, we were a part of the swinging scene. During the week, Nicholas was connecting with other couples on the website, swapping photos and making arrangements. We had started taking coke and he would be watching porn for hours. Nicholas soon hooked up with Toby's dealer and it wasn't long before he was purchasing a half-ounce of cocaine every weekend. The weekend was all about having fun. We had carers for all the children. Respite from Friday to Sunday every other week, sometimes every weekend. We dressed up sexy and went to swinging parties. We took loads of coke, drank alcohol and then had sex, soft swinging to start with, girl- on- girl fun only, while the husbands watched. Our lives revolved around the swinging lifestyle for several years. We didn't keep it a secret. We were very open; our friends and family all knew what we were doing. Our slogan was, "Couples that play together, stay together." I felt that at least we were open and honest about our lifestyle. It was fun meeting new people and something we could do together as a couple.

But I began to notice something about Nicholas that I couldn't understand, that made me feel very uncomfortable. I realise that everyone embellishes or exaggerates a bit from time to time, but Nicholas was telling outright lies, regularly. I don't know why he felt he needed to lie to impress others, but I didn't like it. Nicholas always had to have the best of everything; he liked to "keep up with the Joneses". What he liked best was showing off his stuff to impress others. He was always trying to "one-up" whoever he met. Jane called him "two shits" as a joke, she would say, "If you told Nicholas you took one shit, he'd say he took two." No one in my family really warmed to Nicholas. Probably because he acted like he was better than everyone else and lied a lot. Nicholas was smart, no question; he scored at a genius level on IQ tests. But he looked down on people, quite literally being 6'4". His attitude made people feel inferior and his prideful arrogance turned people off.

My brother Art told me about a time he met up with Nicholas for a drink in the pub for quiz night. The table formed a team and people introduced themselves, Nicholas told everyone that he was an Astrophysicist. Art said he almost choked on his pint. To his embarrassment, Nicholas was found out because someone else at the table was an actual Astrophysicist!

On countless occasions, upon returning from one of our parties, I would ask why he needed to lie to people. Of course, you can tell strangers you just met at a party pretty much anything you want, but why would you? It was like he lied to feed a need to be accepted.

A story Nicholas told over and over again to people we met was from his youth, before I met him, so it could be true, but knowing what I know now, I highly doubt it happened. Nicholas said he'd had some run-ins with the law when he was younger, then he told the tale. He was in a Nightclub and was about nineteen years old. Sat at the bar, minding his own business, when he noticed a guy beating up a girl, he smashed a chair over her head, so Nicholas intervened. They started fighting and Nicholas knocked him out. When the police arrived, Nicholas was arrested and taken to an interrogation room. Then in walked the chief inspector of the Kent Constabulary! The woman Nicholas had rescued that night just so happened to be the chief inspector's daughter. In gratitude, the constable told Nicholas that his criminal record would be completely expunged, giving him a fresh start in life. He made up so many stories, but he told them very well.

I couldn't prove whether the story was true or not, but I had heard enough of his bare- faced lies over time and often questioned whether any of his stories were true or not. "You can get to the bottom of a thief, but never to the bottom of a liar." Mum used to always say, sometimes, I would pull him on his lies when we were alone, but it would only lead to an argument. Nicholas was very good at twisting words and manipulating conversations; he was the king of gaslighting, always making me question myself. So, eventually I thought, does it matter? Are these battles I really want to fight? So, I rolled with it and stopped questioning him.

We were returning from a swinging party in Brighton. It was held at a private house with a big pool. Drinks were available, but you had to purchase a raffle ticket, then exchange the ticket for an alcoholic beverage. Drugs flowed freely at these parties, but there was one time where no one had any cocaine. In his search, Nicholas met a guy that had some Ketamine. We drove back to London and when we got home, Nicholas laid out the ketamine like lines of coke. We did one line each and both felt like we were going to die! I couldn't move, I couldn't speak. I felt like I was sinking into a hole. It was the worst experience I've ever had taking drugs; we took just one line, and we couldn't move. So, the next morning I took what was left of the ketamine and flushed it down the toilet! I then found out later it was used by vets to tranquillise horses! What were we thinking?

****

Dick had been sentenced to serve time following the court hearings. As he sat in prison for domestic violence and violating his restraining order, his parents filed for access to see the children, as their Grandparents, they had rights too. The Children and Family Court Advisory and Support Service (CAFCASS) report recommended that Dick no longer have contact with the children. Cafcass interviewed

181

Gabriel privately, so I didn't know what he said until the report came out. In the interview, they asked him, if he could have one wish come true, what would it be?

He was around eight years old and his answer to that question, "That Daddy would stop saying that he would kill Nicholas." The report concluded that it would not be in the best interests of the children to have any physical contact with Dick. Furthermore, if Dick wanted to mark special occasions, like birthdays or Christmas, he could only send cards, letters or gifts to my parents' home, where we would collect them.

One weekend we were dropping the kids to my parents for a sleepover; Gabriel had affectionately labelled Mum, "Nanny Nut Nut" by this point because they always had so much fun, and he thought she we a little nutty at times. It had been agreed that Dick's parents could visit the kids at my parents' house and quickly Dick's dad became nicknamed Silly Grandad. My parents felt I should consider allowing Dick to visit them, so as not to miss out on birthdays or Christmas. I didn't want to appear to be vindictive and given that Mum and Dad would be supervising, I agreed. It also felt like I was finally in control, setting boundaries and deciding where and when visits would occur.

After dropping Gabriel and Mary at Mum and Dad's that Friday, I rang on Saturday to check up on the kids. Dad had answered and when I asked to speak to them, he said, "Oh, your Mum's just taken them out. They'll be back in a minute." It was late afternoon and after hanging up the phone, I felt something just wasn't right. That doesn't sound suspicious, does it? But Dad is a terrible liar, and I could sense in the tone of his voice that something secretive was afoot. So, without telling them, Nicholas and I jumped in the car and headed to Fulham.

We arrived, walked into the living room, where Mum and Dad were sitting, I said to Dad, "Where are my kids?" Dad was startled, speechless; he had been caught out in a lie. He had let Dick's parents take Gabriel and Mary and keep them overnight, without my permission. He phoned Dick's Dad and Timmy brought Gabriel and Mary back.

Dad was red- faced and angry at the situation. When he got off the phone he glared at Nicholas and suddenly went for him. Dad threw a wild punch which Nicholas dodged. They wrestled, fell to the floor and with my dad on top. Nicholas freed his hands and twisted Dad's nipples to get him off him. This was the first and only time I had seen my dad go for anyone, let alone start a fight.

Shortly after, Timmy dropped the children off, we snatched them up, loaded them into the car and drove off. I was so angry that my dad had lied to me, that he attacked Nicholas and disrespected my authority as Gabriel and Mary's mum. Giving them to Dick's family without asking me was a huge violation of my trust and Dad knew he was in the wrong, but he never apologised. We didn't speak to my parents for a while afterwards. After a few months I allowed visits to continue as Gabriel missed his Nanny Nut Nut so much.

****

Whenever we travelled to either drop -off or pick -up Gabriel and Mary from my parents in Fulham. I began to feel very anxious; nauseous, churning feelings in the pit of my stomach. The feelings always seemed to ramp up as we crossed over Wandsworth Bridge. I was being triggered, but I didn't know anything about that at the time. I didn't know how to process what I was feeling. All I knew was I was getting increasingly nervous and jittery the closer we got to Fulham. It was getting worse each time.

Eventually, it was too much for me. So, Nicholas was now doing all the dropping off and picking up. One time, he was parked outside my parents waiting for Mum to bring the kids to the car. It was a warm, sunny day, the car window was down and as Mum helped load Gabriel and Mary into the car, Dick darted out from around the corner with a glass bottle in his hand. He broke the bottle and then whacked Nicholas in the face with it, with the children in the car. Blood was everywhere, the kids were screaming. Dick ran off and Nicholas called me as he drove back from Fulham trying to stop the blood streaming down his face. He arrived home and we immediately went to St George's Hospital to get him stitched up.

I was in the room with Nicholas, chatting away with the staff, trying to change the subject from the cut on the face. I was telling them that our little Abel was on oxygen, and we had all kinds of hospital supplies and machinery at home and that our home was almost like a little hospital. As I was saying how I thought I would make a good nurse or even a midwife; my attention turned back to his stitches and the blood trickling down his face, I felt woozy and the next thing I know I was on the floor. I had fainted; at the sight of the blood whilst saying how I could see myself a nurse, ha!

****

Nicholas was spending a lot of time with Toby, doing

steroids and working out at the gym to get the perfectly sculpted body. Toby told Nicholas that Egypt was one of the best places to get steroids as they were openly available at any pharmacy to buy over the counter. He told him that if they were discovered at customs when you returned to the UK, the steroids would just be seized. He could also buy Viagra in Egypt, which, given the impact steroid cycles have on sex drive and the difficulty maintaining an erection, steroid users typically took the two hand in hand. Not to mention everything in Egypt cost a lot less than it did in the UK. Toby assured Nicholas they couldn't be arrested because they were bought legally from a pharmacist in your name. Nicholas thought it was a great idea, so off we went to Egypt for a late honeymoon.

We stayed at a very nice, four-star, all-inclusive resort in Sharm El-Sheik, Egypt. There were three or four pools, daily classes you could join, a fitness area, nightly entertainment, and of course, all-you-can-eat food and drink. It was very nice. After we checked into our room, we walked a short distance down a hill to a row of shops to buy some snacks and other bits for our room during our stay. I was standing at the check-out dressed in a bikini and a long sarong covering it as it was extremely hot. The man at the register suddenly reached out and grabbed my breast! I was in shock; Nicholas was standing right there; he was just as shocked as I was. He grabbed the man's wrist, and said, "Oy! What do you think you're doing?!" The man got defensive, they exchanged words, but Nicholas didn't want to get into a fight in a foreign country. Once we said we would call the police, the man finally muttered some sort of apology and we walked back to our room, both fuming about what had just happened. I was shocked and angry that a stranger would do such a thing. There was a lack of respect for western women in some countries. I'm fair-skinned with long blonde hair and now big breasts after my boob job, but that's not an invitation to grope me.

Nicholas was already on edge from his steroid regime, and he quickly became obsessed with finding the best deal to take back to London. Much of our honeymoon was consumed with finding pharmacies, visiting them and comparing the best deals. One evening after Nicholas had finally completed his research and made his purchase, he took some of the steroids and we went to a pool party at the resort. We had made some friends at the bar; I had made plans to meet up with an elderly woman whom I had met at the resort. She was a lovely woman on holiday with her two Grandchildren; a girl about thirteen and a boy about sixteen. It was the boy's first-time trying alcohol on holiday with his Grandma. They were a cute bunch. Nicholas connected with a group of British squaddies on leave, they were all drinking, laughing and joking about getting drunk. Nicholas and his new best mates decided to head out into the night to party more, but I chose to stay behind with my friends and enjoy the evening's entertainment. I wanted to get an early night so I could be up early to sit around the pool, topping up my tan and reading my book. Holidays were the only time I would get to enjoy a good book, life at home meant I rarely had any time for myself, and I wasn't taking the time I had for granted.

At the end of the night, I took myself off to bed but hours later, Nicholas hadn't returned. As I waited for him to get back, the time went by very slowly, I didn't get much sleep as I was getting worried; maybe I slept for a few hours, around 7am I went straight to the reception desk. No one had seen Nicholas.

Just as I turned to walk back to the room, there he was. "Where have you been all night?" I quickly realised that Nicholas was off-his-face. He raised his voice, and we started arguing, which was something we didn't really do, he was normally very level-headed. As we were arguing we moved towards the pool area, and he completely flipped out. He went into a rage unlike anything I had ever seen before - He was totally out of control, throwing deck loungers into the pool, screaming and yelling and stomping around! I'd never seen aggression like this from Nicholas, it scared me, it was worse than Dick! Much worse. he had "roid rage" from mixing the steroids and alcohol.

We went back to our room and the arguing carried on, he started smashing everything up, he was drunk and now in total roid rage mode. I ran out of the room and into one of the restaurants that wasn't yet open. I was shaking, I hid myself away, crouched down in a corner so I couldn't be found. I was petrified. I was in a foreign country and my husband had gone completely mad! I fumbled with my phone trying to call someone but no matter who I tried to call, it wouldn't go through. I realised I had to add the area code for the UK to the number. My hands were shaking like a leaf to the point I could barely add the +44 to a phone number. I finally reached Nicholas's Mum, Karol. I was crying my eyes out; my voice was quivering. I tried to explain everything to her through my tears. She told me to stay put and she would call me back. I was shivering, shaking, sobbing; curled up in a ball in the corner of an empty restaurant. Karol called me back and said she had contacted the hotel to stay where I was, and that a member of staff was coming to get me.

A well-dressed man walked in, then I was taken to an inner office behind the reception at the front desk. I was in bits; I wanted to run as far away as I could. I wanted to hide; I wasn't just fearful but embarrassed. I started saying, "I want to go home! Book me a flight home! Get me out of here! I want to go home!"

I realised I didn't have my passport. I told the man we'd handed them to the reception desk when we checked in. After I stormed out of the room, Nicholas had gone to the reception and asked for our passports back, and they'd given them both to him. The hotel manager tried desperately to make amends. He agreed to book me a room in a nearby sister hotel until things could be sorted out. So, I moved to another hotel and stayed there, alone, by myself, on my Honeymoon, for three days, wondering what the flip just happened. I had nothing with me, just what I was wearing. I didn't feel safe going back to the room with Nicholas there, so Karol transferred £100 to the manager. He gave me the money and suggested I use his driver to take me into town to get some essentials before being moved onto the sister hotel free of charge.

Over the next few days many calls were made back and forth to friends and family in the UK. I wouldn't talk to Nicholas, so they were relaying to me what he had said. He refused to return my passport until I agreed to meet with him. I said that he couldn't do that until he had sobered up. In the meantime, with the money Karol transferred, I was able to get by for a few days. If I needed anything the hotel manager provided me with security and his own driver so I could get out of the hotel.

I just wanted my passport back so I could go home. I didn't want to meet him. I didn't want to see him or talk to him. I wanted nothing to do with him. Karol did the best she could, relaying messages and talking to us both, trying to break the impasse. Sitting poolside at a resort hotel in Egypt sounds wonderful, but I was all over the place inside. I ended up with a nice tan, but it was anything but peaceful. I was on my Honeymoon, but yet, I was alone. I was able to use the hotel's business lounge computers to get access to my emails, as calling the UK was getting very expensive, I had to change all my log-in details because Nicholas knew all my passwords. I messaged Linda, Mary's carer. We had become very good friends and her support at that time was something I'll never forget. She was so supportive, so reassuring and comforting.

After three days, I was feeling better within myself, so I relented and agreed to meet with Nicholas. I have no idea how much Karol's phone bill was; it must have been hundreds of pounds with all the international calls to Egypt from London to both Nicholas, me and the hotel manager, trying to broker an agreement. Karol assured me Nicholas was sober, he wasn't drinking, hadn't taken any more steroids and he was very remorseful, he wanted to sort things out and make things better. I'm sure he was also very embarrassed to have caused such a drama.

The meeting between us was arranged and it took place in the hotel manager's office. Nicholas seemed back to his old self. He was calm, he said he was sorry. He broke down crying, saying how much he loved me and that it would never happen again. I immediately got this sick feeling in the pit of my stomach. it was like I was back with Dick and the cycle of abuse was playing out all over again. I did forgive him, we tried to get past the ugliness and enjoy the remainder of our Honeymoon. I tried, but it was the worst holiday of my life; 'the Honeymoon from hell'!

****

After returning to the UK, it wasn't long before we moved into our new house in Brixton, built especially for us. It was a disability-friendly house with a wheelchair lift and the whole house was wheelchair accessible. Abel's cerebral palsy meant he was now in a wheelchair and needing oxygen full-time, the previous five storey house in Streatham had become impractical.

The house in Brixton was new and purpose-built; two - storeys, a wheelchair lift and hallways wide enough to accommodate a wheelchair. There were two bathrooms, a full bath upstairs and a shower/wet room on the main floor. It was also much bigger with five double bedrooms, a massive living room, a large kitchen dining area and a huge back garden for the kids. The driveway could fit up to three cars. It was perfect for us and met every demand that came with the kid's disabilities.

Raising the kids was relentlessly difficult. By the weekend, we were ready to cut loose and still very much a part of the swinging scene. Nicholas oversaw it all. I would go along with whatever he wanted. I had started to feel like his pretty, trophy swinging wife. His toy, I didn't feel in control of any of it. This was however our way of life for many years until I began suffering severe lower abdominal pains.

It felt like extreme menstrual pain, but it got so bad I took myself to Accident and Emergency. The first thing they wanted to do was a pregnancy test. I knew there was no way I was pregnant; I had been fitted with a birth- control device called 'the coil'. I peed in a pot and waited. Minutes later the nurse told me that it was positive, and I was, in fact, pregnant. How could this be? How could I take care of another child, when I was already struggling with the three I had? Would I be able to carry this baby to term after having two premature pregnancies? They scanned me anyway, and sure enough, I was pregnant. This time wasn't like the other times though, it was an ectopic pregnancy; the fertilised egg was lodged in one of the fallopian tubes, and I needed surgery. I was scheduled for a laparoscopy where that fallopian tube would be removed.

It all happened so quickly, the day after the surgery I was discharged, not feeling very well at all. The pain in my stomach was excruciating and when I went to the bathroom there was a lot of blood with big black clots in it. It got worse before it got better, blood was pouring down my legs. I wasn't too concerned because I was told I should expect bleeding after the surgery, and it did subside in the end.

About a week later, the hospital called me to ask if I could come back in for another pregnancy test and scan. "Why?" I asked.

The responded, "We sent the tube we took away to the lab to be analysed and we haven't found the foetus in the tube we removed. We need to make sure you are not still carrying the ectopic pregnancy; it can be life-threatening. Please come to the hospital right away."

So, I took myself back to hospital. It wasn't such a bad thing as I was still experiencing excruciating pains. My pregnancy test was negative, the large clots and extreme bleeding I experienced at home was a miscarriage. They had however, removed the wrong fallopian tube. The pain I was still experiencing needed to be addressed so I was sent to the gynaecologist and diagnosed with endometriosis. The recommendation was to have a partial hysterectomy, taking away my womb but leaving my ovaries in place to avoid early menopause. I had the surgery. A hysterectomy at the age of thirty-three.

Three weeks had passed, and I was still recovering when the horrific pain returned. I could barely move and was rushed back to hospital. They found a cyst the size of a cantaloupe on one of my ovaries. They didn't know if it was cancerous and needed to remove it to be sure. I went back into surgery, this time for a full hysterectomy, removing my ovaries and forcing me into early menopause.

I was devastated, although I didn't want any more children at the time, having my ovaries had meant if I did change my mind, I couldn't. Now the kids are all grown up, I do wish that I could have had another but, right there and then, after my operation; I felt less of a woman.

Going through early menopause wasn't easy, I was unable to take hormone replacement therapy because I was at high risk of developing cancer, which was determined after lots of genetic testing. After having the surgery, followed by weeks of recovery meant our sex life was on hold, which was difficult for Nicholas's high sex drive. I spent a lot of time painting, reading and playing Scrabble. At the weekends when the children went off to their Grandparents, he would just sit doing lines and drinking lots of brandy. We obviously weren't going swinging anymore so we'd go to our bedroom around 10pm but he wouldn't sleep, he would sit watching porn and sniff Cocaine all night.

I would think to myself, is it normal? Is it normal to think about sex that often? The way Nicholas was? It was like each new thing he tried; the next thing had to be even more extreme; even the porn that he was now watching was getting progressively stranger. Well, for a married man anyway.

It took about three months before I felt I was ready for sex again, we were no longer swinging by this point, Nicholas didn't seem interested in me, He was working away from home a lot, travelling, and when he was around, his attention seemed to be everywhere but being intimate with me. I was flirty and dressing sexy and I wanted to have sex, but he just wasn't interested. The rejection caused me to become very critical of myself. I was feeling stressed and anxious and was losing a lot of weight. The less he was home the more I started to feel like I was a single mum, I suspected Nicholas was having an affair because he had a very active libido, yet we weren't having sex. I figured if he wasn't getting it from me, he was getting it from someone else. This wasn't paranoia; Nicholas had been unfaithful to me previously.

Back when I was attending South Bank University, completing a three-year interior design course. I wanted to put my creativity to use and hopefully make a living from it. This is where I met Gina, a lovely young Brazilian woman. She was also learning interior design; she was in all my classes. It was a full-time course, so we saw each other almost every day; she also taught Brazilian dance to children on Saturdays. We hit it off and quickly became friends, when she broke up with her boyfriend, she needed a place to stay, so I suggested she move in with us until she got herself sorted. It wasn't long before the three of us became intimate... But it all went sour when I found Nicholas and Gina were spending time alone together and trying to keep it from me. The phone was in my name as Nicholas had declared bankruptcy and couldn't get anything in his name, when the bill came in the post it was pages long; I found hundreds of phone calls and text messages between the two of them. He took her out on dates, sent her flowers and they slept together. I was infuriated! Our motto was, "People who play together, stay together." I thought it was safe to be open and honest, but Nicholas had broken that agreement. He and Gina were lying to me, excluding me and being secretive. His sex addiction was getting out of hand.

I found myself wondering who it could be this time.

****

The rejection and broken trust devastated me. I developed an eating disorder and was diagnosed with "eating disorder not otherwise specified" (EDNOS) because I didn't fit all the criteria of either anorexia or bulimia. I was swaying from one to the other. I was exercising incessantly; thousands of abdominal crunches, hours on the treadmill, as well as starving myself, eating only a handful of boiled sweets. I was determined to become attractive to my husband again. But despite my efforts, he still wasn't interested in me sexually. When Nicholas was home, he watched hours of porn, and I felt like he was comparing me to these super-sexual female nymphomaniac porn stars. I felt I had to become whatever sexual fantasy he wanted to fulfil just to get him to look at me but, nothing was working.

Little did I know at the time I was entering the discard phase. Discard/Rejection: when the narcissist gets bored or decides the person is no longer useful enough to them, they'll often end the relationship and 'discard' the person. Sometimes, this ending is final. Other times, a narcissist will use hoovering to lure the person back into the relationship and repeat the cycle.

Things just started getting crazier after that. Nicholas was doing copious amounts of cocaine; his porn selection was going in a bizarre direction. Then he wanted to start wearing my clothes! He started wearing my underwear, things that were silky and satin. Things were starting to spiral out of control.

****

In 2008, we were sitting up in bed one morning watching Sky News, when we heard about the case of a nine-year old boy named Owen Johnson. He was left disabled with cerebral palsy when he was deprived of oxygen in his mother's womb due to errors made by hospital medical staff during his birth. His family was awarded £8 million by the Birmingham High Court. The details of Abel's birth sounded so familiar to this case, we decided to contact the young boy's solicitor and started a case on Abel's behalf.

Valentine's Day 2009 - about six months later, there was a knock at my door. It was a police officer, he was here to deliver the news of my Grandad Rubens passing, Mums' Dad. I couldn't believe that yet again, it had been left to me, I hadn't had contact with him in years.

He and my Nanny Barbara had divorced when Mum was young, she remarried and went onto have more children, but there were still bad feelings between them. It turned out that Grandad Rubens had several thousand pounds in cash in his home when he died. His next-door neighbour claimed it was her money, so the police had to hold it until everything was sorted out, which took about a year with the help of solicitors. Then, in the middle of this process, the executor of his estate quit, leaving Nicholas and I to take it over. We couldn't make everyone happy. In fact, nobody was happy. All anyone wanted was their share of the inheritance. The ugliest part of death is what it does to families when money is involved.

When the estate was finally settled, we had received enough for all of us to take a month's long holiday to Australia, where we stayed with Diana and her family. I had always wanted to go to Australia, ever since the Adamses had moved there. So, off we went, we travelled on Boxing Day, 26 December 2009, to Brisbane, Queensland, Australia.

It was also a chance for Nicholas and me, to repair our marriage. Things were not good. We weren't having sex, my anxiety was sky high, as well as the eating disorder, incessantly exercising and OCD. I couldn't continue to live this way. We had to do something, and I was thinking, maybe something as drastic as moving across the world for a fresh start.

Thankfully, the Australia trip was fantastic! It was summer down under, it was beautiful, it was such a great trip for the kids. Starting a new year in the tropical heat of Australia was a dream come true for me. Gabriel was around fifteen, Mary was around eleven and Abel was about eight when we went. It suited Abel so well with his cerebral palsy and hyperactive airways; normally, when the temperature fell below 15 degrees, his airways would close, and he would need nebulisers and oxygen to help him breathe. At times he needed to go to hospital; in the UK, he was on oxygen most of the winter, so going to Australia was great for him. We spent time at the beach, we went fishing, had cookouts, played in the swimming pool – which was great physiotherapy for Abel. Everyone had a great time. Mary loved the Warner Bros theme park; we even went to Water World and swam with the dolphins. It was truly amazing.

We started to talk about the possibility of moving to Australia. It would be so good for the kids and our marriage was struggling, we thought a change of scenery and a fresh start might help us get back on track. Nicholas started to look for job opportunities, whilst on the holiday, Nicholas left for a day and met with a corporate head-hunter. In the back of our minds was the case we had filed on Abel's behalf with the solicitor. We thought it best to get that sorted first and make plans to move to the other side of the world later. I was so ready to get out of the UK for a fresh start, away from all the bad memories, all the traumas. I just wanted to be happy again.

This was a very exciting time! Nicholas was working in IT, and he said a corporate head-hunter was chasing him with jobs in Australia, which had full relocation packages, paying for the move and everything. So, he started applying for jobs in Australia. He was looking at houses that we could rent at first and think about buying later; we were all so excited, especially the children. The houses he was showing us all had tennis courts and swimming pools; you get so much more for your money than what you get in London. But there was a lot of work to be done this end to make the move possible. Since Nicholas was not Gabriel or Mary's biological father, we had to get Dick's permission or a court order saying that I had full parental responsibility of the children for them to move out of the UK. This wasn't going to be an easy task! I contacted a solicitor as I had no idea how best to contact Dick, who was in prison again, this time for another domestic violence conviction against another woman. He relished the fact that I needed his permission to move Gabriel and Mary to Australia. He tried to make it as difficult as possible, not because he longed for his kids, but to make trouble for me. He refused to write a letter saying he would give permission, so we had to go down the court route, which was going to take some time.

Nicholas told me he'd been offered a position at a company near Brisbane in Australia! He showed me the emailed job offer on a company letterhead email as well as pictures of a beautiful house, the one with tennis courts and the swimming pool. Wow, I thought! Could this really be happening?!

I was waiting on the courts to say that I had been granted full custody, full parental responsibility for Gabriel and Mary. In fact, the whole process was dragging on and on, the whole thing was getting very frustrating. Gabriel put off applying to college, anticipating that we would be living in Australia, but the process continued to drag, and he missed the deadline to apply for college. When Nicholas and I spoke about the move, I would ask him to ask his new employer certain details since they were sorting out the move and relocation. He would blame the company for the delay, saying they were dragging their feet, but he assured me everything was on track.

Finally, the day of the court case came. I remember it so very clearly. Nicholas and I had an argument just beforehand, so I went on my own. The court granted me full parental responsibility for the kids, allowing me to take them out of the country. I was elated! Finally, we could make this happen! When I got home, I shared the good news with Nicholas and the children, although he didn't seem as excited as I was. I asked him to email his employer to start the visa process as the company would be sponsoring us and now, we had everything we needed. His response was, the person responsible for the visa application, was away on leave. He even showed me an email confirming so.

My frustration was rising while Nicholas was away on a "business trip", I went into the office and onto his computer to find the mail address for the person at the company in Australia. I wanted to introduce myself and share our good news so that they knew to go ahead with the visa application. Hoping that it might speed up the process, I found the email that Nicholas showed me with the name of the company. When I tried to email her, it bounced back. I put the name of the company into the search bar and hoped to find an alternative method to reach them, but nothing. There was no such company. I thought, it can't be, so I opened some other tabs, desperately hoping i would find it somewhere. I didn't find the company, but what I did find, that day on his computer, changed my life forever.

I had found a full profile with photos on a dating site called Gaydar. No wife should have to see what I saw that day. I confronted him when he got in, he said nothing; he just left the house, got in his car and drove away. His lies were starting to unravel, that's when the gaslighting started. He told everyone I was going crazy and lying, but I had all the evidence in black and white and in colour. I threatened to tell all his secrets, two days later a policeman turned up at my door with a gagging order – who gets a gagging order if they have nothing to hide? This was when I realised, I was married to a narcissist.

Chapter ten

Who can I Trust?

"It is better to trust in the Lord than to put confidence in man."

Psalm 118:8

I have been let down by so many people throughout my life, it caused so much pain and an ingrained sense of mistrust. It hurts knowing that the people who are supposed to be there, to help you, to support and protect you, are the ones causing the damage. It makes it harder to see danger when it's near, struggling to know the difference between a friend and foe. The constant battle of why me? The fact this wasn't limited to those close to me but extended to people in authority, made it that bit harder to comprehend. It seems like you always have to fight, the fight to survive, to be understood and in some cases believed, the fight for help and support. I will say the one thing that I do have in me, is that fight; to never give up and to always find a way to overcome whatever I am faced with. I long to use my lessons, my journey, my suffering, to help others, as part of my calling and my reason for writing this book - I know I am not alone.

Millions of people are being let down by the systems we have in place, the same systems that promise to protect us, to get justice for victims and hold people accountable for the impact of their actions. My family were let down by multiple agencies, as are many. It's time for them to rethink, it's time to witness and unless we speak out, nothing changes. If you haven't experienced it, it might seem hard to believe, I truly hope you never need to suffer the way so many do. Putting faith and hope in the hands of authorities you believe will hear you, see you, only to be told their hands are tied.

Over the years my list only got longer; the Social Worker that overlooked my abuse as a child, hospitals making irreversible and life changing mistakes, educators failing to diagnose disabilities that impacted my learning, the Police and their insensitive approach to my abuse, GP's and even leaders of the church - I could go on.

The fight's I have faced were often tiring, exhausting and left me feeling more broken. some of the medical challenges I have faced have been avoidable, it leaves you mistrusting and carrying the feeling of defeat. The body keeps score - believe me, mine did.

It wasn't until I was in my mid-forties that I understood the full extent of how badly I was let down by the children's Social Services where I was living. I didn't fully understand until I received my SAR report. I was advised to get mine after speaking with the safeguarding officer who was dealing with my father's case with the church. They were able to obtain some of my father's records and reports from his childhood; getting a report can be bittersweet. I know this was the case for both me and my father. In some ways getting a SAR report helps answer questions that you may have been longing for, but it can also open doors and leave you hurt, angry and frustrated.

I also had many disappointments with the NHS throughout my life. The first was in Charing Cross Hospital as a teen when I had to get my wisdom teeth pulled out. I was supposed to be in and out in the same day, but I had an allergic reaction to the anaesthesia. I woke up in intensive care with tubes in my nose and was in hospital for three days. I think this is where my fear of hospitals started. The feeling of helplessness, not knowing if you will live or die but this was just the start. Later in life it got much worse, to the point I almost lost my life many times. I had to have many major surgeries to recover from the blunders the NHS had made.

Trying to get answers for my daughter Mary was my next disappointment and I know from working with families that have Autistic children, how tedious the road to diagnosis is for too many of us. I knew there was something not quite right; she didn't talk until she was six or walk until she was three and she never slept. All she would do was scream and cry, and when she did start walking, it was always on her tiptoes. She wouldn't play with others, she used to line up everything, from books to toys – it was like she didn't know how to play. Without a diagnosis we couldn't get support or help for her in nursery or school; she had to be home schooled for three years while waiting for a statement of educational needs. We even had to get a solicitor involved to make sure the education system wasn't shrugging us off, which is more common than you would want to believe. It took years to get her diagnosis of Autism, ADHD, Pica, PDA, epilepsy and complex learning disabilities. She had lost out on three years of schooling in a mixed setting with peers by the time we received her placement. I didn't want any other parent to endure what I had to, so, I set up a support group for parents with children with disabilities. I would help them with the statement process so that their children could get the support they needed.

Abel was left for too long after my waters broke, prematurely on Father's Day and by 10am the following morning, when the doctor examined me, it was clear that he felt something should have been done sooner. Despite feeling the contractions and the loss of fluids, the midwife insisted I was not in labour. This was my third baby, and I now knew all too well the look of panic and uncertainty spread across a doctor's face. He was overheard by Nicholas asking the Midwife from the previous day why she had left me so long. Three months in hospital and multiple procedures later he was released and allowed to come home. My home became a hospital, and it wasn't until I took him to the GP with concerns for his progress that I was made aware of the lasting impact his traumatic birth had on him. Cerebral Palsy. The way we received his diagnosis, it was not only late but extremely insensitive, the GP couldn't believe I didn't already know. I thought he was Autistic. Such an important piece of information and basic to any follow up care of a neonatal surely?

My ectopic pregnancy - the operation that was supposed to save my life, a partial hysterectomy, enabling me to continue the production of eggs, Instead, they removed the wrong tube and left me with no choice but to have a full hysterectomy, forcing me into early menopause at thirty-three. It became difficult to go to the toilet after my surgery, at one point I had gone twenty-eight days without going. I later discovered they had damaged my bowel during the surgery causing a prolapse and I now needed surgery involving a surgical mesh. Prior to my surgery I was wearing my red wristband, stating I was allergic to latex, they fitted me with a latex catheter - I then went into anaphylactic shock, they had to resuscitate me with shock paddles on the ward and I was then put in intensive care and monitored for a few days, postponing the surgery I had gone in for by a few weeks. When I returned for the surgery to my bowel a few weeks later, I was first on the list that day and told it was a forty-five-minute surgery; in total it took them almost five hours, goodness knows what took them so long or how much mesh they had to use.

When I came around from the anaesthesia, I was suffering with the most excruciating pain in my left leg - it felt like it was on fire and going to explode. I couldn't work out why a surgery for a prolapse on my bowel had left me with pain in my leg, it turned out my leg was left in stirrups, without frequent movement and had caused compartment syndrome; an increase in pressure inside a muscle, which restricts blood flow. It can be serious and need treatment as soon as possible. Compartment syndrome develops when swelling or bleeding occurs within a compartment. Because the fascia does not stretch, this can cause increased pressure on the capillaries, nerves and muscles in the compartment. Blood flow to muscle and nerve cells is disrupted. So, I was rushed back into surgery to save my leg and my life.

I almost lost my leg. In total had to have five surgeries as well as extensive physiotherapy. I was left in a wheelchair needing to learn how to walk again. I still suffer pain today, more so in cold weather and if walking long distances. But there was no way I could just sit back and do nothing; this was just after Nicholas had left, I was a single mum with three children, I was determined to get well and learn to walk again.

When I first got home, I couldn't do anything for myself; carers were coming in three times a day to help clean, dress and help me with all my care needs. Weeks later it all stopped, so I called them. They couldn't see the whole picture. I asked for more hours to help the children so I could have the time to do my physiotherapy and go to the many appointments to have my wounds dressed. This was impossible if I had to take the children with me, but they said no, as it was me that needed help, not the children. I was passed from department to department, all of them fighting as to who would pay for the care of our family. In the end I got no help, leaving me helpless, unable to cope. I couldn't take any more, I was asking for help everywhere I could, but nobody was hearing me. I felt so bad that I couldn't be the Mum I was or take care of the children as well as I would have liked, due to my own physical disability. I felt helpless. Where was the accountability? I hadn't caused the complications I was now facing. At this point, I didn't understand the care system or how it worked: it's the healthcare system and not the social care system that pays for your first few weeks of recovery at home after a surgery. If care is still needed after that, social care takes over the funding – yes, again, it's all about the funding.

Thankfully my brother George stepped in and was sober at the time, otherwise it pains me to think the fight I may have had to face, begging to be heard for my children's sake.

I was still in lots of pain and struggling to eat as I couldn't pass any food through my bowel. I had now started to link food with pain. So, I avoided food as much as possible or would purge what I ate so I didn't have to suffer the pain. Weight was falling off me; my hair was falling out and my toenails were falling off. The pain was like nothing else. My eating disorder at this point had nothing to do with my body image, it was all to do with trying to control the pain. Years later I sat watching a Netflix documentary called "The Bleeding Edge", which showed four medical devices that should never have been used in a human body; surgical mesh was one of the devices highlighted in the show. The same mesh they had used to repair my bowel. This was when it made more sense to me; out of the fifteen side effects listed I had thirteen, the only two I didn't have were sepsis and death!

It explained how the mesh can come through into the vagina.

This is called vaginal mesh exposure or extrusion. It can cause pain, vaginal discharge or bleeding, vaginal infections, pain or problems having sex. The mesh can also come through into the bowel, the bladder or the tube coming out of your bladder (the urethra). This is called Hernia Mesh Migration. There can be pain with sexual intercourse, which your partner may also experience due to encountering loosening vaginal mesh material. Vaginal bleeding that isn't related to your menstrual cycle. Persistent pelvic pain. Worsening incontinence, discomfort with urination and other urinary symptoms. I had to then have another major surgery. I am now left with a permanent ostomy bag, no bowel and at times have to self-catheterise to pee.

Migration can also lead to several complications, including fistulas, adhesions, abscesses and bowel obstruction and can also cause infections. Symptoms of mesh migration include pain, nausea, fever, chills, vomiting, swelling, redness, skin irritation, fluid build-up and weight loss. The symptoms of prolapse mesh failure are so hard to live with; your body is, in effect, trying to expel a foreign object which has imbedded into scare tissue. I was in and out of hospital with symptoms for years and never ever once did anyone tell me it could be mesh- related. The most common complaints of mesh erosion involving the lower gastrointestinal tract are faecal incontinence, tenesmus, painful defecation, and rectal bleeding. Vaginal mesh erosion is usually initially managed by trimming of the mesh, but often (up to 60% of cases) requires re-intervention. I'm now left with the choice of another major surgery which carries many possible complications or living in extreme chronic pain for the rest of my life. I was told there is a 70% chance of life-threatening complications if I have more surgery to try and remove the mesh. After watching the documentary, I was so angry, so hurt that nobody had told me that all my pain and extreme suffering could be the mesh, which should never have been placed inside a human body! Who could I trust to get answers and not cover ups?

Complications from surgical mesh used in transvaginal pelvic organ prolapse (POP) repair include vaginal mesh erosion, pain and organ perforation. The Food and Drug Administration in 2016 reclassified mesh for transvaginal POP repair as a high-risk device and has said complications are "not rare". In April 2019, the agency ordered all manufacturers to stop selling POP mesh because they had not proven its safety or effectiveness.

One review of several studies estimated that as many as one in four women implanted with mesh during transvaginal POP surgery may suffer complications. After it had received more than a thousand reports of complications, the FDA, in 2016, reclassified surgical mesh for transvaginal repair of pelvic organ prolapse (POP) as a Class III device. The classification means mesh for transvaginal POP repair is among the riskiest medical devices. The most reported complication is vaginal mesh erosion, which occurs when the plastic, net-like device wears through vaginal tissue and becomes exposed.

Complications may happen immediately after surgery or many years later. I've gone through a "prolapse mesh nightmare". I wouldn't have believed it if someone had told me years ago that I would have needed my bowel removed which, as my ex-husband Bob put it so nicely, left me "shitting in a bag" for the rest of my life.

"Mesh has caused me catastrophic damage both physically mentally and emotionally. I have been suicidal – chronic pain does that to you. I can't have full sexual relations without experiencing pain. Until I took control back of my mind, body and spirit through inner healing and trauma therapy."

"I was not the fit, active, life-loving person I once was."

Seven manufacturers have paid out nearly £8 billion to over 100,000 women. The NHS caused me to have CPTSD and I am now terrified of going back to hospital. I have sought alternative methods of managing my pain and pray I do not find myself facing another situation whereby medical intervention is required. I hope my life doesn't fall back into their hands; how can I trust them after all that I have been through.

****

As a victim of crime, you're the very last person to know what's going on. There is very little support for victims of crime; most often police officers have no idea of the effects of trauma on the mind, body and spirit. In fact, they are often re-traumatising the victims because of their lack of training and awareness of trauma. Having to give detailed statements is to relive the incident all over again. I fully understand this needs to be done, but victims are left with very little or no support at all after giving evidence and are often left in a limbo state for years until the case comes to court. The hardest part for me was reporting my historic rape!

It was about a year before I married Nicholas when my parents had a knock at their door only to find an army of police officers. My younger brother George had been arrested for burglary. At this point in his life, he was using drugs very heavily but wasn't living with my parents at the time; when he was arrested, they asked for his address, and he gave them Mum and Dad's.

Officers went to my parents' home, after explaining why they were there they requested entering the property to look around. The police explained that George had been arrested for burglary and he was currently being held at Fulham Police Station. My dad promptly informed them that he didn't live there, and asked if they had a warrant. It was at that point the police officers tried to push their way through the door. One of the police officers grabbed my dad pulling him down; my mum was right behind him. Then another police officer pulled out his truncheon and swung it in Mum's direction, hitting her over the head, knocking her out. She was rushed to hospital and needed fifteen stitches in her head. Dad was then arrested and held in the cells for a day and a half. My parents were awarded compensation for the mistakes made that day; my dad was awarded compensation for wrongful imprisonment and Mum for the injuries that she sustained. I think it took almost a year before she would leave the house following this incident; any time she heard a police car or saw a police officer she would panic. The same people expected to serve the public, to keep the peace and ensure our safety are too frequently abusing their power and doing the exact opposite.

Then there was the reporting of my rape, now considered to be historic.

Reporting the childhood rape against me by someone who currently is still working in our community wasn't easy at all. But it's something I felt I had to do to move forward. All my life I carried such an intense guilt, thinking how many more young girls he might had been able to hurt because I wasn't brave enough to come forward sooner. I had been in therapy for some time with the most awesome therapist, Ed, who helped me greatly to get prepared for the hard task ahead. I had a knowledge and a background in safeguarding, so I felt ready, I needed to do it. I also had the beautiful Beverly, my dad's Safeguarding Officer, supporting me, letting me know what to expect, helping me as she was previously a Police Officer.

I have to say I was very surprised at the Police response; it has been most upsetting at times and, it's quite alarming how they handled my case. For months appointments kept changing, be it location, times or dates. The first time I went in, they wanted me to give my statement to two male officers. I asked if I could at least have one female officer in the room. This took more time to sort out, leaving me with more time to dwell on the enormity of the task ahead - I felt the anxiety rising up inside of me with the thought of having to give evidence, to have to share something that I had kept hidden away for so long – a dirty secret that I had lived with for over thirty-five years. I had to relive everything all over again in a three-and-a-half-hour video interview in Brixton Police Station. I must admit, when I left that day, I felt lighter, like a weight had been lifted.

All the back and forth, only to get a call from the officer dealing with my case two months later, (which I recorded) to tell me they were not going to interview him, but his name would be stored on record in case anyone else came forward. She said because I never wore a school uniform, they couldn't prove I was underage, and it would be my word against his. She explained the case would be difficult to prove, but I still couldn't understand why they wouldn't even get him in for questioning. It was harrowing having to reiterate and recall now as an adult what that man did to me as a fourteen-year-old. I have been told that the man that groomed me as a child and treated me like a piece of meat was free to walk the streets despite all my efforts.

I had provided the police with five witnesses; three from my childhood as well as Bob and my nurse friend that witnessed the interactions between us at the time of my father's passing. I sent them screenshots of communications between Bob and Owen, where not once does he deny what he did to me. Owen was willing to have a chat with us about it. Still, they were not going to interview any of my witnesses and collect statements – no statements? Why? There was a very dangerous man in our community and the Police were not concerned. They even asked me to go and take a photo of the house where he raped me. Did they not care or understand how triggering that would be to a survivor of rape? Instead, they tried a range of techniques in attempt to close the report without remedy. A rape had occurred, and the Police had sought to protect the perpetrator.

They asked me how I would like them to deal with it. I'm not a Police Officer, I don't know how it's supposed to be dealt with. I thought to myself what a strange question to ask a victim of rape. I felt dismissed, like they didn't care or believe what I was saying to them.

Weeks later they called me back to let me know they had tried to get in contact with him, but they were only able to speak to his daughter. She asked them not to pursue the case until after August, as he was having cancer testing and was experiencing heart problems.

Why were the Police giving such consideration to someone who didn't think twice about stealing the souls of young girls, without any regard for the damage that he caused? The police attempted to ask me to allow leeway for the questioning of my abuser, who may be a danger to others, because he was being tested for cancer. They didn't even speak to him directly; it was on the word of his daughter, and they weren't even asked to prove he was unfit for questioning. I was now insistent. I persisted and emailed the officer in charge of my case, and at that point they got him in for questioning that Friday. Almost ten months after giving my video statement.

In total, I had three different officers in charge of handling my case by the time they had agreed to interview Owen. I was being passed on, it felt as though I was the one being interrogated, like they were looking for a hole in my story. I was sent on a wild goose chase to track down old colleagues from the hairdressers in addition to the witnesses I had already provided. I was being asked to investigate my own rape, which meant having to explain it repeatedly.

Eleven months after my initial report, I received a call from the investigating officer who had conducted Owen's interview. On that call he disclosed that Owen did not deny having a relationship with me but obviously, he had denied my age at the time. He then proceeded to ask me the same questions I had answered multiple times. Why was he taking sides? How many times did I have to repeat myself for my account to be accepted? Why on earth he would think anyone would make up a story like this and causing nothing but upset to their own life was beyond me. At the time of publishing this book Owen is still working in our community and the case is still open. It may possibly go to CPS but is likely to get thrown out despite him admitting to having a relationship with me. When I have witnesses that can corroborate, I was below the age of 16.

I have been left feeling like a statistic; it is clear to me that the Police have failed to recognise this as a crime, they are more concerned with protecting the Paedophile.

It is estimated that 1 in 4 people in the UK by the age of 18 are abused, yet only 1% of cases go to court. The systematic abuse of women and children in this country is something that all reasonable and rational people would be against, yet we pay a set of people to protect Paedophile's and facilitate these crimes against us.

This unwillingness from the Police to manage my report of child rape has left me with many questions. It is widely recognised that Paedophile's get worse with age. It pains me to think that this offender has possibly abused others in our community. A question the Police are seeking to ignore and shut down, but a very real possibility.

There has been growing recognition in recent years of the ways in which being a victim of sexual violence is synonymous with experiencing multiple forms of victimisation and re-victimisation. I've felt shamed and faced abandonment and rejection from my family for being brave enough to come forward, just like how I felt in the Church when I defended the victims, I will talk about that later. It's like it is such a dirty topic that no one knows what to do, or how to react, or what to say, so they say nothing, do nothing, then shun or avoid you. When all any rape victim wants to hear is, "It wasn't your fault. I believe you!"

I had been given lots of advice from my dad's Safeguarding Officer, who also used to be a police officer. She had explained to me the full process; she even said to me, "Sabina, if you were my best friend, I would advise against it." International research has identified various ways rape victims have felt re-traumatised by their contact with the various agencies of the criminal justice system, as well as in their own informal networks, by the media and potentially by any persons responding to their coming forward that they have been raped. Police services around the world have been criticised for failing to believe and investigate fully the allegations made by rape victims, whose experiences for coming forward have dubbed it the "second rape".

In recent years, feminist advocates and rape support groups have challenged state responses to rape, resulting in significant changes being made to law, policy, training and practice. These developments have occurred within the wider context of the victims' rights movement, as governments around the world have sought to find ways of enabling the justice system to be more aware and cognisant of victims' needs but unfortunately, so much more needs to be done.

****

Social injustice is everywhere. The issue is complex and multifaceted, it is a problem that affects millions of individuals and communities globally. The scope is broad and calls for targeted interventions, but it cannot be ignored that we have in fact come a long way. Like healing, change doesn't happen overnight.

I believe we all have a part to play in the fight for change. It goes beyond individual acts and often stems from systematic inequalities, but we can better understand by examining our personal experiences and those of others. Understanding the various ways in which social injustice presents is essential in addressing the issues effectively. Recognising the issues means we can work towards dismantling the structures and systems that are failing us.

For our future, our children and those that follow when we leave, it is important that legal frameworks are established to hold individuals and institutions accountable for the injustice they perpetrate. Activism and movements have historically played a pivotal role in driving change. Awareness is such a powerful thing, educating yourself to reach a higher understanding empowers the ability to do something, no matter how small.

Together we can make a brighter future X

Chapter eleven

George, my little brother

"Blessed is he who has regard for the weak; the LORD delivers him in times of trouble. The LORD will protect him and preserve his life; he will bless him in the land and not surrender him to the desire of his foes. The LORD will sustain him on his sickbed and restore him from his bed of illness."

Psalms 41:1,3

Saturday was laundry day when I was growing up. Mum did all the washing on Saturday and all the ironing on Sunday. That is, until I was around ten years old. She taught me to iron, and from then on, I did most of the ironing. We had a twin tub washing machine that connected to the kitchen tap. One tub was for washing clothes and the other was the rinse and spin tub.

We had a black and white cat named Lucky. George, only young at the time thought the cat was a bit stinky. So, he put Lucky in the rinse and spin and closed the lid. It was a Saturday so in went the clothes and Mum not knowing he was in there put it onto spin. Suddenly, all you could hear was a screeching wail as the cat spun around at 1200 rpm! Mum quickly stopped the cycle and let Lucky out. After a top-to-bottom shake, Lucky came staggering, punch- drunk into the living room where we were all sat huddled around the only electric heater in the house watching the TV. Lucky snuggled in with us as we pet him, we could smell something strange, Lucky's tail was so close to the heater it was singeing. He really did live up to the name Lucky more than once and absolutely took advantage of his nine lives.

When we moved to Tamworth Street, at the front of the house was a tiny little box-shaped room, which was Art and George's bedroom. It would have worked well as a walk-in closet; it was too small for two growing boys to share. It could only fit a single bed, so the boys had to sleep in bunk beds. The room was so small, the boys could spread their arms out and touch both walls at the same time, and they could even turn off the light without getting out of bed.

When I look back on that room now, in my role as Chaplain in Brixton and Wandsworth Prison, the cells are bigger than the space that two young boys were forced to share. For Art, who was thirteen at the time, it was the perfect space to lord over and bully his nine-year-old little brother. It was a little bit beyond sibling rivalry and, "boys will be boys". Art took it a bit further. He bullied George and to this day, there is resentment and bitterness between them. So much so that both didn't attend Dads' Mass after he passed away that the Archbishop conducted at Southwark Cathedral in the possibility of bumping into each other as if they are ever in the same space there is always altercations.

George was a character. He, like my dad, developed an addiction to cope with his pain. To us kids, Dad had always been that way with money, but George was just a kid and to watch his fate meet him the way it did after Nicky died was tough on everyone. At fifteen years of age, George was using Heroin to medicate his pain. To the best of my knowledge, he is still using to this day. Causing him a life of turmoil, failed rehab stints and prison sentences. Every time he relapsed, it was like he took a part of me with him, I felt such a responsibility to help George, especially when everyone else gave up on him, but addiction just isn't that simple. I think I wanted his wellness, wholeness and healing more than he did.

The first time George stole from me, I had not long had my first child and moved into our new home. I had been saving up for a while, I wanted to surprise my husband and intended on buying a beautiful vintage leather topped pedestal desk for his birthday. I tucked £350 into an envelope and popped it in Gabriel's pram, ready to take to the antique store. I was so excited I had been saving up to get this for him for some time, he always had his eye on it when we would visit the antique store where both our Fathers worked together selling antiques in the stall next door where the table was, that was a lot of money at the time. George and his friend popped over, I was busy, and they offered to take Gabriel for some fresh air to settle him. I didn't even think about the envelope. Later, I remembered and when I went to check, you guessed it, the envelope was gone. George wouldn't steal from me. I looked around the house and did so for months, I convinced myself it must have fallen out of the pram when they took the baby out. But I was so wrong. George had learned to lie very well; it's the nature of addiction but years later he admitted to me, that he had stolen it and went on a two-day crack binge with his mate. It was the first time, but far from the last.

My daughter Mary was obsessed with her DVD player, she took it everywhere she went. She adored it and if she didn't have it, then there would be without a doubt a huge meltdown. Pretty common in children with disabilities to create these types of attachments, so I made sure we packed it wherever it was needed. Mary went to stay with Mum and Dad one night, the next morning she couldn't find it anywhere. She was frantic and Dad was fuming, George and his friend had been over that evening. Whilst Mary lay sleeping in the box room, one of them had gone into her room and taken her DVD player.

There was a time that George came to live with us. I know what you're thinking, after he took Mary's DVD player. But I always love the sinner not the sin, I always gave him grace, I was always forgiving. He did actually manage to get it back for her. Her Autism makes change extremely challenging, so the offer of a new DVD player was out of the question. It had to be that DVD player. George went back to the person he had sold it too and he bought it back for her. But that isn't why I let him live with me. Out of all his attempts to get clean, this time he had been sober for nearly eighteen months. I was divorced by this point, a single mum and sick at the time myself after my compartment syndrome. George stepped up, he helped take care of us; Abel with Cerebral Palsy, Mary in her entirety and I was learning to walk again. He really did show such compassion and provided crucial support at the time. He was doing amazing. I began to suspect he was starting to dabble back in the drug taking. I went to his room and found paraphernalia and I was crushed. I didn't want him to relapse, I had really hoped this time would be different. He went missing for days; this time taking my car.

I gave him so many chances. After marrying Nicholas. We'd purchased a video camera with the money we were gifted at our wedding. I couldn't wait to capture my little Munchkin, playing Mary at her school Nativity. We were all seated, the camera was rolling. Mary was having difficulties on her school bus at the time. "Mummy, I didn't hit or bite anyone on the bus today! I was a good girl today, Mummy!" she shouted into the audience, so completely proud of herself. I was so grateful to have that on camera. A few weeks went by, and we wanted to watch the footage back. It was gone.

No where to be found. A beautiful childhood memory, irreplaceable.

Around the time of Grandad Rubens passing, George was using heavily. The stealing was no longer secluded to family members, he was shoplifting and committing burglaries. He'd been caught during one burglary and received an eighteen-month sentence. We were not able to have him released for the day to attend Grandad's funeral and that broke Mum's heart. I wrote a letter to George while he was in Prison, despite all the pain he had caused, I wanted him to know the good qualities I saw in him. Prison was good for one thing; he got clean. But the day of his release, he went straight home to Mum and Dad's and started using again. This time a concoction of drugs and not just the one. They call it a snowball, Crack Cocaine and Heroin. He injected himself in the locked bathroom and overdosed; his body couldn't take it. He is lucky Mum heard the noises he was making as he lost consciousness. When the ambulance arrived and gained entry to the bathroom George had to be resuscitated. They gave him something to bring him around. Mum was distraught.

George lived with us on several occasions. I could never leave him out on the streets. There have been times when we picked him up from bin sheds, where he's been homeless, living on the streets and with a needle sticking out of him. It truly does break my heart - I pray every day for his freedom and release from his addiction. My sweet little brother was the one that found me after my overdose, he was living with me at the time. His girlfriend was with him. I felt so bad that they had to find me like that, goodness only knows what that does mentally to a person. I sincerely ask for their forgiveness. After much therapy I learnt how to put in boundaries and I found my "NO", which I now know is a complete sentence. You don't have to explain anything:

"Let your yes be yes and your no be no". We are called to be kind not nice; niceness just enables.

Recovering from a family members addiction.

Addiction affects everyone involved in the addict's life. Watching a loved one sink beneath the weight of their addiction has an undeniably profound impact on the entire family and unfortunately extends beyond a household. Whether it be those they steal from to fund their habit, other crimes committed to secure their drug of choice, a workplace commitment that is severed by unreliability or friend's that helplessly watch their demise - addiction does not simply affect the addict.

From feeling responsible, to anger, despair and helplessness, experiencing a loss and grief for an individual still breathing or possibly attending a funeral because of the inevitable, addiction is unforgiving. It doesn't just impose an emotionally burden but usually expands to financial and social complications, and with the addict comes chaos and deceit.

Being subjected to a relationship with an addict is, to put it simply, exhausting and traumatic. It becomes the elephant in the room and families often try to ignore it, struggle with understanding the severity of it or possibly make desperate attempts to cover it up. The fear of the situation at hand and also the opinions of others is an overwhelming place to be, one that can feel impossible to navigate, especially alone. It is important to realise, you are not alone. Some believe that 1-3 people will suffer from a form of addiction in their lives. The reasons and the degree of an addiction of course vary but still, the numbers are undeniably huge. In my opinion the why and what doesn't really matter, the impact it has does and resolution is key, for self-preservation of everyone involved.

It is important to engage in specific preventative support systems and adopt healthy coping mechanisms and boundaries to ensure you are looking after yourself. Look into the support networks available, suggest to others impacted by the addiction to do the same, sometimes saving the addict isn't possible but limiting the damage done to those around them can provide a sense of control.

Whether it be your first time facing the addiction or a part of a long and tiring journey, making sure you have the right processes in place for you and for them is crucial. Ultimately, you need to decide what the right thing to do is. It is a journey and not always an easy one when trying to support an addict in recovery. If you have reached a stage where you have researched the addiction, staged an intervention, encouraged and supported recovery through therapy and other means but still find yourselves getting nowhere, then you will need to consider a few things; Are you safe? Is the addict putting your family in financial jeopardy? Are they committing crimes and putting others in danger? When considering these factors, it maybe the addiction has reached a point whereby you need to involve the appropriate authorities to protect yourself and your family. Be it the police, a rehabilitation centre or possibly housing support programmes to ensure the addict is supported but your home is protected.

You will find lots of articles on how to identify addiction, how to stage interventions, charities and programmes that can support the addict, along with those affected, and also, stories of hope online. This is a good place to start. Remember, addiction causes collateral damage and ensuring you are limiting the impact it has on you and others is one thing you can control.

George is one of the nicest people you will meet when he is clean, he has the biggest heart, so caring, he would do anything for anyone, but in his addiction he is so hard to be around, it's so very heartbreaking, I wish he could see in himself what I see in him, a lost little boy who's hurting, I long and pray for his freedom every day. He has such a special place in my heart. Working in rehabs and prisons I see it's possible to get well and turn your life around. The key to recovery is dealing with the root of the trauma that's causing the pain needing to disassociate from and self-medicate to numb the pain. I believe 99.9% of people in prison are there because of unprocessed trauma

again, I would really like to see all children at the age of eighteen when leaving school be given the ACE score test and put straight into therapy if they are above a 4, I believe it would save the government millions of pounds in the long term.

Stay safe and remember you are not alone x,

Chapter twelve

Billy Jones, my Unrequited Love

"Hope deferred makes the heart sick, but a dream fulfilled is a tree of life. Unrelenting disappointment leaves you heartsick, but a sudden good break can turn life around."

Proverbs 13:12

There was something so very special about Billy from the first moment I met him. I met him first at my housewarming party I had when I lived with my sister, soon after I met Dick; he lived only a few doors away from him on Bramber Road. Tim, Dick's other best friend, also lived on the same street and they were thick as thieves.

Billy had such a sad story; his Mother was taken from him in a tragic accident. Lots of people in our community felt the shockwaves from her tragic passing. She had popped to the shop not far from where they lived, and as she stepped out on the zebra crossing, she was run over and was killed. Although not the same, I craved for my living mother's love, I felt his longing and the loss of his mother's love; he was one of four children, a Mummy's boy, the only boy, he had three beautiful sisters. The pain he must have had to go through at such an early age pulled at my heart strings. He was a young teen when he lost his mum, which was announced in the local paper. I'm sure she would be very proud of the man he is today; You don't find many men who are willing to raise three children on their own. The relationship between him and his children's mother was not healthy at all, he didn't have it easy, but I've always admired his fight to keep on going and I always will.

Billy is also one of Art's best friends. My Dad loved Billy. They would often play chess together; not many people could beat Billy at chess, he was very good, but my Dad gave him a run for his money (most often money was involved because they both loved to gamble). Billy reminds me so much of my father, kind-hearted and caring. With a difficulty receiving love.

When dating Dick and while I was married to him, Billy and Tim were a big part of our lives. We spent lots of time together; we would all often go away fishing for the weekend. The three of them were like the three musketeers, always together when they were not working. Billy would come and get his hair cut, as did Tim, but Billy seemed to need his hair cut a lot more often. They would both end up at our house after a night out in the pub, to carry on drinking, smoking or doing lines. We would be up talking and listening to music for hours, they would often stay over on the sofa beds in our living room. Nothing ever happened between Billy and I while I was married to Dick, unlike Tim, who kissed me once when getting his hair cut when he was drunk. He wouldn't have normally dared but Dick was in prison at the time, and he begged me not to tell him.

Billy and Tim were both making sure I was OK while Dick was in prison for the fight in the pub that they had ran from. They both felt responsible for the fact my husband was in prison for something he didn't do and was taking the blame for them. They would pop over with money for me or to get a haircut and to see the kids. Both of them are Godparents to our children. After my split with Dick, I didn't see Billy or Tim for many years. Billy did show up at my wedding to Nicholas; he told me many years later that he wished he had been brave enough to stop the wedding and that he'd always had feelings for me, but never acted on them. It was the same for me.

It wasn't until after the break-up with my second husband, Nicholas, that Billy and I started seeing each other on the down- low. I was always his big secret which ended up making me feel very used.

I always tried to understand that he had young twins and an older daughter, for whom he had fought for full custody and raised as a single Dad. He didn't have many people to help him with the kids so he couldn't come to mine, it was always me going to him. I was at his beck and call. I was willing to take any of the breadcrumbs of what I thought was love. I couldn't help myself; I admired him for being so strong, in raising his children by himself, I had never met a man so capable. He always wanted the best for his kids. In the evenings, he would have a drink and then call me asking me to come around. I would do whatever he wanted, when he wanted. I was even willing to take on the motherly role to his children, but he was too worried and uncomfortable that Dick, his now ex-best friend, would find out so we had to remain a secret.

I had again found myself in another situation where I was being mistreated by a man. I continued the relationship with him for a few years, on and off, in the hope that someday things would change, and he would let me in, but he had great commitment issues. I wanted so badly for us to be in a relationship, most of all, I wanted to show him that someone cared, that someone loved him. At first, I would have to leave before the children woke up, but after about a year he allowed me some contact with them. I took the twins shopping one time to Kingston and got them iPads. He would tell them my name was Sophie, to avoid anything getting back to his sisters about me. It felt horrible, I just wanted it to be normal and have a normal life but try as I might, nothing seemed to work for us. His guard was always up, he knew what Dick would do if he ever found out.

He would promise me the world when he was drunk. He would tell me how much he loved me, how much he wanted us to be together, but in the morning, he seemed to be embarrassed and would usher me out the door, scared of being caught out by a knock at the door. I told him countless times that I would be willing to help him raise the children, even if that meant us all moving to Ireland, where his family were from, for a fresh start.

So, there was me, enjoying our time together and then the next morning he would come to his senses and sometimes made me drive home at 5.30 in the morning before the children would wake up. I would be hungover, but he didn't care, he just wanted me gone! I would feel so sad, time after time I felt rejected driving home, often listening to love songs, crying my eyes out all the way. I felt completely used and abused. He would say, "Get out, get out, I don't need the stress." Then he would nurse his hangover for a few days, then we would go through the same performance. Sometimes the kids would spend time with their Mum. These times would last a little longer and I would get to enjoy the next day after sometimes arriving at 11pm. I don't think I ever met up with him when he was sober. never once did he ever take me on a date. He would always ask me to bring or collect something on my way which I always had to pay for.

He was in and out of my life and it was so confusing for me. I was so ready to commit to him and he just wouldn't budge. I've often wondered if he thinks he is undeserving of love, but I was so willing to prove that wrong. I was hurting and to get back at him, I got back with Dick just to make him jealous. I know, big mistake! When I did get back with Dick, I told him the truth about everything, I told him I was in love with Billy Jones. I couldn't live with any more lies. I felt I had to tell him everything. I told him the truth about him not being Gabriel's father. He was devastated, but Dick begged me not to tell his Dad. Timmy worshipped little Gabriel, they used to spend a lot of time together; they would both go to watch Fulham Football together. They had season tickets. Timmy used to take him to school every day. I agreed Timmy didn't need to know.

One night we had a massive argument and his Mum called. She was her usual horrid self-conducting another one of her attacks on me, I was very drunk and fed up with it all; I blurted out that Gabriel wasn't even Dick's son. Both Cathy and Tracey (Dick's sister) heard me but they both kept quiet about it for Timmy's sake. It had been eating me up inside, keeping the lies. I now say I would rather hurt someone with the truth than comfort them with a lie, the truth always comes out in the end. It was a massive relief for me to finally let go of such a huge and heavy secret. It wasn't fair, especially now, as Gabriel was aware and having regular contact with his real father. It was not fair to expect Gabriel to keep this a secret too, I had to ask him for forgiveness for doing that to him.

When I shared the truth with Dick, he admitted to me that he had another child, a daughter, with someone I knew growing up in Fulham – someone he had an affair with, and that the child didn't know that he was her father. He showed me a photo of her, she was the spitting image of our daughter Mary. He didn't want anyone knowing as the Mum was still with her partner, who believed he was the Father. He also told me he had had a relationship with Billy's sister, which despite everything, still hurt a little as we were good friends. Fulham really like an episode of EastEnders. I was so happy to get away.

We booked a hotel. Dick wanted to know the exact nature of my interest in Billy Jones and the exchanges that we had had between us. He was getting drunk and demanding answers. I was frightened and felt guilty for the part that I had played in what was now a great big mess. I reached a realisation in my life from covering up so many issues in my childhood, again as I said I would rather hurt someone with the truth than comfort them with a lie. The truth always comes out in the end and hiding costs so much. I was no longer prepared to do that. The truth must have angered him further. He was firing questions at me and becoming increasingly aggressive, calling me vile names. He was getting right into my face. I was taken right back to the domestic violence of our marriage. What was I thinking? Why on earth did I go back to a crazy man, just to try and get a response from Billy? I couldn't stand it anymore; I wasn't going to let him hurt me again. In fact, I didn't want anyone hurting me ever again, all I wanted was to be loved, accepted, adored.

I went into the bathroom of the hotel room, I took a razor from its packet and tried to slit my wrists. I could end my life and the pain that I was constantly in forever. He was banging on the door as I shouted, "Leave me alone, leave me alone." He managed to get through the door; he saw the blood and he called an ambulance. The ambulance crew calmed me down. I only had superficial wounds. I managed to avoid the big beating that I could tell was about to come my way from Dick and stay alive. They bandaged me up and we stayed the night in the hotel together as we had both had too much to drink.

The next day we both drove back to my house, where I tried to end it with Dick. I could not trust him and the enormity of what I had done by allowing this monster back into my life was dawning on me. I was stuck in the cycle again, but now we both had new ammunition considering the revelations from the previous evening.

On Valentine's Day, I sent Billy a Moonpig card. I really loved him and whatever way I tried to tell him he always knocked me back. I tried to make him jealous, it didn't work. I told him that I did not need him to provide for me that I could support myself. That did not work. Lavishing him with expensive gifts. Did not work. I once bought him a Porsche design Cartier watch. I never got anything in return from Billy. Never once did he ever take me out or do anything nice or special for me, not once did he ever pay for anything. Not once did he thank me for the bottles of wine that I used to bring with me on my visits. He would ask me to pick things up for him on the way such as wraps of Cocaine or Weed, never paying for any of it. He didn't appreciate that I would go out of my way to make him happy. I was his booty call. He treated me like a call girl. I felt like a sexual tool. It was still attention, but it made me feel more disgusted with myself. He was not prepared to go through all the gossip of Fulham and everyone knowing our business of him going out with his ex-best friend's wife, even though it was over ten years since our divorce. He would refuse my calls when he was sober but call me relentlessly when he was drunk. I would then get dressed in sexy lingerie and head right back over to his house for the little crumbs that he offered. Don't get me wrong, I know he cared about me, but I don't think Billy knew how to love a woman, possibly because of his root hurt from losing the only women he loved growing up his Mother. Maybe he couldn't allow himself that kind of love in fear of losing it like he did as a boy.

My brother George was at our house in Brixton with his girlfriend. He was living with me at the time and had made a serious attempt at knocking all the drugs on the head. He was starting a clean and sober life. Of all my siblings, I am George's biggest supporter. Not only because he is the baby of the family, but because we are closer in character. Sadly, the drugs make him behave manipulatively when his habit is active. When he is clean, I love being around him. That evening when I got home, I was heartbroken. The children were away. George, his girlfriend and I spent the evening playing Jenga and having a drink. George is a very loving soul; he was lavishing his girlfriend with love and as it was Valentine's Day there was romance all around me. That was all I wanted but having split up from Nicholas and a brief reuniting and traumatising fling with Dick, Billy Jones was now also ignoring me.

I went to my bedroom. I took a bottle of vodka with me. I felt so alone, so unwanted again, it was too much. My childhood wounds were being poked, although I was not able to articulate this at the time. I unpacked every medication that I had and put them all into a pile. I had Pregabalin, Oxycontin, Zopiclone, Paracetamol. It took me twenty minutes to pop all the pills out of the packets onto the bed. I was determined that I was not going to fail this time. I downed the lot with vodka. As I took each pill, I could feel the pain get less and less and I knew I was serious about making my departure from this world and getting away from all those that had been so cruel to me.

After four days of being in a coma on life support, I came around. Everyone was so angry with me. I could hardly speak. I didn't know what was going on. I was still in so much pain and I had no understanding of what had just happened to me. I had just met God. I tolerated all the anger that was being thrown my way while I tried to make sense of it all.

Just before my attempt, I had purchased a ticket to Australia to visit Diana. I thought getting away for a few weeks might clear my head a little. So, about two weeks later I was at the airport about to board a flight to Brisbane, Australia. Just before I boarded the airplane, I called Billy, and I told him I would always love him and that I forgave him. He told me to enjoy my trip. I think he may have felt a little responsible for what I had done. I think both my brothers had words with him when I was in the coma and on a life support machine for four days them not knowing if I would live or die, by this point they both knew I was so deeply in love with Billy. They didn't want me getting hurt by him anymore, so I think they both told him not to have any contact with me. I was feeling very strange and out of sorts, fragile and vulnerable, but I knew I would get real love and care from the Adams' when I got to Australia. Diana was also pregnant with her son. I so couldn't wait to see them all.

When I landed in Australia, I was journaling lots, trying to make sense of what I had just been through and my experience in the coma. Across the road from where Diana lived was a park. Soon after I landed, I was jet-lagged and decided to go for a stroll in the park to process everything. I wanted to try and write down this amazing experience that I had just been through, which had left me feeling most peculiar. I was in such dire despair and on top of that, God wanted me to forgive everyone that had ever hurt me. Everyone! It was a tall order; how do you start to forgive such dreadful acts of abuse? Was the experience even real or was it just a dream? The flashbacks, they were so real to me, not a single person was left out, I saw every single person that had hurt me. My uncle, my husbands, my Mum, friends at school, Owen, my siblings, the Doctors at the hospital and the other people that had hurt me throughout my life.

The next six weeks in Australia changed my life forever. I was taken on the most special spiritual journey. And I will never look back. Forgiveness had started, but it had to start with me first.

Chapter thirteen

My third husband, Bob the Priest

"Beloved, never avenge yourselves, but leave it to the wrath of God, for it is written, '"Vengeance is mine, I will repay, says the Lord."'

Romans 12:19

I was first introduced to Bob through a friend; Henry, the leader and founder of the online bible school I attended for four years called "Christian Leaders Institute", which has over 560,000 students around the world in over 200 plus countries. Henry was American and is based in Grand Haven, Michigan. He was visiting students around the world, and his last stop before his return home was England, so I offered to host him and his colleague, a teacher from the school. They stayed with me for four days, and I showed them the sights of London. While he was staying with me, he asked why I was still single. I think at that point in my life I was happy. I had found purpose and value. I was studying to become an Ordained Minister, and I was working in the Prisons and in the Drug Rehabilitation Centre. I think I was also still possibly man- hating. So, I wasn't really looking for a relationship., I had signed up to match.com, and Christian connections going on a few dates, but I wasn't actively looking for anything serious. I was trying to deepen my relationship with God. If I was to get into a relationship with anyone I wanted and was looking for a Godly man.

One evening, while sitting around the kitchen table, Henry looked up my profile on match.com. As he was reading through it, he kept saying, "You can't write that in a dating profile." I think I had put something like, "I hate liars", so he pretty much rewrote my whole dating profile, changing things to say, "I prefer transparency". I think Henry saw himself as a bit of a matchmaker. After he went back to America, I got a message from him saying, "There is someone I think you should meet. I'm going to give him your details so expect a message from him. His name is Bob, he has just started working for me and recently completed a Master's in Theology."

Bob contacted me over Facebook a few days later; back then I had a sort of OCD, where as soon as anyone messaged me, I had to reply as soon as I'd seen it, every time he messaged me, I would reply very quickly. Bob was fifteen years older than me, and he had been divorced for around nine years; he had two daughters, four sisters and he was the only son. He seemed nice enough, so I keep talking to him. Around that time my Mum was in palliative care dying of cancer, so chatting to Bob in the evening was a great distraction.

We started video Skyping and chatted almost every night. Some nights, because of the time difference, my nights turned into mornings, and I would see the sun come up. There was a five-hour time difference. A few weeks into our chats I said to him, "You have never asked me out on a date." He was in America, I was in England, how could we possible have a date? So, we arranged a Skype date. He said he would call me up at 9pm UK time. I got myself all dolled up. I put my hair up and makeup on to look beautiful. I did the full works ready to impress, as I would have done on any first date.

When he got online, he was still in his sweaty gym kit. I thought to myself, he hasn't made much of an effort. After seeing me, he excused himself, hung up and made more of an effort, then called back. I had wine and canapés ready to enjoy my first- ever Skype date. We would talk for hours. Bob then found a questionnaire online; it was titled '273 questions to ask someone before you get married.' It covered about twenty different relationship topic areas such as, work, family, health, education, sex, past relationships etc. Each day one of us took it in turns to choose a category subject, and we would start asking each other the questions so that we could get to know each other a little better. I asked the reason why his marriage didn't work, he admitted to being addicted to porn and not showing his ex-wife enough love and attention, hence she went looking elsewhere. Although he took some blame, he did point lots of fingers at her being the reason for the break up going into great deal how she had treated him and hurt him, it sounded very much like a pity party pointing blame and not any responsibility, I felt very sorry for what he had been through by the hands of his ex-wife and close friend of his that she had been in a five year affair with behind his back. I do remember one of the questions being, What's one of your worst qualities? His answer was that he was a bad procrastinator. I had to Google what a procrastinator was because I had never heard of it before. He was being honest and that is what I wanted in anyone I dated, honesty. Little did I know that would come back to bite me in the bum. The total opposite to me – I'm a doer, I get things done and try not to hang around doing so.

Unbeknownst to me, I think our mutual friend had wrongly informed Bob that I was a Millionaire. Bob had not been in a proper job since his divorce from his first wife; he had just spent five years doing his Master's in Theology, which should have only taken three, leaving him in great debt from student financing – over $75,.000.

We were coming to the end of asking all the questions. I joked as to what we should do next. He laughed and said, "I suppose we get married." Was he being serious? Oh yes, he was. So, I said yes as it seemed we both wanted the same thing, to be doing Ministry with someone we love as a couple, we both seemed to have the same views as well as principles and values, we didn't believe in sex before marriage as we were both going into Ministry and wanted to do things right in Gods eyes. So, I sent over a few thousand pounds for him to start planning and paying for a wedding. And I went looking for a wedding dress. Although I had never met him yet in person. He pulled me in with the God card; saying he felt God wants us to be together, God told him "he was to be my ghost writer".

I said my final goodbyes to my Mother at her funeral on my 40th birthday then ten days later, I flew to Michigan to meet Bob for the first time. At first the idea was to stay with my friend Henry and his family doing some work with him at Christian Leader's Institute Headquarters in Grand Haven. I took Sam, one of my best friends, with me. He was a Youth Leader in the church I was working in, where I was running a pastoral support drop-in clinic doing some counselling.

I landed on the Monday. Bob asked me properly in person to marry him and we were engaged by the Wednesday. We quickly found ourselves preparing for a wedding. On Friday, my now friend and founder of the school married us. Sam walked me down the aisle and gave me away. He was the only friend or family at my wedding to Bob, it was a beautiful day; all Bob's family were there. Bob had planned everything down to a tee. One of his grandparents was Scottish, so his Dad paid for us to have a bagpiper play as a wedding gift. Bob wore the Stuart clan tartan kilt for the wedding to show his strong Scottish roots.

One of Bob's friends allowed us to hold our reception on their roof top terrace. Where you could see the beautiful musical fountain display at night that all lit up, it was so romantic. The next day when we got home to his apartment, he had all his sisters and daughters surprise me by filling our room with 100s of balloons, I felt swept off my feet, I was hooked, I felt like I had hit the jackpot. little did I know he would feed off of that romantic gesture for the rest of our marriage together, leaving me always wanting to feel that way again but I never did. looking back in hindsight It was classic love bombing.

Bob's family were so beautiful. I could not believe the idyllic life they led. The family house was on the lake. Bob's Grandad had built it himself; it was so peaceful, just perfect and so tranquil. I stayed in America for three months and then we had to decide if we would stay in the USA or the UK. Bob came back with me first on a tourist visa, as it wasn't worth applying for a spouse visa if he didn't like the UK, he had never had a passport before so wasn't well travelled. We both felt there was much more Kingdom work to be done in the UK. Bob lived in a bible-belt area where Sundays were the busiest day for traffic, everyone was going to church – some churches even had to have police to direct the traffic. Nothing like London in the UK, where only 4% of the population say they are Christians, let alone actively attending a church.

Bob arrived in the UK at my five-bedroom house in Brixton. On his first inspection of the house, Bob asked where the rest of it was. It must have been very disappointing for him to see how we live in England, there is a big difference between a five-bedroom house in the USA and the UK and that he had not married a millionaire. Bob got over his disappointment when weeks later went to visit my family in Birmingham that Christmas; it was our first Christmas without Mum.

We spent our time making home visits for our church together as Pastoral Support Workers, which was when he realised how big our house was in comparison to a lot of others in the UK. At that point, he started to make himself at home. I was already established in Ministry as a Chaplain in Brixton and Wandsworth Prison and in an addiction rehabilitation supported housing project, so Bob became a BOGOF, (buy one get one free) – he joined me as a voluntary worker in all the work I was doing.

When we first started Skype dating, I told Bob I had a calling to write a book. Bob told me that he felt God calling him to be my ghost writer for my book. He had been in media and radio and studied in communications and he loved to write. As I am dyslexic this was music to my ears, and I thanked God for the gift of Bob. So, the idea was that Bob would type the book up for me from my dictated voice notes, but let's not forget Bob's honesty – "his procrastination".

As the plan was for him to start writing my book, I started to pay ALL his expenses. I ended up paying all of the bills the whole time we were married as he did not want or feel the need to ever get a paid job to support us as a family or himself. I paid for all the visas, all the holidays, his phone, even bringing his daughters on holiday to the UK. At one point I was even paying a fifth of his parents' mortgage, as they had to re-mortgage or lose the family home. to pay off their aunt's part of the inheritance of the house built on the lake by this Grandfather. The family didn't want to lose the house, so it was decided that the five siblings would split it, keeping it in the family. Bob didn't have a job, he never had any money, so it was left to me.

Years I went without birthday and Christmas presents. His procrastination was now clear for me to see; nothing was being written, he wasn't working, he was freeloading, sponging off me, his wife. It made me feel so very used. I was starting to wonder if he would ever fulfil anything he'd promised me. I also thought to myself, how on earth could we move to the USA if he would have to sponsor me as his wife, with no way to support me, with no funds, or savings, or job and his student loans.

The plan was for the book to be written, then to move back to the USA to be with Bob's perfect family. Fulfilling my dream of now having a loving Godly family that accepted me and loved me, to live in a house on a lake with a white picket fence. I hated living in the UK, there is just too many bad memories for me here. He would always say, "I'm so happy I can share my family with you." He knew all my story; after all, he was helping to write it… well, he was meant to be, anyway. He knew that's all I ever wanted; He sold me a fairy tale, and I paid dearly for buying into it. I trusted him, after all he was an Ordained Priest. Why would I not believe what he was saying to me?

****

We would run a drop- in clinic every Tuesday at the church and would help anyone who needed it, whatever the problem; we had received complaints from nine different people within our church of sexual abuse – young boys/men that were classed as vulnerable adults were being manipulated, groomed and abused. The accused where a part of our congregation.

I immediately compiled a case to bring up with the leaders, from our victims and witnesses highlighting the matter directly to leadership making a safeguarding report to ensure the issue would be dealt with appropriately. It ended up going to the general London union of the church and the Uk union and the police.

We were met with a wall of silence. We had just presented a serious and urgent issue to people that were not prepared to do the right thing. We were ostracised and shunned from the church. People were told not to talk to us, not to question the decision that had been made; this was a church I had called home and family for over ten years.

This is the truth of abuse. People protecting perpetrators to keep up appearances. Individuals who weren't subjected to the pain, denying victims of justice to save face. All I wanted was to do my job, for the victims to be heard and the abusers to be held accountable for their actions. I was devastated by how the Church had swept everything under the rug. I was disgusted that the fear of losing people, money and reputation was held in higher regard than the justice the victims undoubtably deserved. I was astonished that the priority was to protect themselves rather than the vulnerable young men that were subjected to such advantageous abuse of power.

I must say, being the more outspoken of the two, I carried more of this burden than Bob. I was carrying the torch for those victims, day and night. It left me exhausted, deflated, completely confused and let down. It was all too much for me and in the end, it resulted in my diagnosis with complex post-traumatic stress disorder (CPTSD) and burn out.

The deep feelings of disgust took over my body and I couldn't eat, when I tried, I couldn't keep the food down. It had quite literally hit me in the gut. The Church had failed to acknowledge or resolve what was going on and I had taken it to the Police and higher up in the Church as far as I could. When presenting my safeguarding reports to the police with all the information I had gathered, I suffered my very first panic attack. I couldn't breathe. I thought I was going to die. An ambulance was called, and I was admitted shortly after for treatment. I ended up in hospital having to be tube- fed, which continued for over year and a half – on a slow drip feed. I was now immobilised, dependant on a tube to feed me. Bob was supportive but didn't get why I was so triggered.

I had reached burnout, I was taking care of everyone but myself; throughout the last four years of our marriage, I needed to have major surgery. I think this suited Bob very well; he could become the martyr, supporting me which meant that he didn't need to get a job after all.

I often had to remind him often that before he met me, I was a single Mum with three children, two with extensive disabilities, while I had spent time disabled myself, in a wheelchair and learnt to walk again. I didn't need Bob, I wanted Bob. I wanted and needed for him to keep his word and fulfil the promises he had made to me.

I wanted him to be a leader, a Godly Biblical Husband, with morals, principles and values. Ironically, he wrote and taught with me a twelve-week course on these topics in Prisons and Rehab, to teach what it is to be a Godly man. I even tried to inspire him by paying for him to have a radio slot every other Sunday, so he could teach on biblical principles and values. The show was called "Principles for Life". It's a joke if I think about it now. I feel like a fool, looking back at all his lies, empty promises and hypocrisy.

Following my major bowel surgery, just over four years into our marriage, I became so very zealous and focused on my healing. I rebuked the idea that I would be like this forever and I got to work. Bob actually said to me one day, "I didn't marry you with a tube in your nose and shitting in a bag." So, I guess you could say, I became obsessed with getting better, so conscious I was no longer attractive to my husband. There was one point I was on almost 120 tablets a day, all of which carry side-effects of their own. I was desperate to shake the groggy like state I was constantly in, I spent all my time researching, searching for answers, alternatives. The medication may have been helping me in some senses as I was in horrific chronic pain after major surgery, but I could feel it, I wasn't the Mum, Nana or Wife, that I was before, I felt alone, lost like none understood.

I paid for the flight and off we went to America, back to his hometown. We spent a few months out there; I'd consulted my GP, but our laws didn't expand this far then and not too far from where his family lived, I could legally explore my options, we now had a plan in place. I completely removed any Pharmaceutical prescriptions, and I switched solely to Medical Marijuana. It took away my pain, stopped the nausea and helped me eat enough that I was finally gaining back the weight I had lost. I was regaining my functions, I mean, a lot of my issues were from the side effects from the medications and now I had found the perfect substitute. I was so glad I was no longer reliant on high doses of opioids or subjected to their horrific side effects and thank God to this day I didn't develop an addiction to any of them, knowing what I know now. They were limiting my life and I had gotten it back. And started intense therapy to address my CPTSD.

I was getting better and stronger. My consultant had said to me that my surgery would be "lifesaving but life changing." I'm not sure they expected it to be framed as such a positive, but they were right, after a couple of quite worrying years and fighting back against my trauma and physical limitations from surgeries, I embarked on a new journey. I studied to become a Psychodynamic Psychotherapist in the field of trauma, and after forty exams, I was ready to move from the Ministry world into the trauma field and Healing Ministry.

It's amazing what determination can award you, all whilst Bob, well, did nothing. He literally tagged along for the ride, procrastinating, watching TV and smoking drugs all day, for the best part of the last three years of our marriage.

****

When Dad received his diagnosis, I knew I had to ensure comfort in his final months. I had to be strong and put my own stuff aside, so I was able to provide my Dad with the care and company he needed. Having Bob for support was a great help, it is never easy for anyone seeing their parent decline and reliant on assistance. Bob and I moved in with him to take care of his needs as he refused always to go into hospital and at the end hospice care. It was hard work and heart breaking and dad didn't make it easy one bit, thank goodness for Bob I don't know how I would have got through it without him.

I was asked to go for multiple tests, as a result of my dad's diagnosis as it was due to the sexual abuse he had gone through as a child, and I was abused by his brother who was abused by the same man that abused my father. After my initial screening my consultant said I would need a biopsy that would require I go under general anaesthetic. Of course, these things take a little bit of time and I had delayed the process as I was caring for my dad, and he was my immediate priority.

Having to move back into my old family home was not easy. I was advised not to by my therapist because of the re-triggering; the night terrors returned with a vengeance. I had flashbacks of Mum beating me, abusing me emotionally and harrowing memories of the sexual abuse I suffered from Uncle Rob.

The past had already come back to haunt me, being home and caring for Dad meant I had to go to the shops or the pharmacy to collect medication almost daily. In doing so meant I would also have to pass Owen on his fruit stall. All I wanted was for Dad's last few months on this Earth to be peaceful and full of love, the saying 'no good deed goes unpunished' comes to mind; I was being tormented by my past in every angle I turned, all I wanted was to do the right thing. Passing Owen, the impact the whole experience of seeing him and being home was having on my body was something I wouldn't wish on anyone., it made things even harder for Bob and me. I was back living amongst every one of my biggest triggers, but I had a job to do, and I couldn't give up on my dad.

I would walk with my head down passed Owen, shaking like a leaf at times. Even though I had come so far, returning to Fulham had sent me right back. In one of my nightmares, I would dream I had printed his photo onto a poster, labelled Paedophile in bold red letters and stuck it on every shop window and all of the stalls. I was projecting, I wanted to so badly for so many years to make sure he couldn't do to any young girl again, what he had to me.

I had asked a friend of mine who was living in my house at the time who was a nurse, if she would come to Dads' with me for a few days and help care for him.

She was my daughter's age, a beautiful girl, in the way she looked and carried herself. Her support was everything, she gave me the confidence to conduct his care at home and having her around made things a little easier for the days she was there.

We walked down to the pharmacy together, one sunny day, arm in arm, engrossed in conversation, as we passed his stall with my head down shaking inside as I always dd. Owen looked up at her and went on to say, "Hello, gorgeous." Confirming to me, despite being twenty plus years on, he hadn't changed at all, still preying on young women. I turned, disgusted, as I looked at him, I hissed, "You have days, possibly weeks, before my Father takes his final breath and then, I'm reporting you to the police, you Paedophile."

I was shaking, he responded, telling me, "I think we need to talk." I carried on walking, I couldn't stand there a second longer, we went straight to the pharmacy and hurried home. I told Bob what had happened, he was proud of me for facing him after all these years and for defending the unwanted remark he had made to my young friend.

I didn't stop to think it would happen again, but the next day, as me and Bob walked through the market, sniggers and digs were made by the workers on his stall. One of Owen's employees shouted out, "Priest's are the biggest Paedophile's of them all."

Bob froze, said nothing as always. I was forced to respond in the only way I knew how, honestly, I shouted back, "Yes, I know." As I've said I believe my Father was murdered by a Priest;

I was so embarrassed, knowing that my own husband didn't defend me. Not even a simple, "Don't talk to my wife like that". I spotted two policewomen crossing the road towards us, right in front of Owen's stall where we were stood. I reported it, right there and then. I told them about my Dad and that I would follow up with a full statement once he was at peace. I now had a crime reference number; I had taken the first step. It meant I had to tell my dad, he was still occasionally walking down to the betting shop to play the fruit machines and I didn't want him being approached by someone at the market, it had to come from me.

The time had come to register Dad's death at the town hall, I walked straight from there to the police station. They scheduled me in for a video interview, I had also submitted a report detailing my safeguarding concerns to the Market Management team. A few weeks had passed, and I was lying in bed at home flicking through Instagram and a promotional reel came up posted by Hammersmith and Fulham – featuring Owen. Despite my reports, they had picked him to feature on the advert, I couldn't believe my eyes. They were celebrating him rather than bringing him in for questioning.

****

Bob received a letter from his daughter. A three-page email to be exact, expressing hers and her sister's disappointment and pain of what a terrible Father he had been. This pained me, I knew he needed to sort this out with her, my Father was sick, in the last of his days, Bob wasn't getting any younger and he hadn't been home due to covid for years, I couldn't bear the thought of anything happening to him without putting it right with both his daughters. And seeing his aging parents again.

After my Dad's passing, I was extremely conscious that Bob hadn't seen his family for a long time. Conscious that he too was a Father, a son and a brother. Even in my grief seeing how short life could be and never knowing what tomorrow will bring, I wanted him to be able to be with his family, to hug them tight for a little while, because we just never know what is around the corner. He'd been looking after me, we'd both looked after Dad in his dying days and once I had reached a point in my recovery, Covid 19 was now limiting travel and made visiting impossible. Although we would eventually be moving over there, I wanted him to have that time with his family alone without me as that's what his daughters were expressing in the letter, it was the right thing to do. Especially after reading his email from his daughters.

I told Bob I wanted him to go home to visit his family on a holiday, I gave him my reasons for this and that it was important he go there and fix things with is daughter, hug his parents tight especially as his aging Mum had Alzheimer's. I asked two things of him; that we continue our prayer and devotion time and take communion together in the morning as we did every morning together and that he would FaceTime me when he was visiting members of his family, so that I could say "hi" and see the smiles on all their faces since I couldn't be there with them. I was feeling like an orphan at this stage in my life, both my parents were now gone and my relationship with my siblings severely damaged due to my Father's death and the payout wanted by them from what the Church had done to my father. I was grieving, but I found solace in knowing I had a family with Bob waiting for me to join them later in the year.

So, I was awaiting my biopsy, grieving the death of my Dad and loss of my siblings, awaiting my video interview with the Police, but ultimately, I knew I needed to do this for Bob.

I booked his ten-day round trip for him to see his daughters and sister in Michigan and then on to Tennessee to see his Mum and Dad, in the February just weeks after losing my dad. We had agreed that when he got home, we would put sole focus on the book, and then we would make the trip together in May. I was trying to remain positive; I knew I'd get through the things I was facing and ultimately, Bob would be home in 10 days.

****

That call from him never came. The day I put Bob on that plane, was the last time we ever said our prayers together, the last time I saw him. I didn't get to see his family's excitement to have him home like we had agreed, Bob didn't keep his word, he never came home. He ghosted me, I had no idea what was going on.

Instead, I received an email, two hours after his flight was due to return home, simply saying, he was staying there, he wasn't returning. That was it, complete silence for weeks, he didn't return my calls or reply to my messages. I started to convince myself that my Dad's passing must have scared him, made him feel like he couldn't be away from his family for any longer, after all it was his first real loss, whereas I had done this before. Then I realised, he used to say, "Communication is key" or often, "Nobody's a mind reader." I realised I was excusing him, we were due to fly out in May, and given it was my idea he went home in the first place, if he wanted to extend his say, he could have just said and I would have tied things up here and joined him when I was able to. but I was getting radio silence.

The first few days of silence, I was concerned for his health, for his wellbeing. As time went on, I began to see what I didn't want to. I tried everything to get a reply, even his family were ignoring me. At first, I was frightened to reach out too far, to protect his honour, I hoped he would come to his senses, speak to me, work through whatever it was with me. I tried my best to hold it in, but I couldn't do that forever. It had nearly been 12 weeks at this point, I reached out to connections of his from people we knew at Church in the USA and family members, he must have instructed people not to respond, it was clear everyone but me knew what was going on.

I was stuck in what felt like a trance, not wanting to believe what was happening, wanting to wake up from what was a literal living nightmare. It still shocks me to be core even typing this out, I just never saw it coming. It's been nearly a year, and by the time I publish this book, sightly over a year, since I heard his voice, felt his touch or seen the colour of his eyes. For ages I would smell his clothes and cry myself to sleep. I grieved the loss of him more than my Father.

As an Ordained Minister, there is a standard of morality to live up to, he was falling very short on this occasion. As he had been falling short providing for, protecting and promoting me as his wife. Where were the loving Christian family that had welcomed me so warmly? Married me? Prayed with me? And said loved me? I felt abandoned and rejected, what made it worse was Bob knew these were my biggest triggers alongside being lied to or called a liar. He was purposely going for my Achilles heel, but why?

****

A little over three months after he left, Bob agreed via email to speak with me on the telephone. He did try to change our appointment, I stuck to my guns, I tried to begin the call with prayer, as we had always done but he refused. I asked if we could take communion, he refused that too, I asked that we stick to facts and feelings as there was no avoiding that we needed to get a few things clear. My biggest regret is taking the lead, after hearing how I felt, his only words, "We should get a divorce." Then he hung up the phone. I video recorded the call. Well, I guess this wasn't either of our first rodeo's and I decided immediately after his insensitive display of contact, I had to focus. I no-longer needed an explanation. I needed to return to my calling, finish my book and continue my healing.

After eight years of marriage, Bob left me without any explanation, which nearly took me right back to a point where this book starts. But I will never allow a man to reduce me to that point ever again. I so remember the guilt that I felt when I woke up from my near-death experience. That my children possibly may not have had a Mummy to look after them. I felt so selfish to have ever put them through that. I now have beautiful Grandchildren. I'm so very thankful and grateful that my son Gabriel has inherited his Father's kind and sweet nature and is a brilliant Father as well as a fantastic son and brother. The thought that I wouldn't have been here to see it all is one I will never risk again.

I poured my heart into my morning devotions, focused on body work for my trauma and reading scripture. I would post daily videos to help and guide anyone that may also be struggling, sending out messages of hope. I had to stay grounded, I had to keep it together. Trust me when I say, I had to use every tool in my box to get through it. I was taking cold showers and ice baths to help with my nervous system, I was conducting my teachings on trauma. I had to hold onto hope. I was doing daily yoga mindfulness and meditation, there was no way I would relapse into a CPTSD episode I had come to far, I had to stay focused on what I was being called to do.

I focused on my calling; my dad's death would not be in vain. I knew I needed to finish the book before I could start the Harmony healing foundation, so that's what I did. I had asked Bob to send over whatever progress he had made with the book, I waited weeks without response, only to find what he did eventually send me over, was useless to me. It made me even more determined. I got to work, I was ready to do what he couldn't and, in five months I had my first draft, completed. It's ignited something inside me. Despite the days where the pages rolled into one, the spelling mistakes, the grammatical corrections - It is my story, dyslexic or not, who better to tell it, than me?

It has almost been like desensitising therapy, having to write and rewrite something repeatedly. Having to detail some of the most pain wrenching times in my life. I guess that was Bob's parting gifting, getting out of my way and helping me realise I could do it. I now believe that the book was finished in God's perfect timing.

****

(11th November 2023 – WhatsApp)

(18:09, Bob) Hi Sabina. I'm in London meeting my kids who were on holiday in Denmark. I've come by and must have missed you. Are you free for a chat?

(19:20, Bob) Sorry I missed you. I've collected some of my things and Louis.

Months after the painful five words, "we should get a divorce" I received two messages from Bob. Now, I am sure you are wondering, who's Louis? That's my dog. No, I am not joking, my estranged ex-husband, went to my house after months of no contact and left with a couple of clothes, books and my dog.

(23:26, Me) I am at Belles, how long r u in London?

(01:04, Bob) Have left London. Was due to fly out in the morning but have to delay flight to sort Louis paperwork.

(01:04, Me) What's going on? Don't you think I deserve answers?

(01:16, Me) You have just stolen my dog? That you abandoned 10 months along with your wife and Autistic stepdaughter.

(01:22, Bob) I caught a quick flight over to collect my things and the dog you said was mine.

Wow, I thought. My friends couldn't believe it either. No heads up he was coming, pretended like he wanted to speak because he knew I wasn't at home and then proceeded to take the dog with him. Speechless.

He did a really good job avoiding answering questions and told me how his sister's had failed to tell him quite how bad his parent's health had gotten. Then continuously accused me of forcing him to go there, after the previous message thanks me for encouraging him to repair his broken relationship with his family. Failed to acknowledge that radio silence is no way to treat your significant other, married or not. Then proceeded to tell me I was in the wrong for not waiting for him. I suggested we tried couples therapy, like the therapy we ourselves had conducted for others, I asked him what he believed God's plan was for us, I told him, despite it all, that I still missed him terribly.

I found out he was staying with my son. That hurt a little, I was proud of my Gabriel for staying neutral and ensuring Bob had somewhere to stay as he came to the UK. Grateful that although he didn't immediately let me know, he did tell me that he had offered to host him for a few nights. which turned into weeks while he sorted the paperwork to take my dog to the USA while he refused to meet or talk to me.

I sent Bob his chapter in this book, in one of the messages he told me that what I have written in this book is only my truth. If only he would answer my questions talk to me or meet me and not ghost me, then maybe I could see his. He provided me with some constructive criticism.

(00:45, Bob) I don't know where you get the idea that a husband's responsibility is to promote his wife. Where does that come from? Where in the Bible does it say anything about a husband promoting his wife? Please point it out to me.

If I didn't protect you or provide for you, if I sponged off you for 8 years, why do you want me back? You should be happy I am out of your life finally. Go find someone who will do your bidding.

And although I am not posting it all, the one that shocked me the most.

(01:06, Bob) Do you remember telling me about the last time Dick struck you? You told me you said to him that he would never see the colour of your eyes again. Well, that now applies to you. You will never see the colour of my eyes again.

It gets quite mean from that point. My reply.

(06:30, Me) I love you, that's why I can't move on. Thank you for clearing a few things up. Please can you advise when you are returning to USA.

The last message he responded to was a pictured quote I sent to him. Explaining the silent treatment; "the victim often reaches out to the abuser in an attempt to resolve the situation. All attempts at communication are met with contempt, anger and deafening silence. The passive aggressive behaviour is usually repetitive form of emotional abuse which the narcissist will practice time and time again while blaming the victim for this behaviour."

I followed it up with one line.

(11:09, Me) Fact you abused me. I forgive you. His reply. Copy and paste.

****

Yes, when I was ill, Bob took good care of me. I would never be able to repay that kindness, but in sickness and in health were our vows and promises we made before God. We wrote our own vows, and, in my vows, I spoke about the widow's mite, how she gave the very little she had to the Lord. I was even able to obtain a real antique widow's mite, which I presented to him as I spoke my vows to him. I was promising I would give him my all, which I did.

It saddens me, to think, that because of my first two husband's, Bob was able to appear as a man he was not. He seemed perfect, he really was my dream husband. I gave my all to him, I spoke all of his love languages, I provided so much, I put him on a pedestal. I couldn't see what he was doing, I was too caught up in what was to come, the dream I had for us, the ministers I wanted us to be, I didn't see the advantage he was taking. I guess the flags I was looking for were violence, sexual or drug abuse. I didn't notice him slowly chipping away at me. He had flags, I see that now, hindsight is but a wonderful thing.

I didn't think a man that seemed so kind, loved the Lord and looked after me in sickness, could be hiding such a cold and dark secret. We seemed so perfect to onlookers, from the outside looking in, we were a beautiful display of God's work. Couples from the Church would later say to me,

"What hope do we have if this can happen to you?" that was hard to hear. The truth is, I was holding on to something that wasn't there, I painted a perfect picture of him and that's all I saw.

I now see it all. The way he used our relationship with God to manipulate me, the lies he told and the way he spiritually abused me. Our marriage now seems so very far from biblical. The way he walked away speaks volumes, his actions speak much louder than any of the words he ever spoke over me. The way he would subtly make me feel inadequate, reminding me his family were perfect and mine, far from it. The way he fed lies to my family about me, to feel better about himself. In our time together, we only ever had four arguments. All a result of him leaving me to defend myself, once when a leader of the Church spoke badly and was very rude to me after whistleblowing the abuse in the church, the time in Fulham with Owen and twice when my brothers were lashing out at me, despite his presence, never providing or protecting. I see now, it wasn't because he was timid but a lack of passion to fight for us.

I thank Bob for being a teacher of hard lessons, for showing me new ways of forgiving. I thank him for leaving me with priceless lessons to pass on to victims of abuse and trauma, in my work and the foundation. I thank the Lord for removing him from my life and sending me Angels in his place. I am so pleased to now give Bob his own few paragraphs in this book. Something I never thought would be the case.

I keep Bob and his family in my prayers; may they be truly blessed. I never wanted it to end the way but it did, I ask for their forgiveness, that I couldn't be the wife Bob needed. I forgive them all, I thank them for the happy times together. But I can see clearly now that Bob has gone, he was the rain, and I was the sunshine.

Even when it doesn't make sense, remember this, there is already a plan for us, trust that you are on the right path.

Chapter fourteen

My final letter, Dear Husband

It is only fair, that the people mentioned amongst the pages of my life are given the chance to read their chapters before the books release. No malice or harm is intended upon them in the writing I share with you all. The lesson, I hope my story delivers, is to not feel shame when sharing how you have been made to feel. To stop covering for and protecting those who have hurt you. The only person you owe anything to, is yourself.

I took from the lessons of my own healing, I put my words into an email, in a last attempt of communicating with him. I attached my final edit of the book, as I felt that is the right thing to do.

In essence, he decided how his chapter played out, they all did.

****

Dearest Husband,

Please find attached to this email the final edit of the book.

As much as I tried to prevent a Bob Chapter in my book, which I have been transparent with you about, you haven't replied to messages I have sent to you. You have refused to give me a reason as to why. Sadly, I have been left with no choice other than to speak my truth. I'm trying to be transparent with you, I want to be honest with you, I think it right to share with you your chapter of the book before it's submitted to final manuscript.

Thank you for all the wonderful times we shared and including me in your loving family. Thank you for the lessons that you taught me. You could be an amazing teacher and I choose to see your God given gifts that you can use to build his kingdom, not tear it down. I pray for you every day that the Spirit will touch your heart and you see yourself the way me and Jesus see you, when you look at your reflection in the mirror. You were my world, you were a gift from God, and I so wanted it to work, but it didn't work, but it has changed my life for the better.

I ask your forgiveness for not being the wife that you wanted or needed. I longed for nothing more than to be your perfect wife and make you and God happy. Forgive me if there was anything wrong that I did but was not aware of, I so wish we could have communicated and worked it out. You were given every opportunity to do the right thing. You wrote your own chapter especially its ending.

It saddens me that we don't have the dream you promised, to be teaching the word of God as a couple and bringing about a revival by His Holy Spirit, bringing love and healing and wholeness to God's broken world, like my Spiritual Mentors John and Carol Arnott. You said you saw us as the next John and Carol and bringing a wave of healing revival, but I now realise that God gave me the calling and it was my calling, not ours and I shouldn't have delegated that out, but I had to write the book myself, which I did. I have recognised the lies that I have lived in especially never feeling worthy of your love and have renounced partnering with the lie that I'm not good enough to be loved or have a family that love me unconditionally and have replaced it with the knowledge that I will always be good enough in Papa God's eyes and He loves me unconditionally and would never reject or abandon me. I now understand and shall be preaching about the valuable lesson I have learned about never allowing anything to come between my relationship with God or removing my eggs from my God basket and putting them elsewhere. I now understand that true worth, acceptance, love, identity and value, come from Him and only Him. He is Lord of Lords and King of Kings, and he is a just God.

There are always consequences for actions, a ripple effect and I long for my legacy to be a loving teaching healing one. I long to leave a legacy of love, I pray you felt my love for you IT WAS REAL. We are called to be kind and not nice, we shouldn't enable or tolerate bad behaviour in His kingdom, and I look forward to sharing my testimony with other victims of abuse and thank you for helping me to find my voice and face my fears as my name suggests. To find the warrior princess within me and tackle some of the hardest things in life when I never thought I would be alone. This has turned into the most positively transformational event of my life. I grieved the loss of our marriage more than the loss of my Father that had just passed away, weeks before you left me, and as I was reporting historic rape and having cancer screening. You have taught me the difference between religion and relationship which is what the next book will be about, which you will highlight greatly in to explain the difficult lessons that God has taught me through the process of being your wife. Your abandonment brought me closer to God as I fought my battles on my knees and in his SPIRIT, in my war room consciously putting on the full armour of God.

"For we wrestle not against flesh and blood, but against principalities, against powers, against the rulers of the darkness of this world, against spiritual wickedness in high places.

13   Wherefore take unto you the whole armour of God, that ye may be able to withstand in

the evil day, and having done all, to stand.

14   Stand therefore, having your loins girt about with truth, and having on the breastplate of righteousness;

15   And your feet shod with the preparation of the gospel of peace;

16   Above all, taking the shield of faith, wherewith ye shall be able to quench all the fiery darts of the wicked.

17   And take the helmet of salvation, and the sword of the Spirit, which is the word of God:

18   Praying always with all prayer and supplication in the Spirit, and watching thereunto with all perseverance and supplication for all saints;"

My first goodbye is to me not being or feeling important, my opinion being irrelevant. Goodbye to the days of being last and feeling sorry for ever thinking I should make myself less than for anyone else!

Goodbye, to the days of me trying to impress you, to feel accepted by you and not broken. All I ever wanted was to be your teammate. You just don't understand how that works.

Goodbye, to having to cover up almost everything you ever did or didn't do. To keep your honour. The best part about this is that the 3 pairs of eyes (Father, Son, Holy Spirit.) saw it all, they saw me attempting to make up for your shortcoming, they won't be broken hearted any more. They saw it all. They know what a disgrace you have been to His Church, with your hypocrisy and not being able to practice what you preach. Hallelujah!

I'm happily waving goodbye to all your lies too and you can no longer patronise me with them. A part of me felt sad for you. But I don't feel bad for you anymore at all. It was all lies. You were a wolf in sheep's clothing... An attack on my Spirit that attempted to dim the light within me.

Goodbye, to asking you to help – help with anything that comes with the honour of being a married man to a Godly wife who went above and beyond to support you and to my own detriment. Goodbye to being put in the position of coveting what sisters around me had in their husbands that lived by biblical principles but were lacking in you.

Goodbye, to walking on eggshells. Everyone hated it! I'm perfectly content with never biting my tongue again and moving forward and speaking my truth. I have realised that unbeknownst to me I had partnered in your procrastination and allowed Gods light within me to be dimmed, by you. I learned to speak my truth and without a shake in my voice because for the first time in my life I now feel safe and accepted and loved in the truth. The truth really does set you free.

Of course, goodbye to all the good things too. There had to be some good for me to accept your proposal, right? It was good in the beginning, and we made some nice memories. Sometimes they sneak up on me and take my breath away. The man I fell in love with and who I thought was my knight in shining armour, that I was so desperately longing for. That man is long gone though as he was just an illusion a figment of my imagination that you sold to me.

Thank you for teaching me to know my triggers and the balance that this has brought to my life. I realise that you can't give what you do not have, so thank you for teaching me to love myself in your absence so that I could give to others from my overflow. Thank you for reminding me of the importance of Forgiveness, Repentance, and most of all, Reconciliation with the Father and putting my eggs back into my God basket for his Glory. Reclaiming the woman that I was before you met me and furnishing her with the gifts that you gave me has been spiritually promotional. I thank you for helping me to reclaim the little lost girl inside of me that was desperate to be loved and for helping me to rescue her from any harm so that she could feel safe. And thank you, for your abandonment, leading me on a journey of self-discovery and liking what I found and being able to pick up that hurt little girl and show her how to have an awesome life.

I shall need a forwarding address to be able to engage in your request for divorce proceedings. As your wife, this is quite concerning that I do not know where you live and is an insult to my character, you have expressed to a lot of people around me that for some reason, you won't discuss with me. Instead, ghosting and gaslighting, ohhhhh goodbye to the gaslighting too.

I am so proud of Gabriel, that he was gracious enough to host you whilst you were in the UK to collect your things without notifying me or arranging to spend time with me so that we could talk about the bizarre events that led us to this point. I was shocked that you went to the house while I was away and ransacked it, leaving only the certificate of your pension that you had been in receipt of during the later part of our marriage from United States Social Security and Pension and which I knew nothing about. In light of the Pension Statement, I do think you could have contributed to

. the running of the house a little as it was quite expensive and a burden for me to have to do this on my own and some support from you could have made a real difference in our marriage. I do think that relocating the dog to America without telling me or allowing me time to say goodbye was not a very nice thing to do and I hope you will take care of him.

Maybe one day I will come to understand why your loving Christian family did not intervene in any way and help us to reconcile our marriage. I ask myself the question, would they host me if I turned up at their door in the same way that my son hosted you when you turned up at his door. That answer leads me to the understanding of the difference between Religion and Relationships. Is it too much to ask you as an instrument of God's church of healing, restoration and love to respond to your wife now with compassion, humility and grace.

If you have any issues with my truth as expressed in your chapter, I would be more than happy to discuss that with you.

With love and understanding,

Rev'd Sabina Harmony

(Your soon to be ex-wife - THAT WAS YOUR CHOICE.)

Chapter fifteen

My Journey of Forgiveness

"If we confess our sins, he is faithful and just and will forgive us our sins and purify us from all unrighteousness."

1 John 1:9

The most wonderful part of my healing journey was not long after my near-death experience, after I had arrived in Australia visiting the Adams'. It was only about ten days after I got out of hospital; it had been a long flight and I had jet-lag. I didn't get much sleep. So, I went for a walk in the park across the road from where Diana lived. I was journaling, trying to put into words to paper, explain how I was feeling and what I had just experienced. I was on a mission, but I had no idea what I was searching for. As I was walking back from the park, just across the street from Diana's house, I saw a big sign. I had to get close to it to read it fully being blind in one eye. When I got closer to it, it said "loving Jesus, loving life". I thought to myself, I'm not loving life right now. But, for some reason I felt an urge to write down the contact information. It had been some time since I last went to church; because life had become so difficult having two disabled children, it was almost impossible to take them with me. Mary would have massive meltdowns and Abel was on constant oxygen and could not go out the house if it was cold because of his hyper- reactive airways. When we first moved to our house in Well Close, Streatham, the church helped us a lot by throwing a paint party, so we could move into our new home where it would be clean, safe and dust- free for Abel and his airways. When we got the keys to the house it needed so much work, but thanks to the church we got in much sooner than we thought possible.

I got to Diana's and took out my iPad. I started to pour out my heart into an email. About an hour or two later I got a call from a lady called Glenda; she seemed lovely over the phone; she said that night they were having a youth trip out into town to do a treasure hunt. I had no idea what that entailed, but I was invited to join them. I thought to myself, cool, at least I will get to see a bit of the town, and I'll meet some new people. So along I went. I was off on a treasure hunt, but what was I going to be hunting for?

It was a Friday night youth meeting. When I arrived at "Burpengary Baptist Church", Glenda was setting up some chairs into groups of four. When everyone had arrived and taken a seat, they explained what the treasure hunt was all about. There was only me and another two young girls, around sixteen to nineteen years old. We were told to sit and wait on the Lord in silence and write down if we receive any feelings, words or images. After about ten minutes of sitting in total silence, Glenda asked people to share if they had received anything with the group so we could help each other when we went out into the town on the treasure hunt. I was a bit lost. I had no idea about what it was like to get a Word or image from God, but I went along with it. It seemed like the other two girls in my group knew what they were doing. They were both jotting something down on the pieces of paper they were given; it obviously wasn't their first treasure hunt.

It was at this point I was a little bit freaked out. I had written down on my piece of paper "a pink bag with white daisy flowers on it." The other two shared what they had written down, and the first girl said, "I got a picture of a lady with lots of tattoos, and she has lots of pain in her heart." I was wearing nothing that showed any of my tattoos and I have many. I was wearing long sleeves and pants so none of my tattoos were visible; I had more than a lot of pain in my heart, but I didn't think anything of it at that point, until the second girl started sharing what she had received that I became really freaked out. She went on to say, "I don't get pictures or words, I get feelings." Suddenly she started rubbing her left leg vigorously she said, "I can't feel my leg."

It had only been about six months after my compartment syndrome and learning to walk again. I still had numbness all down my left leg – even to this day – as they had to cut through my tendons and nerves to save it. I had five operations in total. She raised her hand to her face to cover her eye then said, "I can't see out of my left eye." I had been blind in my left eye for over nine years following a golfing accident just before I married Nicholas. I didn't say anything to the girls that night, I had never done, seen or been a part of anything like this before.

After people shared what they had been given, we loaded into cars and were taken into the town. It was a beautiful evening. We walked along the beach and stopped for a cold drink at the kiosk. There was a lady sitting on the bench, she had a pink bag with white plastic daisies on it! This evening couldn't get any weirder. I really thought someone was playing tricks on me. One of the girls then said to me, "Sabina, there's your treasure hunt, go claim your reward." I had no clue what she meant by that. I asked her how? She took me by the hand very confidently and showed me how it was done.

We both walked up to the lady with the bag. I was very sheepish. She then said to the lady very confidently, "We are on a treasure hunt from God. Before we came out tonight, we prayed, and God gave Sabina a picture of a pink bag with white daisies on it. I want to let you know that Jesus loves you, can we pray for you?" The lady was taken aback, a bit like I had been. She said yes to prayer and then burst into tears; she couldn't stop thanking us. She had been touched by God – by the power of the Holy Spirit. I was still a little weary and said nothing about the blind eye, numb leg, lots of tattoos or pain in my heart. After that it was time to go home. I was very moved by the experience, so I decided to go back to the Church on Sunday morning for the service.

On Sunday when I got to the Church it was packed. It had a very relaxed family feel to it. There were sofas as well as chairs; it was very homely. I'll never forget that day for many reasons; before the service started a man came up to me and he said, "You have a Jezebel spirit." I thought to myself, how bloody rude! Is he calling me a prostitute? I had no idea what he was talking about when he said that. The worship had begun, the band were playing a song called "Break Every Chain". My whole body started to shake and then all of a sudden, I just broke down and I was sobbing like a baby. Glenda then came and stood next to me; she held me like a mother would hold a child; it was the most beautiful hug I had ever received.

The worship music stopped, then a lady called Diane Pearce started to preach; she was a guest speaker so didn't attend the Church but was well- known. She was a Prophetess. She said, "I had a whole sermon planned ready to give to you all, but I feel I'm not to give it today. I feel the Holy Spirit has others plans." Then she looked over at me and said, "Can you stand up and come over here," ushering me to the front. This wasn't what I was used to in a Church service. When I got to the front, she laid her hand on me and said, "One day you're going to be standing here doing what I'm doing." I thought to myself, that's never going to happen, I hate public speaking or reading aloud... there's no way I can do that. She then continued to speak over me and asked everyone in the Church to gather around me to lay hands on me and to pray for me. It was a very moving service.

Years later when I did deliverance training, I found out what a Jezebel spirit was and was delivered from it. It turned out that man was the lead Pastor of Burpengary Baptist Church; because there was a guest speaker that Sunday, he wasn't preaching that day. That man is truly an anointed preacher and Pastor. it was as clear as day and night that he had a very deep relationship with God. I was hungry for more. So, before I left, I grabbed one of the Church notices that were being handed out telling people what was going on over the next coming weeks in the Church.

That evening after returning from the service I had such a headache; I didn't get any sleep all night. I was tossing and turning. The next evening at the Church they had a bible study. So, along I went. There was only about ten people there; the chairs were set up in a circle and someone led the bible study, the young girl who had been there on the Friday – the one that got the picture with the girl with tattoos and a pain in her heart – sat next to me. After the bible study the man leading it said he was having trouble with his back that day and would we mind if we prayed healing over him, again this was a completely new concept for me.

He put his chair in the middle of the circle then everyone else put a hand on him and started making funny noises. I now know this is referred to as "praying in tongues". The man sitting in the chair said, "Does anybody else need prayer?" I sheepishly put my hand up, and he ushered me forward to take his seat. He then asked, "How can we pray for you this evening?" I explained that I hadn't slept the night before, that I still had a headache, and I needed a good night's sleep as I still had jet-lag. I explained my headache could be because of my blind eye and the pressure of being on the twenty-four-hour plane journey. They all laid a hand on me and started praying in tongues; some were praying in English. I heard them praying for my headache, a good night's sleep. Then right at the end, the young lady from the Friday night service gave like a PS prayer; she prayed, "Lord, I pray vision into Sabina's blind eye, give her eyes to see." I walked out that night thinking I'm not expecting miracles, I just want to have a good night's sleep. I went home and slept like a baby.

When I woke up the next morning, I really did think I was going a little crazy. I could see out of both of my eyes! I was in shock. I woke up after Diana and her husband had left for work because of the jet-lag, but I could see, and I didn't know what to do or who to call. I grabbed my iPad and called home to my Dad, who was looking after the children. I told them I could see. I covered my good eye and was asking them to hold up fingers, I would tell them how many they were holding up. After I got off the phone, I called Glenda from the Church and explained everything to her. She suggested going to get my eye checked out at the opticians. I put the phone down then I called Mum and Dad Adams. I told them I needed an emergency appointment at an optician, and asked if they knew where I could get one. They called me back within ten minutes and said they had made an appointment for that afternoon; they would collect me and take me in the car. When they came to collect me, Mum asked if I was OK. She thought I had done something to my good eye and that I couldn't see anything at all, hence asking for an emergency appointment. I said to her, "No, I'm fine. The thing is I can see out of my blind eye." I wanted to know what was going on, would I lose my sight in that eye again? I needed answers.

I got to the opticians and this sweet little old man called me in; he looked like he should have retired years ago. I explained to him why I was there. I told him my crazy story, that you could only believe it if you could see it with your own eyes. I told him that I was totally blind in my left eye from a golf accident, and I had been blind in that eye for the past nine years but last night someone prayed for me to see. He started to examine my eyes, taking test after test, looking at the back of my eye. The tests took about forty-five minutes. It was a very in-depth appointment; when he had finished the tests, I asked him, "Will I lose my sight again? What's going on?" He went on to say:

"I have to tell you something, Sabina. When I was a young boy, my parents became missionaries and I felt that they abandoned me to work for God. I've chosen all my life because of that abandonment to follow no religion or have faith. But all I can tell you is it's a miracle. You now have almost 20/20 vision in what was your blind eye. I can still see the crack down the back of your eye going through your centre of vision, you shouldn't be able to see out of it, but you can. Jesus has healed your eye." He was crying. I was crying and we shared an embrace. I asked how much I owed him, but he said he couldn't charge me for a "miracle".

I had so many emotions running through my body, like excitement and butterflies at the same time. For the rest of the holiday, I spent as much time as I could at the Church. They had a great Ministry called "Heaven Sent", which was a hotdog van, they would hand out free hotdogs and just talk to people about Jesus on the streets. They would keep calling me over, asking me to share my miracle testimony of my healed blind eye healed.

It was almost time for me to leave Australia. I had been there a month, but Glenda asked if it would be possible to extend my stay for an extra week and would I like to attend a special week's ministry training called the International Leaders School of Ministry (ILSOM), with special guests being flown in to host it called John and Carol Arnott. Gosh, it was the most powerful teaching experience of my whole life. Carol almost didn't leave my side for the whole week; she was so loving, so kind, so caring. She held me in times of worship, praying over me, laying her hands on me, it's like she knew exactly what I needed and what to say to bring me comfort. She too also gave me a prophetic word. "Sabina, you're going to be doing what I'm doing. God has given you a heart for healing."

I have so much respect for the Arnott's Ministry and whenever I know they are in London I always try to go. They are known for The Toronto Blessing, also known as "The Father's Blessing" or "The Renewal," which began in the storefront facility of the Toronto Airport Vineyard Fellowship in January 1994. They carry such an anointing and Carol is such an inspiration to me. I look up to her so much, John's awesome too, they Minister in the Holy Spirit beautifully together; they make a wonderful team. I was so hoping for me and Bob to be ministering just like the Arnott's, but it looks like Papa God had other plans. It's now just me and Him. And I'm OK with that. My forgiveness journey started in Australia after my blind eye was healed; to me, it was like affirmation and confirmation that my near-death experience was in fact real, God was real, Heaven and Hell are very real… choose wisely! Our actions have consequences! Choose forgiveness ask for his forgiveness, we are here but a blink of an eye, where do you want to spend eternity?

For me, forgiveness came fully with my Mum in the very last week of her life, while she was in palliative care in the Trinity Hospice. I didn't leave her side. Listening to the worship song, "Oceans" as she gave her life to the Lord, was so beautiful. She wanted the song on repeat all the time; it was truly peaceful. I knew she was now saved, I know I'll see her again, where I know it will be very different and that brings me a great sense of peace and comfort. Now, my beautiful Daddy is with her.

I love my siblings so much, more than they will ever understand. I pray one day they forgive me as I forgive them. I keep them in my prayers every day; we are all on a journey. But most of all I know my parents would want reconciliation between us. I pray one day that's possible, but everyone deals with grief differently. I pray it's just a matter of time. I hope they all know I love and miss them. I long for a family – they are my family. I always wanted to feel like part of their family and hopefully I will one day, even if that's in heaven.

Six days after I married Bob in America (28 August 2015 at 14.02 pm) I sent my Uncle Rob a message on Facebook messenger. Sending this set me free, well at least for a while. I had to see him after that message was sent and as I've said after trauma, you get triggered, so forgiveness is an ongoing process, but it gets easier over time.

I have always tried to use my experiences and turn them round for good. Forgiveness is one of the most beautiful things you will see in ministry. The gift that it gives us is freedom – freedom from shame and guilt. We all have a past; we can't change the past. We need to accept it. My Mum used to say, "We wipe our arse with yesterday's news."

Chapter sixteen

The Writing of This Book.

"My dear brothers and sisters, take note of this: Everyone should be quick to listen, slow to speak and slow to become angry, because human anger does not produce the righteousness that God desires."

James 1:19-20

The spiritual attack I have undergone in the last 10 years whilst writing this book has been undoubtably the biggest battle in my life. Each day I woke up I had to make a choice to be positive and shift the energy around me. Living in the hope that we can get to a better place in spite of all the negative things and situations that surround us.

Of course, my book focuses on abuse and healing techniques. The question for many victims remains, "why would I want to live after enduring such pain?" the feeling of not wanting to fight anymore is oh so real. I want you to know, that in my healing and my journey, I can now confidently say I am living again. When you are stuck amid traumas grasp it can seem so impossible to imagine a life beyond the pain. As I said at the beginning of this book, the rest of my story is still unwritten and that is my favourite part.

Just as I was writing the end of this book, I honoured that dream inside me all those years ago, to be a flight attendant. I did, however, take it a little step further and it is so true that with determination, anything is possible. I knew someone with their own plane, a small, four-seater and we had decided to go out for the day. Due to technical issues and no fault of the pilot, we encountered a terrifying ordeal on the runway. Something wasn't quite right at take-off, it wasn't until the very last second that the plan lifted, we couldn't abort the flight and we were heading directly into the trees. Before my eyes flashed what could have been, the rustling of the leaves against the wings of the plane, the loud crashing of our downfall. It was slow motion for those moments, I was calm and not fearful at all. This time I had no unforgiveness in my heart, I wasn't afraid, and it confirmed I no longer fear death.

It further inspired me to keep on living. To chase the dreams I had almost forgotten, after all, life is for living. So, I enrolled in flying lessons, and am soon to be a qualified safety co-pilot. Keeping to the promise I made, to make five-year-old me proud.

God sent Angels into my life. I had the best time finishing up the book myself – it brought great healing and a feeling of accomplishment. Despite the years Bob spent pretending to help me, when it came down to it, I just knew I had to go at it alone, like most things in my life and my determination meant I had started and completed my first draft in less than five months. It helped me to see that I can do anything if I put my mind to it. I feel a little bit for my proof-readers and the editors, what with me having dyslexia, but I can now proudly say I'm an Author.

I've completed that part of my calling, although it took many years for so many reasons. I'm now super-excited to be moving into the next chapter of my life, the next stage of my calling, to bring Harmony Healing Foundation to life in honour of my Father. A foundation designed to support others, to put my pain to use and to show that healing is truly possible. To heal I needed to feel. I had to go deep into my feelings. I had to connect with my body, with the tiny young me who was hurt so badly in so many ways as a young girl. I had to listen to what my body was trying to tell me for years. I'm now grateful for all that I have been through, as I wouldn't be who I am today without my story. I survived, now I choose to thrive in the love of the Lord. He never left my side; it was Him that gave me the strength on the hardest of days, to keep on going when sometimes all I wanted to do was give up.

I am finally to a point in my life that I don't care anymore about fitting in with the crowd, needing to be accepted. I needed to accept myself first and foremost. I have come so far since I first started my journey of healing following my diagnosis of CPTSD. Trauma doesn't have to be a life sentence. So many people stole so much of my peace, I now choose not to be drinking any more of their poison, the lies that they left behind. I forgive them all. I pray for them all daily that the Lord blesses them in such an abundance that they know it could only be Him showing them such grace.

There is a massive difference between religion and relationship. I'm going to explain a lot more about this in my next book, which I've already started writing: "The difference between Relationship and Religion: My Journey through Ministry". As a woman called into ministry it wasn't easy at all. I will never forget the Prophetic words that Justin Welby, the Archbishop of Canterbury spoke over me on my confirmation day as I was going into my Ordination process. He said to me, "I feel the Lord saying to me to tell you, do not conform, God is going to use you outside the box." For years I did the opposite. I tried to conform. I tried all I could to fit into religion and the Church, to feel accepted by man.

Seeing my life printed on pages of a book has made me realise so much, about myself, my journey and about others. It's one thing to go to therapy and address the things that caused you pain and years of suffering, but to share your vulnerabilities, the details that were once secrets and be so raw and truthful about things that quite often go unspoken, well - I am proud of myself. I think back to five-year-old me, and I want her to know we made it and then we made something of it.

I guess what I am trying to say is, if you are here and you are reading my book, then you made it too. You have navigated your darkest days and despite anything that has happened between the then and the now, you survived. I hope my book helps you to keep on surviving, I hope it guides you to new ways of coping, new ways of thriving and the realisation that like you, we all have secrets and have at some point, for whatever reason, carried the burden of shame. You are not to blame, for anyone else's actions, you are not even to blame for your reactions to those actions. I want you to know, you have got this.

I don't know you personally, I don't know your relationship with God or the weight this world has put upon you. I don't know the horrific things you have gone through or might still be experiencing. But I do know that he hears our prayers, I know that you too can be free from your suffering.

You, my readers, are in my prayers, today and always. I would like to leave you with some parting words and a parting prayer;

"I started my healing journey through prayer and accepting Jesus, To accept Jesus as your personal Saviour is to acknowledge who Jesus is in your own life. It is to believe in Him. John 1:12 says: "But to all who did receive him, who believed in his name, he gave the right to become children of God." John 3:16 adds, "For God so loved the world, that he gave his only Son, that whoever believes in him should not perish but have eternal life."

Are you willing to place your faith in Jesus Christ as your Saviour and receive this free gift of eternal life? If so, follow through with the decision right now. with a a prayer of salvation.

A salvation prayer is a prayer that expresses repentance for sins and faith in Jesus Christ as Lord and Savior. It is a way of asking God for forgiveness and receiving His gift of eternal life. A salvation prayer usually includes confessing that one is a sinner, believing that Jesus died and rose again for one's sins, and inviting Jesus to be the Lord and Savior of one's life.

Lord, forgive me for my sins and save me. Help me to turn away from my old ways and follow Your will. I believe in Jesus and ask Him to be my Lord and Savior. Cleanse me with Your blood and fill me with Your Holy Spirit.

Lord Jesus, I know that I am a sinner and that I often fall short of the glory of God. By faith, I gratefully receive Your gift of salvation. I'm ready to trust You as my Lord and Savior.

Father, I confess that Jesus is my Lord. I make Him Lord of my life right now. I believe in my heart that You raised Jesus from the dead.

Jesus Christ, Son of God, pray for us as we believe in our heart that You are our Savior. With hope-filled hearts, let us seek redemption through faith in Jesus Christ Amen

It's not about a religion; it's about a relationship. Seek and you will find, knock on the door and it shall be opened.

Religion kills. It killed Jesus.

It killed my father and it killed my marriage. its all about a relationship not religion.

To live is Christ, to die is gain.

To be continued..."

Epilogue

"To live is Christ, to die is gain."

As I stand, at the precipice of a monumental chapter in my life, on an enlightening journey around psychodynamic psychotherapy and trauma, healing in mind, body and spirit.

A journey so eye opening, vivid and transformative, it has surpassed even the wildest bounds of my imagination. I went in with caution and came out with a celebration for life and the freedom of letting go, no longer playing tug of war with myself & the past.

I now embark on the very adventure I always dreamed of. This path has led me through an odyssey of profound emotions and changes. I experienced the pain of loss, loss of friends, loved ones and even family, but in their place, found new connections that resonate deeply with my ever-evolving self. Growing an entrepreneurial spirit that is guiding me to build a foundation for healing from abuse and trauma. I now believe experiences are stepping stones to your true calling. I have transformed into a visionary leader, leading in love, compassion, and grace, with listening ears, wanting nothing more than to see captives of trauma set free. To give them tools to reach their full potential.

Love, found its way in a tumultuous journey of healing. I made a choice to become the woman of my dreams, embarking on a mission to help others reach their highest potential, deeply inspired to see chains broken, and freedom found. I was on a quest to understand and experience true love in its most profound sense. The love I encountered initially, was a spark that ignited a deeper exploration and understanding of self, my true self, true love, true understanding, reclaiming my true identity.

This journey tested me in ways I never imagined. I faced moments that I thought would break me, but in each of these moments, I found the strength and support needed to heal and emerge stronger than before. Just as gold is refined through fire, I too will be refined through my experiences, emerging as a golden beacon for others.

As I move forward, I remember; that every challenge, every setback, is an integral part of my journey and growth.

The journey with myself was just the beginning, learning to love myself so I could give from my overflow.

True LOVE, X

Further reading.

Why Has Nobody Told Me This Before? by Julie Smith

Sensorimotor Psychotherapy by Jenina Fisher and Pat Ogden

Trauma and The Body by Pat Ogden and Kekuni Minto

Who switched off my brain? By Dr Caroline Leaf

Attached by Amir Levine and Rachel Helle

*The Body Keeps The Sco*re by Bessel van der Kolk

Mother Hunger by Kelly McDaniel

The Child In You by Stefanie Stahl

The Body Remembers by Babette Rothschild

Trauma and Recovery by Judith Lewis Herman

Internal Family Systems Therapy by Richard C Schwartz

Somatic Internal Family Systems Therapy by Susan McConnel

Coping with Trauma-Related Dissociation by Suzette Boon

Adult Children of Emotionally Immature Parents by Lindsey C Gibson

Healing the Fragmented Selves of Trauma Survivors by Janina Fisher

Trauma-Proofing Your Kids by Peter Levine

Boundaries by John Townsend

*Healing From Trau*ma by Jasmin Lee Cori *Born For Significance* by Bill Johnson *When The Body Says No* by Gabor Mate

Healing Trauma by Peter Levine

Nurturing Resilience by Kathy L Kain *Trauma and Memory* by Peter Levine *Waking the Tiger* by Peter Levine

Boundary Boss by Terri Cole

The Invisible Lion by Benjamin Fry *Slay the Bully Rebecca* by Zung Ezq

The Complex PTSD Workbook by Arielle Schwartz

Gaslighting by Dr Stephanie Sarkis

Survivors by Maggie Oliver

The Myth of Normal by Gabor Maté

The War in Your Head by Bill Johnson

The Supernatural Ways by Bill Johnson

Good Morning, Holy Spirit by Benny Hinn

Shifting Atmospheres by Dawna De Silva

I Believe In Miracles by Kathryn Kuhlman

Nothing Is Impossible With God by Kathryn Kuhlman

Preparing For The Glory by John Arnott and Carol Arnott

The Bate of Satan by John Bevere

Dirty Glory by Pete Gregg

Battlefield of The Mind by Joyce Meyer

Healing Through Deliverance By Peter Horobin

Failing Forward by John Maxwell

Manifesting The Spirit by Smith Wigglesworth

Waking The Tiger by Peter Levine

In An Unspoken Voice by Peter Levine

Developing a Supernatural Lifestyle by Kriss Valeton

The Wim Hof method by Wim Hof

Overcoming Fear by Dawna De Silva